What people are saying about Alon Gratch's international bestseller *If Men Could Talk...* *Translating the Secret Language of Men*

"Written primarily as a codebreaker for women, *If Men Could Talk...* is a serious book with a clever title. Gratch's premise, greatly oversimplified here, is that men behave the way they do because they are in constant conflict with the feminine part of their psyches. Women must be 'detectives,' he writes, to find out what men are really thinking."

— Teresa K. Weaver,
Atlanta Journal-Constitution

"*If Men Could Talk...* follows in the tradition of John Gray's *Mars and Venus* series and Deborah Tannen's *You Just Don't Understand.*" — *Publishers Weekly*

"Filled with advice and stories that are surprising and shocking, this book will change the way you look at your relationships. So universal are the book's concepts that it has already been bought for translation and publication in many countries. . . . Dr. Gratch gives you the tools to listen so you can interpret and understand the inner world of men. *If Men Could Talk...* is men in translation."

— Mardia Stone, M.D.,
African Sun Times

"Few therapists have been able to engage the nonprofessional reader while remaining clinically responsible. Dr. Gratch has done just that, telling each clinical anecdote in a moving, compelling way. He is clearly not only a good clinician but a literate and interesting man."

— Olga Silverstein, M.S.W., author of *The Courage to Raise Good Men*

"Do men want their girlfriends and wives to understand them? Of course. Might this book help foster that understanding? Sure. Is it a cause for celebration that an author is promoting reflection and empathy rather than gimmicks and deceit? Absolutely. . . . *If Men Could Talk...* does not treat its female readers like total idiots. It does not portray men as mere self-obsessed, sex-obsessed, status-obsessed infants. It does not filter all behavior and miscommunication through a political or linguistic lens. Best of all, it does not promise that if you simply wait till Friday before you call that eligible investment banker back, or use an egg timer as a tool to maximize your conversational edge, you will meet the man of your dreams and — after tricking him into doing something he wouldn't ever do on his own — live happily ever after. This book is different. . . . Gratch skillfully explores the roots of men's most painful feelings . . . and movingly documents the ways in which we are warped by them. In doing so, he displays a broad knowledge of literature, history, and popular culture — citing everyone from Freud to John Gray — as well as a rigorous and nimble approach to the causes of the problems plaguing the men whose case studies form the basis of his theories."

— Steve Friedman, *Elle*

If Men Could Talk...

Translating the Secret Language of Men

Alon Gratch, Ph.D.

Little, Brown and Company
BOSTON NEW YORK LONDON

To Michele, Jordan, and Ilana with love

Originally published in hardcover by
Little, Brown and Company, February 2001
First paperback edition, February 2002

Library of Congress Cataloging-in-Publication Data

Gratch, Alon.
If men could talk . . . translating the secret language of men /
Alon Gratch. — 1st ed.
p. cm.
Includes bibliographical references.
ISBN 0-316-17861-6 (hc)/0-316-17868-3 (pb)
1. Men — Psychology. 2. Masculinity. I. Title.
BF692.5.G73 2000
155.3'32 — dc21
00-041234

10 9 8 7 6 5 4 3 2 1

Q-MART

Book design by Fearn Cutler

Printed in the United States of America

Contents

Author's Note

All the cases described in this book are composites. They have been deliberately mixed and altered in order to protect my patients' rights of confidentiality and privacy. All patients' names have been changed as have other aspects of their identities, including their occupation, marital status, age, and family background. I have also modified the details of their experiences and dreams. Any resemblance to actual persons, living or dead, or to actual events is purely coincidental.

Acknowledgments

First and foremost, I'd like to thank my patients, male and female. Without their trust and openness to the therapeutic process, this book could never have been written. Their struggle to uncover their own psychological truths and the courage they bring to it inspired me both at work and in my own personal searches. And I've learned more about psychology from them than from any book, theory, or teacher.

Two individuals who have taught me much about my own development as a man will no doubt recognize their imprint on my thinking throughout this book. Ironically, but not inconsistently with the thesis of the book, both are women: my wife (and colleague), Michele Sacks, and my own analyst, Dr. Betty Hellman. The extent of my emotional and intellectual debt to my wife cannot be expressed in words, certainly not in these public pages. Recalibrated, and for different reasons, the same can be said about my analyst.

My editor at Little, Brown, Judy Clain, has played a critical role in the overall direction of the book from the moment she read the initial manuscript. She brought to the project great enthusiasm and intelligence, shaping it with insights and comments which were thoughtful, creative, and practical. She also encouraged me to be more open about myself, which made the writing process both more challenging and more gratifying. I also want to thank the rest of the team at Little, Brown, particularly Beth Davey, Linda Biagi, Heather Rizzo, Matthew Ballast, Claire Smith, and

Betty Power. I owe a special debt to my agent, Judith Riven. From the very beginning of our relationship, she reinforced my efforts to develop my own voice, never trying to dilute it. She treated me and my text with a firm but gentle hand, and was not afraid to confront me when necessary, always with great integrity and respect. She worked with me and on my behalf with unusual intensity, humanity, and professionalism.

I am deeply indebted to Mark Rosenman and Jane Rosenman for going out of their way to offer advice and assistance which eventually facilitated the publication of the book in its current form. Also, to several colleagues and friends who read the initial manuscript and responded with words of encouragement and/or critical suggestions: Brenda Berger, Eric Friedberg, Morris Shinderman, Beth Dorogusker, Adam Price, Arthur and Evelyn Sacks, George Packer, Anne Berkowitch, and Linda Kane. I'm greatly indebted to two writer friends, Zia Jaffrey and Joseph Berger, for supporting and facilitating my work as a writer early on in my career.

Other friends, colleagues, teachers, or supervisors who have influenced my personal development and work over the years are Itamar Lurie, Ivan Bresgi, Richard Shuster, Ysrael Eliraz, Harvey Hornstein, Joel Davitz, Marsha Levy-Warren, Sandra Buechler, Karen Crystal, Mona Macksoud, Peter Cohen, Andy Grunebaum, and Laurie Grunebaum. I would also like to thank Gordon Churchwell, Judy Siegel, and Frank Schnneir for referring me to various individuals in the publishing community.

Last but not least, home is where we come from. I'd like to express my deepest gratitude and love to my parents, Haya and Avraham Gratch and to my two brothers, Eli Gadot and Ariel Gratch. Without their love, encouragement, and generosity nothing in my life that I value would be here with me today.

If Men Could Talk…

Men Are Difficult

...let me count the ways

Men are difficult. On the surface, they often seem distant and elusive. Or loud and obnoxious. And when you try to get to know them, it often gets worse — they can become defensive and impenetrable. Indeed, unlike women, who are generally open with their feelings, most men find it extremely difficult to open up to others. But when they finally do, they invariably reveal a dramatic, bold, and amazingly vulnerable inner self. This hidden self, and the challenges it presents for the occasional visitor, is the subject of this book. As I explore the inner world of men, we will come upon multiple sightings of the central paradox on which masculinity rests: the cornerstone of man's gender identity is his feminine, not his masculine, desires.

I am a clinical psychologist working primarily with men, which is unusual because most psychotherapy patients are women. So while many therapists spend their time listening to women complain about men who don't talk, don't listen, or don't understand, I spend most of my time listening to these men. And with a little bit of help, my male patients do talk, do listen, and do understand.

In presenting the inner world of men, I am assuming that women will always be in the business of trying to decode male behavior. For them, it's a practical matter of improving their relationships with men — a high priority for many women. In writing this book I hope to help women to attain this goal, not by telling them what to do, but rather, by inviting them into the emotional and spiritual equivalent of the male locker room. My intention is to discuss my experiences with male patients and to share what I do, as a psychologist, when confronted with some of the troublesome aspects of male psychology. In short, I'm going to tell the "inside story" about men.

But this book is not only for women. As a writer, I'd like to replicate here what I believe I have accomplished as a psychologist — to reach and connect with men. I hope, as they read about other men's struggles to break out of their emotional isolation, male readers will feel understood and moved and that what they read will mirror and nurture their own self-knowledge — nascent, secret, or not fully conscious as it may be.

What brings men to therapy and what they end up talking about in therapy are two different matters. For one thing, at the beginning of therapy many men don't talk at all — that is, about anything significant or interesting. In a sense, men come to therapy *because* they don't talk. Since their unconscious philosophy is that talk is cheap and that actions speak louder than words, they often enter therapy in the same way that they drive: rather than ask for directions, they keep on going until they reach a dead end, are lost, or have an accident. Even then they may avoid asking for help: their backseat driver might do it for them.

In that way, many of my male patients stumble into my office for the initial consultation after some destructive action and/or at the urging of their spouse or girlfriend. In the latter case, they are often "dragged" in because they refuse to communicate or because they communicate chiefly by means of angry outbursts or other unseemly discharges. Sometimes they are forced to come for the same reasons not by an intimate partner but rather by a business partner or a boss. An ultimatum — a threat of divorce or of termination of employment — is often involved.

While some men seek treatment for problems or issues similar to women's — depression, anxiety, relationship difficulties — many more enter psychotherapy with distinctly male dilemmas and a uniquely masculine style. Perhaps not surprisingly, research shows that men are particularly susceptible to such conditions as alcoholism, drug abuse, and antisocial behaviors. But in my consulting room, even men who do not fit into such diagnostic criteria — and most of my patients don't — cannot be mistaken for women.

Many of the men who come to see me on their own initiative are in the midst of a work-related crisis. Being fired or even "restructured" is a traumatic experience for most men. Even a perception of failure, let alone an actual lack of success, can precipitate a crisis. There are other work issues which bring men into my office, for example, difficulty in making business decisions, getting into costly political conflicts, feeling oppressed by the corporation, and being bored or lacking passion for one's work.

Some very successful men come to see me to address the fundamental sense of uncertainty, the oversized survival instincts and the emotional hunger which have served them so well in their drive to the top of their professions. Some of these men come because they realize they will never feel satiated. Others come because of the heavy price they have paid for their success: alienation from wife and children or a lack of personal fulfillment.

Last but not least, many men seek therapy for sexual or what they think are sexual symptoms. Impotence, premature ejaculation, disturbing sexual fantasies, questions about sexual identity, infidelity, and sexual impulsivity or compulsivity are the most common "presenting problems." In this group are those who are so ashamed of their difficulties that they don't even tell you for many months why they came to see you. Then there are those who are so "oversexed" that they do not hesitate to be graphic or pornographic as soon as possible. There is a third group as well — those who guardedly allude to their sexual anxieties by cracking jokes.

It's Not about Sex after All

The idea of writing a book about men occurred to me first several years ago when I noticed that my practice was different from that of many other therapists. At that time, in teaching, supervising, or comparing notes with colleagues, I developed a vague sense that my patients were a rather spirited, colorful bunch and that their problems and inner lives were more dramatic, perhaps even audacious. One obvious difference was that sooner or later my patients would provide detailed and elaborate accounts of richly provocative sexual fantasies. In addition, they would often criticize my shoes, tease me about my ties, analyze my own comments and motives, ask about my favorite color, try to catch me in a lie, and playfully accuse me of manipulating or experimenting with them. They were also openly loving and appreciative.

At first I thought all this had something to do with me, and to some extent it did. But eventually it dawned on me that most of the patients I was comparing mine to were women. Obviously, men are different from women. But could it be that under their dull, cement-like exterior there's a world of riveting, warring emotions? Ultimately what I've learned from my male patients is that given a certain emotional environment, men *can* talk, and that, furthermore, what they have to say is nothing less than inspiring. This, in a word, is both the message and the content of this book.

The emotional environment I'm referring to is not really something you learn in a graduate psychology program. Rather, it's something that the "good enough therapist" brings with him to his therapeutic relationships and, more important, something that any thoughtful and caring person can bring to any important relationship. It combines an attitude of the mind with certain personal tools which spring out of such organic life elements as play, humor, and curiosity.

Philosophically, I do not view the therapeutic process as a specialized medical procedure. If anything, I see it as an extension of natural interpersonal processes, primarily that of love — love defined as getting to know, to feel, and to appreciate the inner world of another person. As a result of this naturalistic perspective, the reader should be able to use in his or her own life many of the therapeutic techniques embedded in the narrative of this book. For example, one of the most critical things the therapist does is ask questions about the patient's way of thinking. And the good therapist asks these questions out of sheer curiosity and interest, not because he wants to change or influence the patient. So those of us who complain that men don't talk should ask themselves when was the last time they asked a man what was on his mind — not in order to extract something from his mind but simply because they valued it. Of course, there are better and worse questions, and ways of asking and timing, and these too are in the content of this book.

Now, whereas you can ask a woman what's on her mind and get an answer, the route to a man's inner world is often more circuitous. And many times it requires side trips into crude or vulgar substations. One patient, a retired police officer, started his first session after vacation by saying: "So I won fifty-five thousand dollars in Las Vegas last week, in black jack." As I was reflecting and expecting him to comment on the fact that he had just about doubled his life savings, he smiled triumphantly and said, "And my wife gave me a blow job this morning." I honestly felt that this second piece of news was much more important to him than the first. But was that because it was about sex or because it was an achievement less predicated on chance and more reflective of his self-perceived masculine superiority?

Yes, men do have sex on the brain, but when they talk about it openly and uninhibitedly, it becomes clear that the male sexual interest is often a mere vehicle for the expression of bigger and better things. To rephrase Freud's famous dictum, we might say that "sometimes a penis is just a cigar." This notion, that through sex men communicate powerful, unconscious feelings, was crystallized for me several years ago while developing a professional seminar about male sexuality. The seminar, which boasted the rather technical title "Transference and Countertransference in Psychotherapy with Male Sexual Disorders (and Orders)," was designed to teach mental health professionals how to help their male patients talk about, and understand, their sexual problems. The seminar participants, most of whom were female therapists, found the material provocative and helpful. But what caught my imagination was the gradual realization that the six or seven concepts around which the seminar was organized were characteristics not only of male sexuality, but also of the psychology of men in general. I then began to reflect, through the prism of these concepts, on all that I've absorbed over the years from my patients (as well as my corporate clients), and on all that I've observed in my own development as a man. Eventually, and consistently with previous theory and research in the field, I reorganized these concepts into seven psychological elements, or attributes, each of which explains why men are so difficult, yet so compelling, to engage.

The Seven Male Attributes

The first two male attributes which I explore in this book explain why it's so hard for men to talk about their feelings. These elements are discussed first because they are used by men as psychological defenses to guard against the emotional pain associated with the other five elements. Our path will thus simulate the progression of a therapeutic relationship, or of any close relationship: from the outside to the inside, from appearance to substance, from guarded inhibitions to comfortable expositions.

The first male element is simple, yet profound. **Shame (boys don't cry)** refers to the most common reason men do not indulge in emotional dialogues. We all know what shame feels like — it's disturbingly painful. What we don't always realize is how destructive it can be. In relationships, for example, men often project their own performance shame onto their partner. They do so by criticizing her appearance, by requesting that she wear certain clothes, or by demanding that she wear her hair a certain way when they go out. In this kind of interaction, the man is trying to get rid of feelings of shame over his own sense of inadequacy by insisting that his partner shine, so that he can feel better about himself in her reflection. The woman in this situation feels controlled and evaluated. Worst of all, she ends up feeling ashamed about her own (bodily) imperfections. When the circle of projection is thus completed (she ends up feeling what he felt at the beginning of the interaction), a terrible fight ensues. She accuses him of being critical and controlling and he accuses her of being sensitive and defensive. Clearly, this type of fight can be avoided if, at the outset, rather than focusing on his partner's performance, the man has the self-knowledge and the facility to say something to the effect of "I felt inadequate at work today." In the absence of such self-knowledge, the fight can still be avoided if the woman, in her own self-interest, comes to the man's help. As we shall see throughout this book, in some respects we can all be our partner's therapist.

While breaking down the shame barrier helps all men to open up, most men have yet a deeper, even more troubling resistance to the language of feelings. This is the second male attribute, **Emotional Absence (I don't know what I feel).** Here, we are on a more complicated terrain where the usual psychological tools don't necessarily work. For example, the rather uninspiring question "How does that make you feel?" which many therapists (and I hate to admit, myself included) resort to in desperation or for lack of imagination, is particularly useless here. The typical male response to such a question is, "I think...," to which the therapist might say, "That's not a feeling."

Men's proclivity to live in their heads and to distance themselves from their feelings is an obvious liability in intimate relationships. But it can also be a subtle yet devastating problem in business situations. For example, one young investment banker was "sent" to therapy by his fiancée, who was concerned about his workaholic tendencies. When he came to see me he had already amassed eight million dollars. But within two years, he gambled it all away in risky investments. Because he was incapable of feeling any fear or anxiety when making business decisions, he couldn't calibrate the degree of risk involved. Remarkably, after losing everything, including his job and office, he was able to use his cell phone (from a bench in the park!) to raise new capital and to bounce back — until his next and final fall, at which point he also lost his fiancée.

As for relationships, whereas the shame barrier to communication can be broken relatively quickly, the problem of emotional absence does not yield itself to a quick fix. What to do when someone doesn't feel? Part of the solution is to look for feelings where they are, not where they are not; to nurture and welcome any feelings, even such unpleasant ones as anger or depression.

The other part of the solution is to learn to accept, even admire, the appearance of strength which comes with that dull male calmness, and to join men's emotional experience in their own domain. For example, in working with a business executive, rather than ask him about his feelings regarding the lack of intimacy in his marriage, I will start by inquiring into his strategy for his upcoming meeting with the company's CEO. From there we'll go into what's important about this meeting, why his career's so important to him, and what is life all about anyway. This will lead to a discussion of what's missing from his life, which invariably will uncover the quiet pains of his marriage.

So you can see that such words as "strategic thinking" and "negotiation tactics," which are practically aphrodisiac for some men, can be a pathway to words of intimacy. This may sound like a manipulation, but it's not. It's not, because I genuinely care about the patient's strategy for the meeting. Not that I am so interested in the business outcome of the meeting or even in the patient's career. What I am interested in is the patient's mind and how it works. And I don't mind starting with the intellectual part: if you can't beat the enemy, join it.

The third male attribute, **Masculine Insecurity (I'm tired of being on top)**, goes to the essence of what men secretly harbor beneath their rugged and guarded exterior. One patient, a driven, hard-nosed entrepreneur, put it this way: "Sometimes I just want to be flattened," by which he meant literally lie down and stop moving, and figuratively put down arms and withdraw from the business wars. But this was not merely an indication of exhaustion or a wish to quit the rat race. Rather, it represented a deep desire to abandon the active pursuit of bravado and to become the passive recipient of care. Consciously or unconsciously, these kinds of wishes — to be pursued rather than pursue, to be the object rather than the subject (of attention), to "be done to," rather than to do — are shared by all men. At the same time, such feelings pose a fundamental threat to men's sense of manliness. Therefore, men must overcompensate by searching for, and always seeking to assume, an ever more masculine stance.

This conflict plays a central role in the psychology of that most common of male afflictions, sexual impotence. On a conscious level, impotence is almost always about performance anxiety, which is why the more the person puts pressure on himself to be cured, the worse it gets. Unconsciously, however, the man's reluctance to be firm bespeaks his wish to escape the pressures of masculinity to a feminine place of softness.

Paradoxically, then, the treatment of impotence requires that the therapist ally himself with the uncooperative penis, rather than with the demanding patient. In doing so, the therapist invites the patient to experience in feelings and thoughts what his body is displaying in action (or inaction). The patient then might uncover such feelings as "I'm tired of having to be successful and provide for you all," "I wish I could have intimate friendships," "I wish I could stay home with the children," or "I wish *I* had a strong man to protect me."

Notwithstanding all the positive changes the women's movement created, it has left us profoundly confused about our gender identity. If the President groped a woman, we ask, was that a sexual assault or a "boys will be boys" type of indiscretion? Or is it a good idea for a woman to be aggressive on a date? Or should I be a successful provider or an available father?

Psychologically, these types of questions represent an attempt to integrate our old, rigid, yet safe, gender identifications with our new postfeminist freedoms. Theoretically we now know that there are no right or wrong answers to many of these questions. We tell ourselves that it all depends on what kind of man or woman we want to be. But many of us are still confused or conflicted precisely about that.

While the women's movement initially attempted to deny that

there were psychological differences between the sexes, it ultimately came to see that acknowledging differences was not the same as accepting inequality. Similarly, after its initial backlash to feminism, the men's movement now seems willing to concede that femininity is not the enemy. These days, I suspect, most reasonable people think that while sex differences exist, they can be bridged through better communication. Now while it's hard to argue with that notion, I'm suggesting we take it a step further: differences cannot only be bridged, they can be integrated. That is, men can learn to accept their own femininity despite the threat it poses for their masculinity. And they can do so without becoming "wimps." And women can, as they often do, play an important role in this integrative process. The good news, then, is that men don't have to choose between masculinity and femininity — they can have it all. And women don't have to choose between a wimp or a bully of a partner. The bad news, however, is that it takes quite a bit of work to achieve this kind of integration. Yet whether you consciously work on it or not, as we shall see throughout this book, men's attempts, failures, and successes at integration, and women's reactions to these, have a powerful effect on both genders — in the bedroom as well as in the boardroom.

Before the women's movement, one of the most common forms of marital discord was the psychological polarization of the traditional couple. This couple had an untenable division of labor in which the husband did the thinking, the wife did the feeling. He was calm and cold, she was emotional and hysterical; he enjoyed sports and action movies, she liked shopping and romantic comedies; he went out drinking with the guys and she played canasta with the girls. This split was untenable not only because it created conflict in everyday life, but also because the partners in this kind of marriage had little in common.

Today, while such relationships still abound, marital therapists see more and more couples struggling with the opposite dynamics. These couples are polarized along the same masculine-feminine dimension, but in reverse. The woman is an assertive, take-charge, action-oriented, bottom-line type, while the man is sensitive, supportive, receptive, and emotional. When these differences become polarized, this newer version of what I call *the masculine-feminine split* is also untenable: the wife complains that the husband is a passive, submissive doormat, and the husband feels that the wife is a control freak and a cold fish.

Clearly, the war between the sexes thrives on extremes, which, amazingly enough, are still easy to fall into. As we visit and revisit the conflict of masculine insecurity, we will see that the techniques used to resolve it almost always involve the integration of the masculine-feminine split *within each gender*. For example, in the case of the "aggressive" wife and the "submissive" husband, the more the wife complains that her husband is passive, weak, or unassertive, the more she continues to dominate him with her demands and criticisms. Unwittingly — and unconsciously — she actually reinforces the dynamics which she presumably wishes to change. What she might want to do instead is to work on facilitating or promoting her own latent or dormant passivity, receptivity, and sensitivity — her own "feminine" qualities. If she is then less directive or aggressive and more emotionally vulnerable, she leaves some room for the husband to step up to the plate. The same, of course, is true for the husband: if instead of whining that she is too bossy or insensitive — thereby subjugating himself even further — he undertakes to work on expressing his own denied, masculine aggression, he will in effect invite his wife to tone down her own assertiveness and raise the volume of her feminine sensitivities. Clearly, the same principle applies to the traditional couple, where the husband is hypermasculine, the wife, hyperfeminine.

Now, unfortunately, in both types of couples the masculine-feminine split is deeply fissured and highly self-perpetuating, which makes my integrative solution an easier-said-than-done proposition. But if it can be implemented in therapy, it can be implemented in life — and by using the same basic strategies.

The fourth male attribute, **Self-Involvement (see me, hear me, touch me, feel me)**, is a direct derivative or one possible outcome of the conflict of masculine insecurity. Merely knowing one is a man is not enough protection against one's own feminine desires — one has to also demonstrate it repeatedly to oneself. But even that's not enough: one also has to show it in Technicolor to the rest of the world.

Obviously, women too need to be seen, recognized, and admired. But whereas female narcissism often reflects our society's interest in physical appearance, beauty, and aesthetics, male narcissism is more about our obsession with strength, power, and achievement.

What greed is to capitalism, narcissism is to personal growth. Healthy, even excessive self-love is the psychic engine for courage and achievement. In its expansiveness and eagerness to please, it even creates generosity. But narcissism has a bad name for a reason. One acquaintance, a highly successful surgeon, casually told me in front of his wife and teenage children, "In the past fifteen years I've cared about nothing except my career, not even my wife and children." It is this kind of brutal honesty that leads us to assume that the main problem with the self-centered narcissist is his lack of regard for others. But interestingly, this kind of man always ends up hurting himself. We all know someone like that: a man in his fifties or sixties who is confronted by, or trying to avoid confronting, the tragic sense that after devoting his life to being the best provider to his family, he now feels estranged from his wife and alienated from his children.

Sometimes, the irony of the narcissistic defeat does not afford the person any success. One patient was a talented actor who, over the years, performed in several Off-Broadway shows. He always received excellent reviews and was therefore completely mystified as to why he could never quite make it in a big way. To me, it was fairly obvious. In his interactions with producers, directors, and other actors he had always put work or career considerations ahead of all and any social concerns. The only thing that mattered to him was being on center stage — literally. Therefore, while everybody recognized his talent, nobody wanted to work with him a second time.

The Greek figure of Icarus defied his father's admonition by flying too close to the sun. His wax wings melted and he fell into the sea. In his quest to feel good about himself, the daring, oblivious, self-centered man sets out to defy reality. His eventual fall, therefore, marks the all-important psychological meeting place of narcissism and masochism. For many men the accumulation of wealth and its outward manifestations are sufficient evidence of self-value. But others seek to enhance their self-esteem by testing the limits of their most fragile asset — the human body. Such men may engage in sexual activities with great youthful exuberance, not for purposes of intimacy, but as a means of conquering the fear of aging and decay. So much like man's primordial fantasy of flying, the male sexual pursuit can serve to deny our limitations and to bolster our illusion of immortality.

Notwithstanding its lofty existential origins, this dynamic presents many practical problems. For starters, denying our mortality only brings it closer to us. This is all too apparent in the tendency of young men to feel invincible and to engage in such risky behaviors as smoking, fighting, and driving under the influence. The "unsinkable" Titanic is another example of the possible outcome of this type of male arrogance. In the sexual realm, when an older man has an affair with a young woman in order to borrow her youthfulness, chances are he ends up feeling like a "dirty old man."

Resolving conflicts arising from men's self-involvement is critical to having successful relationships with men — at the workplace or in the love space. In trying to do so, I believe, much can be learned from the therapist who complements his empathic acceptance of the self-involved man with a confrontation of his grandiose defenses. Loving someone for who he is and admiring his real achievements mandate that we also reject and attack his exaggerated sense of self-importance. Of course, how to walk such a line is the part-art, part-science which I hope to impart to you, the reader.

The fifth male element, **Aggression (I'll show you who's boss)** is also a natural outcome of the conflict of masculine insecurity.

As any marital therapist knows, one of the most common presenting marital problems is the dynamic of the angry, critical, or explosive husband with the wounded, tearful, and defeated wife. In this dynamic, the man's aggression serves to (1) intimidate the "opponent" and catch her off guard, (2) violate her psychic, if not physical, space in order to penetrate and occupy it, and (3) create a wall of bitterness which will psychologically separate him from her. In all three tactics we can clearly see traces of man's fear of losing himself in a woman, a powerful fear which is also an equally powerful wish. As I have said, this conflict, between the wish to be (with) a woman and the fear of losing one's masculine identity is at the heart of the conflict of masculine insecurity.

As with masculine insecurity, the key to coping with male aggression is balance. We must respect emphatic if insensitive male assertion and respond in kind, but reject sadistic, though remorseful, male destructiveness. How to tell the difference between the two is a problem for many women. Some are so used to aggression that they collude with each sequence of abuse-remorse-good behavior-abuse-remorse-good behavior as if it's not going to happen more than twice. Others are so fearful of any sign of male aggression that they cannot see the strength and protection it may one day offer them.

One patient came to see me for a consultation about his explosive anger at his wife. Among other things, he told me that he had had temper tantrums as a child and had always been impatient. At the end of the second session, on his way out, he asked, "So does this help?" In responding, I first said, somewhat defensively, "I don't know, you tell me." But then, smiling warmly (because I liked him), I added, "Let me tell you what I really think. I think what you are saying is, 'This doesn't help,' but I think that's just you throwing a tantrum. You really are impatient." I thus met his aggression with mine, which preempted him from devaluing me as a "softy." But at the same time, the warmth and caring in my tone disarmed him of his need to protect himself with a counterattack. In an intimate relationship, the same applies: the man needs to feel free to dispatch some aggression without fearing that his partner will be destroyed. His partner, therefore, must respond with her own aggression so as to set the limits of what's acceptable. But literally at the same time, she must also try to disarm him with genuine care and affection.

When men are fundamentally and completely incapable of expressing aggression toward others, they turn on themselves. This is what the sixth male attribute, **Self-Destructiveness (I'm such a loser),** is all about. One patient, a warm and charming young ophthalmologist, started therapy because he was unable to form a lasting intimate relationship good enough for marriage. While he was professionally successful, he felt extremely unhappy about his inability to commit to a woman. After a few weeks of therapy, he was feeling so frustrated with his lack of progress that his frustration and helplessness began to "contaminate" our relationship. Just then, as I was beginning to feel frustrated and helpless myself, the patient had a dream in which I was an insecure, "weak" tour guide with an eye problem. And he, the patient, was one of the tourists in my group and was called upon to treat me.

In my mind, the fact that I "caught" his helplessness and became "weakened," suggested that this was precisely the unconscious intention of his frustration. If this makes no sense, think of the power an unhappy child has over his parent's happiness — self-destructiveness is a way of getting back at the other by depriving oneself. If I have a vision problem, how will I guide my patient?

Another way to look at it is that the patient didn't feel "seen" by me, and that his frustration and helplessness were an attempt to correct my vision. As it turned out, this patient felt that he was living the life inscribed for him by his father, and that the only way to say no to him (or to be seen as his own person) was to become "a loser," at least in the sense of not following his father's footsteps into marriage. Viewed in that light, frustrating and destroying me — the presumed therapeutic representative of the marriage agenda — was only a logical if irrational step. And this is the essence of self-destructiveness. We'd rather curse the darkness than light one candle. That will show them.

This powerful dynamic is often at the center of the psychology of such self-destructive conditions as addictive and compulsive syndromes, professional failure, accident proneness, and high-risk, reckless behavior. But it is also to be found in less dramatic problems such as making poor financial decisions, being in a dead-end job, arriving late for job interviews, bouncing checks, speaking without thinking, lying and getting caught, not paying attention, burning the toast, burning the kitchen towel — and, as anyone who has ever dealt with men knows, the list goes on and on.

In their zeal to help self-destructive men, many therapists (like well-intended parents and spouses) learn the hard way how the road to hell is paved with good intentions. Depending on the circumstances, trying to save someone from the brink of self-destruction can be counterproductive and painful. Even the small ways in which men experience themselves as losers are frustrating. The trick is to treat it as a form of aggression against you, which can leave you in an impossible situation. Do you hang in there with a policy of constructive engagement, or do you walk away? Whatever you do, do not assume responsibility for his behavior. This is true if you are a therapist, a girlfriend, or a spouse: if you are a backseat driver, your man will never learn to drive safely.

Finally, if men were truly mute they would communicate through sex. Indeed, for most men, everything is about sex, except sex, which often enough is about shame, emotional absence, masculine insecurity, self-involvement, aggression, and self-destructiveness. **Sexual Acting-Out (I want sex now)**, the seventh male attribute, presents a dramatic condensation and a summary of all the previous elements. As you can see, I ended up with male sexuality, just where I started in my original seminar. The reason is simple. The sexual arena is where men naturally play out emotional conflicts which, ultimately, are not about sex after all.

One startling example: a patient who was emotionally distant but very kind to his girlfriend could be aroused only by fantasies of rape — the absent emotion of rage was only present in his sexual fantasies. Thus, while the content of men's sexual fantasies may suggest a variety of strong feelings, most of what they consciously experience when aroused is sexual desire.

The good news is that the male sexual language is not entirely foreign. It is more like a dialect, but one which can and should be deciphered by both women and men. One patient came to therapy because he would lose his erection when he was about to penetrate his wife. He had no trouble in any other sexual situation or fantasy. In one of the first sessions he presented a dream in which I, as his therapist, prescribed that he insert a banana in his rectum. When he carried out my prescription, the banana penetrated him deeply and came out on the other side, through his penis, which then became hardened and strong. The patient, who had no conscious sexual attraction to men, was worried that the dream could represent a homosexual wish. That was a definite possibility, but I took it to mean that what he needed in order to function as a man was a soft yet powerful dose of masculinity.

Ultimately, only he could inject himself with such a serum. But others, primarily his therapist, could certainly facilitate his growth as a man. In this case, as in so many others, the patient's wife played an important therapeutic role. In her own feminine way, she helped her husband to express his feelings — or, in other words, to talk more like a woman but to act more like a man. And that is the royal road to a man's heart.

A Family of Men

As I have said before, the concepts presented in this book are consistent with current theory and research in the field of clinical psychology. At the same time, I do not believe that it is possible to be fully objective in describing or analyzing human behavior: one's own subjective psychology is always in the way. Indeed, in their book *Faces in a Cloud: Intersubjectivity in Personality Theory*, Stolorow and Atwood show how the psychological theories of such great thinkers as Freud, Jung, Rogers, and Winnicott reflect their own life experiences and psychological makeup.

This can lead to a rather depressive intellectual position: if we can't make objective observations about our psychological universe, what's the point of observing? But before you get depressed, consider an alternative position, based on the paradox that the more we acknowledge our subjectivity, the more we approach objectivity. This may seem rather philosophical but in fact it's a highly practical matter. When you go out on a date, how do you know if the man sitting across from you is x (assuming x is a bad thing on your check list), unless you know you are not too picky? Or how do you know whether to confront your friend about an insulting comment if you don't know whether or not you are an overly sensitive person?

So, in mentally gathering the data for this book, I've had to ask myself about my own masculine insecurity and the extent to which it biases my observations. To start with, I grew up in a family of men. As the youngest of three boys, I came into a world with no shortages of masculine aggression. My brothers were five and ten years older, and they were rather fierce, or at least that's how they seemed from my perspective. There was also some objective evidence, however. For example, the plywood in the hallway door, which finally replaced the glass pane after it broke one too many times. And further, perhaps more inferential evidence: both of my brothers grew up to be very successful attorneys, one a litigator, the other, a corporate lawyer.

My father, a successful businessman, was not as externally aggressive, but he too was pretty tough. Like many men, he spoke little about his emotions. A few years ago, he had a massive heart attack, at home. As my mother tells the story, all he said was, "I'm not feeling well," which was enough for her to immediately call an ambulance. It was thus my mother's interpretation of his minimalism that saved his life.

Now add to this mix the culture and the times in which my family lived while I was growing up. This was in the early history of the Jewish state, Israel, where masculine aggression was a necessary, indeed an idealized ingredient for survival. Imagine this: when the 1967 Arab-Israeli war broke, and warning sirens filled the air of Jerusalem, my fourth-grade teacher sent me home with another ten-year-old, unaccompanied by an adult. Our walk home was suddenly punctuated by machine-gun noises, and before we made it home artillery shells started falling in the area. Now the truly strange thing is that I don't remember feeling scared. I think by that age I was already conditioned to rid myself of an emotion as useless as fear.

The imprints of one's family, I believe, cannot be separated from the influences of culture (or of genetics, for that matter). When I was in graduate school, my mother once said, "Now that you are becoming a psychologist, you should analyze our family." Actually, this is what she meant to say but she made a slip of the tongue, and instead of saying *mishpacha* — Hebrew for "family" — she said *milchama* — the Hebrew word for "war." Now I don't think that this slip reflected her feeling that there was war in our home — we were a very close family with no more conflict than many other families — but rather, that the culture of the family, like that of the country, was a warring one. To summarize, my home and country were somewhat hypermasculine.

My mother, the only female in the family, had no choice but to adjust to this environment. In some ways, in order to stay afloat with the "boys," she adjusted only too well. While she remained warm and loving at heart, she became quite tough herself, at least superficially. She certainly held her own ground in loud political arguments.

Now if you were the mother or the father or even one of the two firstborn sons in a family like that, wouldn't you want the third child to be a girl? I would. And so did my parents, and I suspect my brothers too — although by the time I was born, the latter two were probably already too tough to verbalize or even to entertain such a thought. But in physical defiance of all such wishes and expectations, I came home from the hospital as yet another baby boy, another potential warrior.

Potential, but not actual. As kids often do, I reflexively complied with the family's expectation, at least in some respects. While I was not an effeminate child, and not even overtly feminine, I was certainly not as aggressive as my brothers. Rather, I was sensitive and introspective. I was emotionally more gentle, if not fragile, and at least on the surface, I behaved like a good little boy (girl?). I can still summon up the physical sensation of tears slowly rolling down my cheeks, not to mention the bitter feelings of shame over those tears, when my brothers would tease me. And I can hear my mother's voice, in trying to help me, offering me the same good but useless advice I now give my own children when they are teased on the playground, "Just ignore them!"

So this was one of my conflicts as a child: on the one hand I wanted to preserve in myself and bring to my family a level of emotional vulnerability and expressivity. On the other hand, I was not going to give up on the kind of power and strength which I perceived my brothers to possess. Now, does this sound familiar? Is it not an instance, perhaps the unconscious origins, of my "clinical" ideas about the conflict of masculine insecurity in which men struggle to both express and repress their feminine desires?

Like many other men, my own struggle with this conflict over the years was not always successful or pretty. As a teenager, for example, I unconsciously sought to become emotionally vulnerable not only to preserve a world of feelings but also as a means of "saying uncle," thereby getting my parents or some other powers to save me. I thus "stooped to conquer." At other times I sought to express aggression even more covertly, by using the weapons of observation and analysis in order to "diagnose" what I arrogantly believed was others' inferiority. Was this the unconscious reason I sought to become a psychologist rather than, say, a lawyer? I would hope this was only a small part of a bigger, more appealing picture: being a psychologist was going to provide me with a path, or an identity, where I could better integrate my masculine and feminine identifications. And happily, it did. Yet like all men, I continue to work on resolving this conflict in many areas of my life — with varying degrees of success.

All this is not intended as an analysis of my childhood or family dynamics. There are in fact other, deeper and more complex analyses to be done. But this conflict was fundamental, its simplicity notwithstanding. And it was therefore reflected all through my work as a psychologist, often completely unconsciously.

At the beginning of my career, while completing my doctoral dissertation, I took a job as a police psychologist with the New York City Police Department. I didn't particularly like the idea of working in a paramilitary setting, but it was the only halfway decent job I could find without a degree and license. Nonetheless, I found myself totally fascinated by the defensive nature and emotional cost of the hypermasculinity in that organization — the largest employer of psychologists in the United States (!).

For example, one of the most dreaded situations for the psychologists at NYPD was a police officer seeking help for suicidal feelings. This was difficult not so much because someone was suicidal, but because the psychologist had to make a decision about removing the officer's firearm. At that time, and I suspect it is still the case today, removing an officer's gun and reassigning him to a desk job was likely to induce in him severe feelings of inadequacy. In addition, since there was no way to hide the absence of a gun from other officers in the precinct, its removal was tantamount to public castration and would evoke unbearable feelings of shame. Thus, the psychologist's intervention could potentially push the officer further toward suicide! At the same time, you obviously could not permit a suicidal individual to have such easy access to a weapon. The worst part of this dilemma was that many police officers had their own, licensed firearms at home, over which the department had no authority. So while the department psychologist may have had to remove the officer's assigned gun, the officer might still have easy access to self-destruction.

This dilemma, which stemmed from the emotional value and symbolism of the firearm, was thus a practical, life-or-death consequence of hypermasculinity. A less practical but even more perplexing example was sometimes evident in one of the psychological tests that police candidates had to take before they were deemed suitable to be cops. As part of the rather comprehensive screening process, candidates at some point were required to draw a person on a blank piece of paper. This kind of "projective" test assumes that since it imposes no other instructions or guidelines, the person taking the test projects his own thoughts, concerns, or problems into his creation — much as an artist does. And while it is of questionable scientific reliability, when used in conjunction with other, more "objective" tests (which was the case at NYPD), this type of test can be very useful.

Now many of the police candidates, young men in their early twenties, were under the impression that in this test they should draw a figure of a strong, well-built man, perhaps as a way of demonstrating their own strength. But since most of them were not such great artists, they had to work hard on shaping and emphasizing their man's muscles, with results that were sometimes as comical as they were revealing. In their effort to draw a well-developed upper body some candidates would go overboard, producing a figure of a man with a huge, well-carved, breast-like chest, a narrow waistline, and thus an overall strangely androgynous look.

This illustrates an idea which I will return to later in the book when discussing the *masculine-feminine split,* that is, that opposites contain each other. In this case, when a man is so driven to deny his internal vulnerability that he assumes an extreme or unrealistic position of masculine strength, he ends up precisely in the place he was desperately trying to avoid. On a bigger scale, this dynamic is often seen in alcoholism, gambling, reckless driving, and other male behaviors; to prove their toughness, men go to war, where they die. Women, in the meantime, are the tough survivors. In a way, then, opposites not only contain each other, they also produce each other. In my family, for example, it was the hypermasculinity of my brothers that produced my femininity.

In my dissertation research project I was trying to combine my disparate passions for clinical and organizational psychology. Would it be oversimplifying (and politically incorrect) to suggest that the former, an interest in working with people, was more feminine, while the latter, a desire to work with business organizations, was more masculine? I'm not sure, but regardless, even as

I was conducting empirical scientific research, I continued to see the ghosts of masculine and feminine dimensions everywhere. For example, as my dissertation was about the personal development of people in positions of leadership, I had to review the published research specifically on what makes for effective leadership — corporate, political, or what have you. I found that well-known organizational psychologists had analyzed many different factors and, using statistical and conceptual tools, categorized them into two elements, which then received the cryptic academic names of "Initiating Structure" and "Consideration." Now guess what leadership styles were correlated to these "core factors" over the years? Here's a partial list: for Initiating Structure: "task-oriented," "production-oriented," "goal emphasizing," "high performance," "self-oriented," "directive," "autocratic," and "closed." And for Consideration: "relations-oriented," "employee-oriented," "interaction facilitative," "supportive," "interaction-oriented," "consultative," "democratic," and "open."

In my own research — with no clue at the time as to my unconscious motivation — I was trying to determine what kind of personality development would predispose a leader to use both leadership styles or to alternate between the two depending on the situation. In other words, while I was, empirically speaking, following a legitimate avenue of inquiry, unconsciously I was looking to integrate.... Well, I think you know how this sentence ends.

After graduate school, while building my clinical psychology practice, I also worked as an organizational or management consultant. In that capacity I provided consulting and training services in the area of negotiation skills to many business executives. Now in negotiations, depending on the nature of the business relationship between the two parties, one can employ more or less cooperative bargaining tactics. For example, if you are selling your car and you are never going to see the buyer again, you may not volunteer to him that you're selling the car because it's costing you $3,000 a year in maintenance. But in most business negotiations (e.g., when your company is negotiating the fees and terms of a contract with an advertising agency or with a computer vendor), there is a long-term relationship to consider. When this is the case, the parties need to employ more cooperative, "win/win" negotiation tactics — withholding information from the other side, for example, could come back to haunt you. But try to sell this to aggressive business executives attending a negotiation training session! While intellectually they may agree with you, when it comes to an actual negotiation situation they'd much rather surprise, attack, argue with, or strong-arm their "opponent" than apply "softer," relationship-building, dare I say "feminine," negotiation tactics. Listening to the other party's business concerns? Working on developing common ground? Offering free advice? Conceding a minor point to facilitate forward movement? For most of these executives — the vast majority of whom were men — these were boring, mildly disdainful ideas. As for me, once again I would like to think that there is room in the world for both competition and cooperation.

Now is this masculine-feminine dimension all in my head, or is it out there in so-called objective reality and I'm just observing it? I think it's both, and I hope that in recognizing my own subjectivity this book is approaching objectivity. But as you read on, you will have to make your own judgment.

In terms of my clinical practice, it goes without saying that my own history and psychological biases color the ways I perceive and interact with my patients. In terms of gender, the therapist's is always a factor in the development of the patient-therapist dynamics. Am I a different therapist with a man than with a woman? I would say yes, to an extent. Does this limit the usefulness of the advice I might offer female readers about their interactions with men? Once again, to an extent it does. Unless, of course, my advice is that women learn from my very masculinity and act more like a man in their relationships with men. Which, in a sense, *is* my advice, at least to some women. Remember? I am advocating...integration, and not just for men.

Psychologically, not to mention physically, while we are not always conscious of being a man (or a woman), it is not something we ever stop being. In thinking about that recently, I noticed that the four or five books I tend to recommend to my male patients — books ranging from Scott Peck's *The Road Less Traveled* to Tolstoy's *The Death of Ivan Ilyich,* were all written by men. I was never conscious of this before, but now I can see that these books have a "masculine" bent: their narrative is penetrating, challenging, and intellectualized. Compare this to a comment I once made to a female patient (yes, I do see a good number of women in my practice, so I am not all that out of touch with the psychology of women). The patient, a young but successful writer, was a mesmerizing storyteller. But in the sessions, as in life, she used her intellectual gifts to "live in her head" and to avoid intimate relationships. So by way of making that point to her, I said, "I sometimes feel in the sessions with you that I am lost in a Virginia Woolf novel." Here, not only was I unconsciously choosing a female writer as the reference, I was also unwittingly expressing my own fear as a man — the fear of being lost in the mind, if not the body, of a woman.

But while gender is a given, the subjectivity of the therapist does not start or end there. Whereas most people think that therapists are not supposed to have emotional reactions to their patients, the truth is almost the opposite — good therapists pay attention to, and use, their own emotional reactions to the patient as a therapeutic instrument. If I feel angry with a patient who tells me that he doesn't really "believe" in therapy and that he is only doing it because of his wife, then my feelings of anger are not really about me. Rather, they are induced by the patient, and I can use them to learn something about his way of relating to others. But to be able to do so, I must know (1) that I am angry, and (2) that I am not angry because of my own doubts about therapy. In other words, it is only when we know who we are that we can be receptive to knowing another person.

I've said that men are difficult. But this is not to say that women are not difficult in their own ways. It is also not to say that men are jerks, dicks, or perverts as some women believe. My own feeling is that each of the seven challenges of masculine insecurity is a challenge worthy of understanding, tackling, and...loving.

I often see this in couples who come for marital or couple therapy. At the start, it looks as though the man is the bad guy: he doesn't communicate, he is angry and critical, he is distant, he is childish, he is irresponsible, he has a sexual problem, he spends all his time in the office, he drinks, he is having an affair, he is on cocaine, and so on and so forth. And yes, he is often skeptical about psychotherapy. The woman, on the other hand, appears to be open to criticism, willing to take responsibility, eager to communicate, and reasonable in her wants and wishes.

But soon enough a different picture emerges: the male acting-out is nothing but a cover for a sensitive, searching soul, while the cooperative, sensible female agenda is a thin veneer under which lies a...but that's for a book about women.

Shame

...boys don't cry

When my son was in first grade, I made the courageous decision to volunteer to be his Little League T-ball coach. It was courageous because, not growing up with baseball in my blood, I hardly had a working knowledge of the game, let alone the right stuff for coaching it. But I figured it was just first-graders — I could handle it. And with the exception of some embarrassing moments — such as when my son's best friend asked me during a game, "Alon, why should I listen to you?" to which I answered, "Because I am the coach!" — I handled it okay.

The truth is, I really wanted to coach soccer, a game I grew up with, was good at, and loved. But in first grade my son was not into soccer, so I was deprived of the "opportunity" to project on him my unfulfilled dreams of being a soccer pro. Then came second grade. My son had a change of heart and became a soccer fanatic. Naturally I was elated and excited about the prospect of coaching his team. Little did I know that coaching soccer would be even more challenging — requiring perhaps a different kind of courage — than coaching T-ball.

It is truly amazing to see how competitive second-graders can be — how much they care about winning and losing in sports. It is even more amazing to see their parents on the sidelines — *they* are crazy. And, of course, the parent coach is potentially the craziest of all. As for me — as much as I told my team that having fun and learning skills is more important than winning, privately,

I desperately wanted my son's team to win. This barely articulated desire was driven home to me one time when, because of a minor medical problem, my son couldn't play. In that game, my coaching style was much more relaxed. My son perceptively observed from the sidelines, "You were not as bossy."

There is nothing wrong with being emotionally invested in competitive sports. But in one of my son's games, I did something which really disturbed me. At that particular game my team was losing badly, and my son, who also happened to be tired and hungry, started crying. And there I was, the psychologist who advocates vulnerability for men, furious that my son was crying. And out of my mouth came the automatic "Stop crying," and the shaming, cruel addition of "Don't you see you are the only boy who's crying?" I was so angry and frustrated that, even though I immediately knew I had wronged my child, I was unable to comprehend what I did until much later.

In my mind, crying was not an appropriate or mature reaction to losing in soccer, so I felt ashamed of my son's tears. And because he "made me" feel shame, I unconsciously returned the favor, and shamed him. Of course, he did not "make me" feel anything — he was just crying. And regardless, if crying when losing is not okay, how could I blame my son for merely mirroring my own competitiveness and emotional sensitivity?

As soon as I understood what I had done, the original feeling which I was trying to rid myself of, shame, came back to consciousness — with a vengeance. But this time I felt ashamed of my own behavior, and rightly so. Yet by virtue of my understanding, I couldn't once again simply get rid of my shame by dumping it on someone else. So what's a man to do? Talk to my child about it? Wouldn't that add insult to injury, burdening him with my psychological analysis in order to alleviate my guilt? Talk to my fellow coaches about it? Wouldn't they think I was crazy? After all, they do pretty much the same thing with their sons and don't seem to feel bad about it. Or perhaps talk to my wife about it so that she could make me feel even worse about how insensitive I was to our child?

Eventually, I apologized to my son for my behavior, and I confessed the entire episode to a friend, who is also a colleague — he was very understanding. And I suppose I am confessing it here as well. But while confession liberates, I can hardly claim that I talk regularly to others, even close others, about my feelings. In that respect, at least, I am hardly an atypical man.

Of course, in psychotherapy one is expected to talk about one's feelings. But even with that expectation or permission, many men find it uncomfortable. Left to their own devices, men would much rather discuss, in descending degrees of comfort, sports, cars, sound systems, information systems, politics, the stock market, work, children, girlfriends, women's bodies, and gossip about friends and neighbors. And yes, they also talk about themselves, but mostly as it relates to their external performance on some task — from making the big sale to fixing the garage door.

But while a man may not talk about his emotional self, if you listen closely, you will find indirect evidence for its existence in everything he says — or doesn't say. You will find it in a husband's reaction or lack of reaction when he comes home to a tearful, overwhelmed wife who says, "I can't take it anymore, my boss was so mean to me again."

"You've only been there two weeks, honey," he might respond, and then add with a slight, hardly detectable tone of annoyance, "You have to give it more time." Now as soon as he says this — even before the wife walks away wounded or gives him the silent treatment or retorts with anger, "Why can't you be more supportive?" — he knows that he screwed up. All she wants is to be heard, comforted, and reassured. So why can't he just do that? Why does he have to correct her thinking rather than simply empathize with her situation and tears?

In *Men Are from Mars, Women Are from Venus*, John Gray explains that when women talk about painful feelings or problems, men take it personally and feel that they must do something to fix the problem. And if they can't fix it, says Gray, they become frustrated. This is certainly true about our hypothetical — yet all too familiar — man above. But what Gray doesn't fully explain is the nature of this frustration. In my experience, it is not just that "Martians" are "fixers," who can't tolerate unsolved problems. Rather, their rush to solution-driven, action-oriented advice is also an instantaneous, unconscious maneuver to cover up and minimize feelings of shame.

It is therefore not true that men are incapable of empathizing with or listening to a woman's pain. However, to do so requires that they allow themselves to feel what the woman feels — hurt, exposed, and vulnerable. "Well, no thanks," they say to themselves. And they say it so quickly, so automatically, that even they don't hear themselves say it. But somewhere in the back of their minds, they know they are avoiding feeling something — something uncomfortably akin to being naked in public.

This internal dialogue is the first suspect when a man speaks (or doesn't) in ways which make no sense. It's a safe bet when men fail to volunteer information or to complete sentences or when they say things subtly or oddly out of context that they are battling with shame.

So when a young money manager having dinner with his girlfriend mentions casually but out of nowhere, "I sold some stocks today," his longer, internal dialogue is, "I'd like to say, 'I feel awful about myself because I sold low and lost a lot of money,' but if I just say, 'I sold stocks,' maybe she'll ask why and I could still say what I feel, or better yet, maybe she won't ask, in which case I won't have to say anything." This thought process often takes place without words and within a fraction of a conscious second. And naturally, unless the girlfriend is particularly attuned or sensitive, all she hears is something slightly odd or out of context, but mostly factual, brief, and boring. "Why is he telling me this?" she might ask herself and miss an opportunity for a deeper, more intimate moment.

Similarly, if a man says, "I had a performance evaluation at work today," rather than "I had a great performance evaluation at work today," his wife should hypothesize that this was not a good evaluation and that her husband is feeling scared, vulnerable, or worried and is shaming himself into part silence. And more often than not, an unelaborated and vaguely suspicious statement like "I have an appointment" is not an indication of a secret affair, but rather of a shame-producing activity, which may or may not be an actual secret.

Shortly after starting therapy with me, one of my patients began to date a woman whom he perceived as more attractive and successful than himself. He was too ashamed to tell her he was seeing a therapist, which for a while posed no particular logistical problems. "I had an appointment," "I had lunch with a friend," and "I took a walk in Central Park" were initially easy enough answers to incidental questions about his whereabouts. But as the relationship got serious and their social lives and schedules became more interdependent, half-truths and simple lies had to be supplanted by ever more innovative scenarios.

All the while, the patient and I talked about this in therapy. We spoke about his shame, and the likelihood — based on her personality and most women's reactions to the idea of "counseling" — that she would be understanding and accepting. Yet, week after week he planned but failed to confront her with the news. Finally, after a year and a half, he couldn't continue with the lies. So even though he felt therapy was critical to the success of the relationship, he abruptly ended the therapy. It was one of the most perplexing and frustrating "terminations" I've experienced.

Amazingly, in all these examples men are motivated by the emotion of shame to avoid feeling further emotional pain, be it more shame, fear, rejection, or inadequacy. As if shame is not just as painful as those other feelings! This strange technique men learn, and learn well, very early in life. They learn it in their boyhood relationships not only with people, but also with objects and concepts. Take their relationship with Barbie dolls. At age four or five a boy is quite likely to play Barbies with his sister, but a year or two later, even if he still plays with them, he would seize every opportunity to announce to the world, "I hate Barbies." Or take their boyhood relationship with clothes. One morning in school a six- or a seven-year-old might be horrified to find out that he is the only boy in class wearing a button-down shirt — "Why did you give me a handsome shirt?" he may wail at his mother at pickup time. Or perhaps most significantly, think about their early relationship with their own tears. A first- or second-grader may feel so bad about crying that he is likely to ask someone to cover for him — "Please don't tell I cried," he might ask his older brother after a fight.

When men feel shame they try to minimize it by not communicating (silence), by communicating the opposite (lying), or by communicating indirectly (evasion). But it is not only that shame is too painful an emotion for them. Rather, shame is also a signal that other troubling feelings are lurking just under the surface. It thus serves as a deterrent and a reminder to not even think about those other feelings.

Now those other feelings do not include all painful emotions. For example, it is apparently okay for men to fall in love, even into unrequited love — or to fall in rage, for that matter. But such feelings, by their very nature, have the potential to motivate men to *do* something: to pursue someone and hopefully to come out on top or to gain some concrete result. The more problematic feelings for them are those which render them passively wounded and vulnerable.

So, if we are to enter into an intimate exchange with men, we must first penetrate through the thick layer of shame which shuts them down. This is relatively easy when the man is conscious of feeling ashamed and is purposely trying to make himself feel better. For one thing, in this kind of situation men are likely to confess. For example, one patient felt so bad about the fact that his first sexual experience (as a teenager) was with a cousin, that fifteen years later he felt compelled to "confess" this to his fiancée on the eve of their wedding. Another man was delighted when, on their second time out, his very attractive date took the initiative and started kissing him. But motivated by the desire to rid himself of anticipated feelings of shame, he stopped in mid-kiss and said, "I have to tell you I once had a sexually transmitted disease, gonorrhea." The fact that this disease was treated and cured years earlier did not stop him from confessing.

Men's compulsion to confess is one of several simple ways they try to cope with shame. Another common device is the use of sarcastic, self-deprecating humor, as evident in the work of many stand-up comics. "I guess I'm not Prince Charming myself" is a statement which benignly disguises the subtext "I wish I didn't feel so ashamed of who I am." Postponing and avoiding doing things is another mechanism. One patient, a hard-working man who had always provided for his family, was laid off through no fault of his own. Nonetheless, he was so ashamed of receiving unemployment that he repeatedly postponed applying for it. Finally, he completely forgot about it until it was too late — which cost his family a significant amount of money.

In his book *Shame,* psychiatrist Michael Lewis explains why these types of behaviors help to reduce or deny shame. In forgetting, Lewis explains, we shift the focus of attention from the shame-producing situation to something else. In confessing or laughing at ourselves, he says, it's as if we are looking at ourselves from an outside perspective. "This other person did it," we seem to be saying, distancing ourselves from the shame-inducing experience.

Now when shame is experienced consciously, as in most of the examples above, if we can find a way to talk about it our work is nearly done. The trickier problem is that many times men are not at all conscious of their shame. While women are often capable of articulating feelings of embarrassment, shame, and low self-esteem, men are more likely to deny or repress such feelings all together. For some men the emotion of shame is so painful that they simply won't tolerate it. Well, what's wrong with that, you might wonder. Isn't this a case of ignorance being bliss? In fact, shouldn't women actually learn and adopt this behavior from men?

Maybe so, except that there is always a cost for ignorance. In this case, the hidden cost is first paid by others — often women — then transformed into another currency and passed back to where it belongs. Let me explain.

In the words of social psychologists, while women tend to attribute their success at a task to others but their failure to themselves, men do the reverse: they take credit for their success but blame others for their failure. Or in my own words: in order to rid themselves of feelings of shame, men project their own inadequacies onto others. And in dating situations as well as in intimate relationships, these others are most likely to be unsuspecting women.

Dating and Relationships: The Checklist

A woman friend put it this way: "All men think they are Adonis. Bald, fat, short, or skinny, they always think they are hot — that's why they are always ready to have sex." From a woman's point of view this theory makes sense. It may also appear to be true to the outside observer of many male-female interactions. But observing the male side of such interactions from the inside-out perspective of the therapeutic setting turns the theory upside down.

Yes, as any sensitive single woman on the dating circuit might suspect, behind closed doors men take out their checklist and debate the merits, or more likely the shortcomings, of the candidate. In my experience, men's typical mental checklists consist of such positives as pretty, intelligent, thin, sophisticated, warm, assertive, sensual, funny, and stimulating, and of such negatives as plain, stupid, heavy, naive, cold, insecure, inhibited, quiet, and boring.

Usually, most women get some positive marks, but at least in therapy, the men evaluating them focus on and obsess about the negative attributes: "She is pretty and she is a lawyer, so she must be bright. But she didn't really say anything smart. She is not interested in politics or in constitutional law, which is what I'm interested in. Come to think of it, I don't think she has any intellectual interests. She likes hiking! Maybe she is really stupid. What do you think?"

To some extent, this torturous evaluative process is to be expected in a dating situation in which both men and women nervously try to figure out, "Is this the right person for me?" Yet with the therapeutic microscope applied, a deeper, more focused picture of it may emerge.

One patient, a sweet, handsome, and eager-to-please medical student, was also blessed with considerable intellectual, musical, and culinary gifts. His career was promising, he had a lot of energy, and he loved Nietzsche, Kafka, and Mozart. He also loved women, or so he said, but had been unable to engage in long-term relationships with them. As he was so eligible, there was no shortage of candidates. But typically, he would date someone for two to six weeks, at the end of which he would lose interest and break it up.

After some time in therapy, this patient and I were able to observe his dating pattern with an absurd degree of predictability. In phase one (weeks 1–2) he would collect data for his checklist. In phase two (weeks 3–4) he would analyze the data, and in phase three (weeks 5–6) he would guiltily plot how to break up the relationship without hurting the woman's feelings.

But the most interesting part would come at phase four — the postmortem. Here, after each breakup, he and I would collect and analyze his data. He broke up one relationship, we observed, because the woman was too "naive." "She was too easily influenced by her friends, and she had this admiring relationship with her boss." Another relationship he discontinued because the woman was "almost too sweet." She loved animals, she loved nature, and she was just not sophisticated enough. A third woman was "too enthusiastic about folk music and didn't appreciate rock and roll, let alone classical music." And a fourth was "too easily swept away by Hallmark cards and the 'spirit' of the holidays."

Clearly, these women, at least in my patient's mind, had something in common, something which never failed to bother my patient. While I was not sure how to define it — sweetness, simplicity, innocence, or naïveté — it didn't strike me as something that would bother most people. Why did it bother my patient so? In thinking about it, I tried to listen to my own experience with the patient.

In our sessions he would often rail about the bureaucracy of medical school, the corruption of the medical establishment, and the cynical lack of care by institutions and people in our society. And while he said he was not worried about his ability to deal with illness or even death as a physician, he several times mentioned that he cried easily at stupid movies, and even at commercials.

In terms of what he told me about his childhood, several things stood out. When he was a young child, his father, who was absent on business trips much of the time, had always promised him great things, like ski trips and horseback riding, but never delivered. And each time, with each new promise, the patient got excited and happy, only to be repeatedly disappointed. But he never got angry. Instead he always tried to please his father — and by extension, any authority figure — hoping against hope that he would finally deliver. In second grade, when he had to write a sentence with the word "you," he wrote, "You are such a great teacher Ms. Dalton."

Later on, this sweet eagerness to please invited or allowed older neighborhood boys to take advantage of him. They had him run errands for them and they made him dance naked in the snow for them. And as a young adult, his brother, a compulsive gambler, had repeatedly persuaded him to bail him out with loans he had never made good on.

In other words, underneath his worldly sophistication he was idealistic, simple, and trusting. He had a fundamentally artless disposition which often put him on a path of vulnerability, humiliation, and loss. Understandably, then, he felt ashamed of this very disposition. And he felt particularly ashamed that because he was so eager to please, he had never learned from his experience.

So it was in order to avoid or repress these feelings of shame that this patient had to stay away from anything reminiscent of his own sweetness, naïveté, and so on. Or more accurately, he first had to find women who had this disposition — he never fell for intellectual, sophisticated types — so that he could see it and reject it in them, rather than in himself.

And this is what "the checklist" is all about. Traits or characteristics that men are unconsciously ashamed of in themselves get projected onto the date. Men who deny their shame about their own lack of intelligence — which may or may not have anything to do with their actual intelligence — are particularly concerned with stupidity. Men who are unconsciously ashamed of their baldness or flabbiness wonder, "Is she pretty enough?" And those who deny their shame about their own social anxiety are worried that the woman is "not outgoing enough."

Interestingly, for many men, making a commitment or getting married does not eliminate the checklist, at least not entirely. Instead, it narrows it to one or two major items which are then magnified and blown out of proportion. For example, a man might be upset that his wife spends hours watching *General Hospital* or *The Young and the Restless,* or that she is not a gourmet cook, or that she has no interests other than the children, or that she doesn't keep the house neat. And often, any one of those issues can lead to constant bickering or even repeated, bitter conflicts with prolonged feelings of anger and despair.

Over the years, many couples have come to see me because of such a conflict. During their first session, the wife in one of those couples said that she was tired of being criticized by her husband, especially about the fact that she was quiet in group situations. "Like when we go out with friends," she said. "I'm the type of person who likes to listen. But it's not as if I don't talk. I certainly ask questions, and I also talk about myself, when I feel more comfortable. But I don't understand why it bothers him. He can talk or not talk and it wouldn't matter to me. He always tells me I should talk more, and that makes me really mad, because it makes me feel self-conscious. My friends don't think I'm too quiet. And the worse part is that I end up believing him and thinking that there *is* something wrong with me and that I *should* talk more."

"The other thing," she went on, "is that he always wants me to wear a certain type of dress or outfit when we go out. And I don't mind doing it for him once in a while, but he is so intense about it. This makes me feel so bad about myself. It brings up all my insecurities about my body and attractiveness. Why can't he just accept me the way I am?"

At this point she pauses, and the husband, red with rage, attempts a smile. "That was quite a distortion, wasn't it?" he says. And regrouping into reasonableness, he explains, "It's true that I think she is too quiet with our friends. I think that makes people uncomfortable." "My friends don't feel that way," she angrily interrupts. "Your friends are not going to tell you if they feel that way, are they?" he fires back. "But never mind your friends." He gears up for the final salvo. "*I* think it's rude, and I also think it's boring when you don't talk — it really reminds me of your mother."

At this point I can see — who wouldn't — that the woman is enraged. But she is holding herself back, and he continues. "As far as the clothes issue — here you can actually learn from your mother. She is so well dressed, everybody always comments about it. What's wrong with me wanting you to look attractive? Isn't that normal?" He turns to me. "Plus, I don't understand why she is so sensitive and defensive." He addresses her again. "Why do you feel that I am criticizing you? I'm just making a suggestion. Or think about it this way, I'm just asking you to do something for me, what's wrong with that?"

For our purposes there are two critical points in this exchange. When the husband brings in the mother, we know something serious is happening. He is being deliberately mean, trying to press buttons and humiliate his wife. But why? Why does he need to drive the point home about her being shy and withdrawn like her mother? Amazingly enough, it turns out that part of this man's family legend was that as a child, he didn't talk. In fact, at age four his parents took him to a child psychologist because he spoke so sparingly. There was nothing wrong with him, the psychologist said, he was just quiet. This shyness continued well into the patient's adolescence, and it was only in college, when he realized he was quite intelligent, that he began to be more verbally assertive. And he overcompensated to such an extent that he became extremely articulate and extroverted. But in his wife, he saw his own boyhood shyness — and he had to crush it.

So to generalize, when a man is mean in an argument, chances are he is trying to deny feelings of shame and inadequacy. The second critical point is this husband's request that she dress up more *for him.* We can suspect that underneath this request is his need, not for her, but rather for himself, to look good. Now based on my analysis so far, you might expect that the husband in this case was unkempt or at least had a big coffee stain on his tie. But no, he was actually good-looking and well dressed. So why did he need his wife to be his aesthetic representative?

Clearly, this process of denial and projection of shame is not as simple or as symmetrical as I've implied. In the above couple, what the man felt did not look good in himself was not his physical appearance, but his résumé. He grew up in an affluent suburb, but unlike most of his high school friends, he went to a local state college — nothing fancy or Ivy. Unlike many of his friends he was also not a professional, although he had done quite well in his career. As you might guess, I realized that he felt ashamed about this only through his silence and evasion — when I took his personal history in a subsequent session, I noticed that his narrative skipped the college years. Also, seeming to answer a question I didn't ask, he volunteered a defensive explanation as to why he didn't go to graduate school.

So this man felt ashamed about what in his status-conscious circle would appear to be an educational deficiency. And in an effort to avoid such feelings, he projected them onto his wife's physical appearance, expecting her to give him a status ride. Unfortunately, this kind of dynamic is common not only in status-conscious couples. In fact, it is probably even more common than the tit-for-tat checklist projection described above. The reason for this is that men are more likely to feel shame about work-related problems than about their physical appearance.

Shame and Vulnerability: Is Offense the Best Defense?

Clinical experience as well as research shows that while women tend to feel shame about issues related to their physical appearance and to feel failure in interpersonal relationships, men are more likely to experience shame in relation to performance, both at work and sexually. This sex difference or, more precisely, how couples manage it, sets the stage for many a fight even in the best of relationships. In daily life, men have many "opportunities" to feel shame about their performance. One man might be in a dead-end job, another may have a boss who is always critical of him, a third may be making less money than his friends, and a fourth might suffer from a bout of impotence. Even the plain old "bad day at work" can cause enough of a sense of failure to trigger shame — as well as the knee-jerk reaction of trying to avoid feeling it.

When he comes home after a bad day at work, the toys scattered in the house, the imperfectly set dinner table, or his wife's "bad hair day" can all present our shame-prone man with the opportunity to criticize someone else's performance and discharge his own shame. Similarly, in going out to dinner with his girlfriend, the man with the critical boss can rid himself of his own feelings of shame by "suggesting" that she wear her hair differently or by "asking" why she's not wearing "the nicer earrings I bought you."

Unfortunately, the woman in this kind of situation is all too ready to receive and internalize the man's projection. After all, she is prone to feel shame about her appearance and about failing in a relationship context, which is what the man so intuitively takes advantage of. But this is just the beginning of the fight. Although the woman shamefully tells herself, "Yes, I'm not that attractive," she is also feeling angry with the man who made her feel that way. So she either strikes back or withdraws in silence.

This makes it evident to the man that he has done something wrong. But unaware that he was motivated by his own feelings of shame about something else, he can only respond by insisting that he did not mean to criticize her. The woman doesn't really believe him, and feeling further aggrieved by his denial, she calls him insensitive or dense. Feeling attacked, the man now retaliates by saying she is too sensitive and defensive. And this is when the fight escalates into a spiral of attacks and counterattacks, when phrases like "You always..." and "You are just like your..." and

"I should never have..." take the fight into the destructive domain of previous, unrelated conflicts. But at the root of that fight are the man's inability to tolerate the emotion of shame and the woman's "overcapacity" for it.

Now lest we see women as the helpless victims here, it is only fair to note that many relationship discords are based on the mirror-image dynamic in which the woman projects her own feelings of inadequacy onto the man by giving him the message that he is not such a great provider. I will return to this when we talk about *the masculine-feminine split.*

Why do men and women feel shame about different issues? Clearly, most cultures reinforce this sex difference by applying to both genders different expectations about performance, physical attractiveness, and social relationships. But why do cultures do that? While a full discussion of this question is outside the scope of this book, I'd like to mention one intriguing theory discussed by psychiatrist Michael Lewis in his book about shame. According to that "sociobiological" theory, it all goes back to the evolutionary imperative of procreation. If shame drives men to perform more vigorously and women to maintain their attractiveness, they are more likely to copulate and procreate.

It is probably the case that many of my own observations about men can be accounted for by such sociobiological theories. But it is also possible that such sociobiological factors are changing as we speak. For example, isn't it possible that the continuous development of the human cerebral cortex — the part of the brain responsible for our most advanced thinking — coupled with the continuous technological revolutions it generates, will make physical sex differences such as size and strength less and less consequential, and that this process will eventually do away even with psychological sex differences? I think it's possible, but it might take a few billion years, by which time books like this will be beamed directly to the reader's brain.

But back to earth for now, let's look at this sex difference through the lens of male vulnerability. Simply put, men feel shame when they experience themselves as vulnerable, weak, or ineffectual. As we have seen, they attempt to avoid such vulnerability by making another person feel it in their stead. But this technique of theirs is not limited to the interpersonal arena. They do something quite similar in the business world — often with disastrous consequences.

A small beverage company is losing market share to its larger competitors and is becoming increasingly vulnerable. In a last-ditch attempt to remain viable, they negotiate to join forces with another small competitor. But after agreeing in principle on a buyout, the other company wants to change the terms — they want more money. In response, the CEO of our company is threatening with litigation, which he knows will flood the other company with legal bills they can hardly afford. The competitor responds with a letter stating that this litigation will drive them into bankruptcy, offering a take-it-or-leave-it acquisition deal, unfavorable to our company. Our CEO now has two options. To accept the less-than-ideal offer, which would give his company a chance to remain viable, or to pursue litigation, which may in fact bankrupt the other party. In analyzing these options our CEO must evaluate the veracity of the other party's claim. If the company is as vulnerable to bankruptcy as they say they are, he should accept their offer. But if they are crying poverty as a negotiation ploy, he should pursue litigation.

Which option will he choose? When he really needed the deal and was in a vulnerable position, he had taken a litigious, aggressive stand. So now, when the other CEO is claiming vulnerability, he can only assume that he too is posing and is in fact aggressive. Who in their right mind, he rationalizes, would admit a vulnerability in the marketplace? So he fires off a letter of litigation and gets his lawyers to work.

What happens at the end of this anti-vulnerability standoff? Well, this case is based on a real situation in which I, as a consultant, tried to infuse some conservative, lower-risk behavior. Unfortunately I failed, and two years later both companies are still mired in costly litigation and the prospect of bankruptcy looms. Clearly, this courtship, in which the pursuer did everything to avoid the appearance of vulnerability, went nowhere. And both parties remained single.

Taking the offensive in order to avoid the perception (and/or reality) of vulnerability is also at the heart of the process which characterizes many international conflicts. I'm feeling weaker than my neighbor so I must protect myself by arming. The neighbor, in turn, is feeling threatened by my build-up and must protect himself by matching my build-up plus. This, of course, proves I was right to worry in the first place, so in order not to be defensively vulnerable, I exercise the advantage of the first strike — we are at war. This is also the precise dynamic of the adversarial divorce, in which lawyers — often with the genuine desire to protect the legal interests of the spouse they are representing — recommend certain unilateral maneuvers, to which the other party must respond in kind. Here too, war is the likely outcome.

This dynamic is not directly about shame. Yet it highlights the defensive aspect of this emotion in men. While a painful feeling in and of itself, shame is also a shield, a defense against feelings of vulnerability. As such, it serves as a signal and a reminder that we must not feel (vulnerability). Though it often masquerades as an offense, it is really men's first line of defense.

Conventional Man

It is a peculiar paradox that while most "deviant" behaviors in our society are carried out by the male gender, men are much less tolerant of deviations from the norm than women. Men are more likely to devalue or even condemn diversity, creative imagination, homosexuality, homelessness, corporate incorrectness, rebelliousness, and all matter of eccentric, unconventional behavior. Male psychologists are more interested in diagnosis and pathology, while women psychologists are more concerned with empathy and feelings. And politically, whereas women tend to support more liberal, tolerant causes, men are drawn to law-and-order, conservative ideologies. The paradox is clearly seen in the gender gap as it relates to our evaluation of figures like Bill Clinton. Men, the polls tell us, are less forgiving of his deviations even though these were stereotypically male and more hurtful toward women.

As with many a paradox, the answer to the riddle lies in the question. The reason men are more concerned with conventionality is that they have a greater potential for deviation. In other words, they have a reason to worry about it. But typically enough, they worry about it by projecting their concerns onto others. They try to keep their own house in order by rigidly defining their expectations of others and of society at large. Yet the truth is that privately, and often unconsciously, men apply the same rigid conventional thinking to themselves. Because they are concerned about their potential for rule-breaking, they harshly criticize themselves for any thoughts or feelings which they deem abnormal.

So far we have seen that men feel shame about not performing. But clinical experience shows that they are also prone to feeling shame about deviating — in their minds or in the outside world — from the narrow conventional path they think they should walk. Since most of us "sin" in our minds, if not in our behaviors, this source of shame is particularly important in situations which require opening up to others. Obviously, it is something to contend with in a therapeutic relationship. But it is also an important factor in other intimate relationships.

For a therapist, a girlfriend, or a spouse, it is all the same: If you want the other to be open about their inner world, you must create an environment accepting of differences. Such an open environment, I feel, cannot be an artificial creation or a product of learned therapeutic tools. Rather, it has to be the outcome of a genuine attitude. But given what seems to be our natural inclination to be critical and judgmental of others, how do we become genuinely accepting?

If you consider that at least in our thoughts, feelings, dreams, or fantasies, we are all potential deviants, it is easy to see that condemning others' behaviors as "bizarre," "sick," or "weird" is nothing but a defense against our fear and shame of our own deviation. By defining others as abnormal, we consolidate our belief that we are normal. And the more we reject our own pathology, the more we need to see others as pathological. This is why accepting and loving oneself is a prerequisite for accepting and loving others. It is also the reason that if you feel too ashamed of the skeletons in your own closet, you cannot expect your partner to put his shame aside.

This kind of reciprocity has an important implication which I often repeat to skeptical patients. Men often feel that if they reveal to others shameful thoughts or feelings, they will be humiliated and rejected. The truth, which I consider the best-kept secret for interpersonal success, is almost the opposite. Rather than humiliating you, most people will respond with care. And they will feel safe enough to reciprocate with their own self-doubts and secret sins. Of course, there are those who would jump at the opportunity to affirm their own strength by picking at your wounds. But one hopes you'd know enough to walk away from them.

Successful politicians know how to use this secret to gain popularity — note their penchant for self-deprecating jokes and for making a virtue out of necessity. In the intimate realm, though, accepting oneself and others cannot be a political or a tactical ploy — it has to be genuine. At the same time, life is not some kind of giant support group. So acceptance and tolerance cannot be based on a naive notion of unconditional love. Rather, they should rest on certain philosophical and psychological assumptions.

For example:

- *Human beings are fundamentally more alike than different from each other.*
- *It is ultimately better to be a member of a club that accepts people like yourself as a member.*
- *Ask not what other people can do for you, but what you can do for yourself; or put another way, instead of looking for the right person, start being one.*
- *The line between mental health and mental illness is thin if*

not invisible (if you don't believe that, consider that even the most so-called abnormal behaviors are common and "normal" among children).

- *Alcoholics and social drinkers drink for similar reasons — it makes them feel good.*
- *The main difference between the "normal" and the "neurotic" individual is that the latter has the courage to question his unhappiness.*
- *Being hypercritical is hypocritical, that is, undercritical of oneself.*
- *Our fear and hate of such "outside" groups as immigrants, Muslims, or gays is based on our need to repress our own "outside" feelings.*
- *It is because he mirrors our own potential imperfections that we can be both obsessed with and forgiving of our President's personal misconduct.*

I could go on and on, but I'm not sure how useful it would be, because ultimately, such concepts cannot be learned from a book. Unfortunately, at the cost of appearing to reinvent the wheel, we need to develop them on our own. It is through grappling with such basic beliefs, not through buying them ready-made, that we can cope with shame.

With that in mind, I will now demonstrate how working with men to overcome shame renders what seems to be unusual or deviant rather ordinary. I will illustrate three techniques, developed over years of search and research: (1) asking stupid questions, (2) laughing, and (3) thinking.

The Man Who Wanted to Be Barbara Bush

The patient was a New Jersey architect in his mid-thirties. He was good-looking, bright, and sensitive. There was a physical and emotional gentleness about him which women loved. But to his great dismay, he had been unable to sustain long-term relationships with them, which is why he came to therapy.

At first he sounded like the typical "commitment-phobic" man. He would get involved with a woman, but after a couple of months begin to feel "suffocated" or "smothered" by her. He would then distance himself, but generally, the woman would respond by becoming even more needy and attached. That, of course, would doom the relationship, although typically, because of his guilt and his fear of being alone, he would not break it up for several months.

After about a year of therapy, during which I listened to two of these relationship cycles, the subject of sexual fantasies came up. The patient, who was generally self-confident and articulate, was suddenly self-conscious, insecure, and vague. He was then quiet for a while. At last he said there was something sexual on his mind that was difficult to talk about.

"Why is it difficult to talk about sex?" I asked. "Come on, it's embarrassing," he retorted as if I had asked the stupidest of questions. Which did not deter me from following up with another stupid question. "What's embarrassing about it?" I asked. But before he had a chance to answer, I chuckled and laughed at myself. "I know these are stupid questions," I said, "but I'm asking them for a reason." I went on to acknowledge that sexuality is a private matter and that's why it is difficult to talk about. "But," I added, "some people are not at all embarrassed about it, and different people are embarrassed about different aspects of their sexual experiences. So to rephrase," I said, "what are you specifically embarrassed about?"

"Well," he said, "the problem is, I think I really like big breasts." Here, I could have said, "So what's the problem" and gone on to talk about normal sexual variations, matters of taste or preference, and so on and so forth. But rather than dismiss his feelings of shame, I wanted to get through them so that the patient and I could learn exactly what they were about. So somewhat intrusively, I asked, "Why do you say '*I think* I really like...'?" to which he answered, "I guess I do, I just feel ashamed of it and don't really want to admit it — to myself."

"Now why do you see it as a problem?" I continued to play

dumb. "Because I can't get aroused without them," he blurted almost angrily and added, "Wouldn't you say that's a problem, Mr. Psychologist?" I smiled and we went on to discuss "the problem." It then became clear why his relationships always failed: he had dated the breasts, not the women. The aura of the large breasts diffused the person of the woman, and when the initial attraction waned, the emerging personality was incompatible with his own.

Now while the patient was hopeful that he could fall in love with a woman who was not necessarily large-breasted, he was still concerned that he wouldn't be able to function sexually if she weren't. But he then thought that since he now felt less ashamed of his attraction, perhaps when he met someone to whom he was attracted for reasons other than her breasts, he could discuss his preference openly with her and "Maybe she'll agree to wear artificial breasts or something like that."

While I had no particular objection to this idea, once again I saw dissolution of shame not as a terminal goal but rather as a means to an end. So I asked some more questions, this time about the details of the patient's sexual fantasies. This quickly led to another cycle of self-consciousness, vagueness, and embarrassment. And once again, I stopped my interrogation, this time to engage the patient in a somewhat rhetorical discussion about the difference between reality and fantasy. What's the difference between seducing a nubile fifteen-year-old girl and having a fantasy about seducing her? Does it ever make sense to feel shame about a fantasy or a thought (as opposed to an action)? Then I asked the patient whether he would feel judgmental about his own fantasies if they were being expressed by his best friend, to which he emphatically said, "Not at all." He finally felt enough at ease to tell me about the deeper layer of his big-breast fantasies.

"The reason I like big boobs is that I can share them," he said. "In my fantasy I am the one with the breasts. What turns me on most is the fantasy of me as a woman, being fucked by another woman. I guess that's why when I'm having sex I can only come when the woman is on top."

As we can see, merely acknowledging and talking about feelings of shame help to open up communications. In a way, the very feeling of shame is a gateway to greater emotional openness — as long as you are not afraid to ask about it. And you don't need to be a therapist to ask stupid questions. What you do need is courage. Or, like Dostoyevsky's Idiot — whose mental slowness and naïveté opened Russia's high society to him — you need to unlearn what you think you know about people. If you make no assumptions about what men might be ashamed of, you are more likely to ask "stupid questions" and to find out what it is that causes them shame.

The second technique, laughing, walks the fine line between laughing *at* and laughing *with* the other person. In one session, when elaborating on his sexual fantasies, the patient said, "If you want to know how perverted I really am, the other day I dressed as a woman and took a picture of myself so that I can use it for sexual stimulation." Then, barely containing his smile, he added, "I wanted to have a woman's face for the picture, but the only mask I found in the store was of Barbara Bush. So that's what I used."

I could barely contain my own smile, and a second later both of us burst into laughter. I was laughing *at* the absurdity of the fantasy and in that sense was noting its "bizarre," problematic nature. But I was also laughing *with* the fantasy, thereby showing my appreciation for its creative playfulness. It was thus both a critique of the fantasy and an invitation for more.

The third technique, thinking, is the one that gets you and the other person to see that his fantasy is not all that bizarre after all. My patient who liked big breasts, for example, grew up as an only child, without a father. His mother, a strong, independent, and idealistic woman, dominated the landscape of his childhood. A successful professional, but a former Haight-Ashbury hippie, she had definite views about sex education. These included nudity at home, casual touching of genitals, and buying her young teenage boy pornographic magazines.

So if we think about this history, would it be a stretch to conclude that the essence of the patient's fantasy was (1) identifying with his mother and wanting to become like her (i.e., a woman), and (2) wanting to be loved by his mother (i.e., by a big woman who's on top of him)? And that this deep and sole emotional connection was sexualized because his mother, in fact, had been the manager of his sexual development? And if we think a bit more, can we fail to see that every man's bond with his mother is based on his boyhood desire to become like her in some sense and certainly to be loved by her?

It is this kind of thinking that ultimately resolves a man's feelings of shame. But in order to work, this technique must be more than a therapeutic tool designed to "make the patient feel better." It must be a genuine and natural extension of the philosophical conviction which views people as fundamentally more alike than different from each other.

Nonetheless, we must admit that on the surface this patient's fantasy was somewhat unusual, though not as uncommon as you might think. Does this in itself account for the patient's feelings of shame? To some extent, yes. Men with unusual fantasies, thoughts, or habits are particularly prone to feeling like "a freak." On the other hand, if we only allow ourselves to, we can all manufacture some rather unusual mental products. So let's employ our natural curiosity and not be scared of the human imagination. And let's take it out of the exclusive hands of the therapist: anyone wanting to know what's on a man's mind must first value how his mind — fantasies and all — works.

As I mentioned before, these techniques are in a sense natural derivatives of love. The question is, can the emotion of love, in and of itself, break through or even heal the emotion of shame? The short answer is yes: the therapist's, the parent's, the child's, the friend's, or the lover's — are all curative loves. The long answer is that a more permanent healing requires that this love be internalized, digested, and then reorganized into a new structure of self-love.

The Silent Treatment

In everyday situations, the man you are dating or having a relationship with may or may not have such sexual fantasies. Chances are, by the way, that he has some sexual fantasies he is not telling you about — out of shame. But regardless, the techniques I used with my big-breast guy can be used anywhere, anytime.

In general, asking questions is an incredibly simple, easy, and effective tool — it's also the best selling-and-negotiation technique because it helps you learn about your customer's or partner's interests and needs. Asking stupid questions is a little more difficult, as it exposes you to ridicule. Except that in the case of shame, as you no doubt remember, some vulnerable self-exposure is actually a plus — and I'll come back to that in a minute.

But what makes asking questions about shame particularly difficult is the fact that it places the attention squarely on the shameful experience, with the potential to make the person feel even worse. "I don't want to talk about it, okay? How many times do I have to say that?" is what you might get in response to interrogating a shamed male partner. So the key to a successful use of questions with a man is, paradoxically, not caring about the answers. You should be asking questions because you are naively curious, like a child, not because you are invested in "the truth," in helping, or in liberating a man from his secrets. So first of all, don't ask when you really want or need to know, unless your intuition is that he is ready to confess. Ask when you have a detached, open, or intellectual interest in the general subject matter (e.g., "What is it that men fantasize about?"). Also, ask in a manner that demonstrates an attitude of acceptance and readiness to hear any answer. And as long as it doesn't feel like nagging, ask in order to push the man to overcome his embarrassment.

The second "technique," laughing, is even trickier. For one thing, what if you don't have a sense of humor? I think most people are naturally endowed with one. The problem is, people are afraid to laugh in tense situations. First, they are afraid of saying something inappropriate or immature, which, once again, is not really a problem in the context of shame. Second, they are afraid of the "laughing at" aspect of humor, the hostility or aggression which is embedded in the punch line. But if you philosophically see yourself as a fellow sinner, you will not be laughing at the person any more than at yourself. And you don't have to be struggling with exactly the same problem as the other in order to feel the camaraderie of mutual self-ridicule.

Laughing with or near the shamed person is great because it acknowledges that there is in fact something to be embarrassed about ("I can't believe you did that") but with a degree of emotional distance and acceptance ("We can laugh about this together"). It places the shame experience in perspective and rescues the person from dejection and self-pity.

Thinking, the third "technique," is also about shifting perspectives. When thinking about or analyzing something, really anything, we question whether what we see is what we get. We therefore question not only the object of our study, but also our very perception of it. Not only do we not take something at face value, we also challenge our way of looking at it, and by implication, our entire system of knowing anything. Thinking is thus an inherently subversive activity, which is why totalitarian regimes try to discourage it. Thinking also leads to understanding — of another perspective — which is why societies at war discourage intellectual introspection: if you understand the enemy, you may not be willing to kill him.

Lest this become too philosophical, let's see how thinking works with everyday shame. Your boyfriend tells you his best friend is cheating on his girlfriend. Your reaction: "What a jerk, I can't believe you hang out with someone like that!" There is nothing wrong with that reaction, except that the message to your boyfriend is not only that you accept no deviations, but also that you accept no deviation by association. There is nothing wrong with that either, as long as you don't expect your boyfriend to open up to you about his emotional deviations — his feelings. If you do have such expectations, the more "intellectual" reaction of "He's such a jerk but I'm sure there're two sides to the story" is a better bet.

These three techniques work particularly well with shame experienced consciously. But they don't really address unconscious, or denied, shame, which must become conscious before it can be alleviated. Now while making the unconscious conscious is the job of the therapist, I believe that this too can be, and is being done, by untrained others every day. Take the case of a marital fight in which the husband projects his unconscious shame over his lack of success at work by criticizing his wife for not exercising enough. If she gets hurt, wounded, or angry, she accepts the projection and his shame remains unconscious. But if she feels untouched by his criticism — which might take the form of cracking a joke, shrugging her shoulders, or saying "Talk to me when you have something nice to say" — he is left stranded with his shame. He now has to come to terms with his unhappiness over his wife's imperfection. And the only way he can do that is to say to himself, "Well, I'm not perfect either — I don't make as much money as I should." Bingo, his shame is now conscious. His next step would be to either work on making more money — instead of working on his wife's workout program — or to accept himself, and his wife, as is.

In short, the principle is to throw the ball back into his court and let him stew in his own juice. This approach, in more subtle ways, can also apply to dating situations. If after a few dates which seem to go really well, the man surprises you with, "I don't know if we are compatible," your best response might be "We must not be compatible, because I was just thinking we were." To decode the exchange: he's saying "You are not good enough for me," and you react by sticking to your own perception, which paradoxically, takes his conclusion to its logical extreme. In effect you are saying, "Sounds like you have a problem, don't you?" which leaves him to ponder who is not good enough for whom.

So far it would appear that dealing with men's shame is a lot of work. But there is one more technique I'd like to mention. It requires no work at all, but it's the hardest to learn. It's silence. Sometimes when a man gets the courage to bring up something he feels ashamed of, it's best not to say anything at all. For example, if your boyfriend tells you that he feels unable to speak up or be assertive with his boss, greeting him with silence — an ignoring, not a loud silence — is like saying, "I'm not impressed by your shame so far. Next?" In other words, if you don't react, the message is "It's not a big deal," which might liberate your partner to elaborate.

However, if you are generally a critical person, or if the man you are dealing with is of the suspicious kind, this may not be the technique of choice for you — the silence will be interpreted as unspoken disapproval. Also, if you are too full of shame yourself, silence will be correctly interpreted as a fear of mutual embarrassment.

The silent treatment technique is also useful with unconscious shame. One patient, a single systems analyst, related a dream in which he was watching pornographic images on his computer terminal at work. "Suddenly the door opened and someone walked in. I tried to 'change the channel,' but the knob was broken. I got angry, picked up the monitor, and threw it on the floor." When I asked him for associations to the dream, he talked about his relationships with people at work, his feeling that he couldn't close the door to his office, and his frustration with computers. He then went on to interpret the dream in terms of his need for privacy and his feeling ineffectual at work.

Then, just as we were about to move on, he said, "I don't think this has much to do with the dream, but I'll mention it anyway. The night before the dream I rented a porno movie." With another patient I might have responded with shock and disbelief, "You don't think this has much to do with the dream?!" But with him, I didn't respond at all. He then reiterated his position, saying, "You see, I don't think I feel bad about watching pornography," and we moved on. The reason for my silence: when a smart man insists on not seeing the obvious, it is less likely that he is lying and more likely that he's in denial. His shame about watching pornography was unconscious.

The advantage of the silent treatment in this case was twofold. First, his unconscious, casual confession about watching pornography (he had never mentioned it before) failed to impress the person he may have perceived as the critical, persecutory arbiter of mental health. But second, it left the ball in his court: he was now forced to wonder about the eclipse of logic in his brain vis-à-vis the dream — all by himself. Sometimes, this is the best way of "driving" the unconscious into consciousness — let it emerge on its own cognizance from the illogical fog of denial. Of course, it is entirely possible that I was completely wrong and that this patient enjoyed "adult" entertainment without shame. That would be another good reason to be silent.

If up to this point I seem to prescribe acceptance and openness as the cure-all for shame, I now want to issue a caveat: don't be so open-minded that your brain falls out. Like guilt, shame can serve a useful purpose — sometimes we *should* be ashamed of ourselves. If the therapist, or really any recipient of intimate communications, has the attitude of "Anything goes," or "I'm perverse, you are perverse, we are both OK," then he is depriving the other of the opportunity to acknowledge and take responsibility for the hostility that may reside in his deviation. It is no coincidence, then, that the various techniques I've mentioned are more neutral than supportive in nature. For example, asking questions is an invitation to open up, not an advanced approval of the answer.

But then again, the time we "should" feel shame is not necessarily when conventional wisdom would have us feel it. For example, one patient started talking about his "favorite" sexual fantasy with great embarrassment. After struggling with a good deal of shame, he finally revealed that the fantasy was based on a sexual encounter he once had in college. He had invited a girl over to his dorm room, and in the course of the evening the girl "begged" him to have sex with her. And the more he hesitated the more she begged, which was a real turn-on for him.

It would be easy for me, and I suspect for anyone, to relate to such a fantasy and to dismiss the shame as unnecessary. But as I listened to the patient's elaboration (here's another good use of silence) the reasons for his embarrassment gradually came to the surface. It turned out that the patient was ashamed because deep in his heart he knew that this was a fantasy about rejecting and dominating women.

What the patient didn't know at the time was that the fantasy represented a sexualized attempt to reverse the balance of power in his early relationship with his mother. It was only when he became aware of his anger toward his rejecting and domineering mother that his shame was resolved.

This case illustrates that in the world of the unconscious, the ordinary and the banal may in fact be more perverse and therefore more legitimately shameful than the "bizarre." It also shows why, in the words of psychiatrist Harry Stack Sullivan, "reassurance doesn't work." Open-mindedness and tolerance can help men to overcome shame — as a communications barrier. This is not the same as sparing them from experiencing it altogether. The latter may not be a realistic goal. But if we are to make progress in helping men resolve their shame, we must descend deeper into their psyches.

Emotional Absence

...I don't know what I feel

Perhaps things are changing," I was thinking, as the third consecutive male "customer" walked into the office. Contrary to what the subject matter of this book may suggest, I generally do not divide the world into men and women. But subconsciously, I must have still expected women, not men, to come see me in the plush but sterile, up-in-the-sky Wall Street office which was mine for that one grim day.

A couple of days earlier I had received a call from one of the partners of this investment firm. He was wondering if I could come and spend a few hours in his office in case people in the firm wanted to talk to someone. They had just received terrible news: one of the firm's most beloved employees, a veteran executive secretary, had been killed in a car accident.

When I arrived at the firm, the partner briefed me and then showed me to his office. "Why don't you hang out here," he suggested. "I told everyone you're here, and I also told them we got these." He pointed to a large assortment of cookies and coffee on his huge mahogany desk. "I thought it might entice people to come by," he explained. I said nothing — about the cookies — but I was privately skeptical. (This is something you might do with children, I thought, but with adults?)

It turned out that this investment banker was a better psychologist than I was, or perhaps he just knew his buddies better. To my amazement, the first person to peek into the office — a full hour after I first seated myself and just when I had begun to contemplate leaving — was a tall, bespectacled man wearing an elegant Italian suit, inquiring about the...cookies. When I invited him to sit down and talk, he said, "No, I really just came for the cookies, but maybe I'll have some coffee too. Talk? What's there to talk about? We all go at the end, don't we?" He then sat down and we spent the next fifteen minutes talking about life and death. He had lost his father when he was twenty-three and his mother just two years ago.

The second man who came in had lost a brother at a young age. He did not come for the cookies but he also didn't think there was much to talk about. Yet he stayed for half an hour. When leaving, he looked me up and down and said, "This is the first time...I mean, I've never seen a psychologist before." "Must have been pretty traumatic," I joked. "I guess you don't look that scary," he said, laughing, on his way out.

The third man was also there just for the cookies. He stated flat-out that he was "one of those men who internalize things and deal with them on their own." With him, the conversation somehow drifted into his and his wife's struggle with infertility in the past five years. He was factual and philosophical about it, but the topic of our dialogue remained strangely close to what brought me to that office — notwithstanding its incongruent panoramic views of the New York Harbor or the cookies — the loss of life.

I do not know what the statistics are, but anecdotally it seems that more and more men are willing to open up — that's the new news. The old news is that how men talk hasn't changed much. These three men, the only employees of that firm to stop by to discuss their feelings about the sudden loss of a coworker, did not talk about their feelings after all. Rather, they talked about the facts of their own losses, their own mortality, and the meaning of life — all thoughts, not feelings. Yet, I was strangely moved. Having done this many times before, I had expected an outpouring of emotions, which is usually the case with the more traditional female mourner. But interestingly, the men's more intellectual approach left me full of emotions, as if I myself had lost someone close. By comparison, women's open emotions in similar circumstances had tended to evoke in me more thoughts and ideas — as if their feelings needed to be structured and contained.

The Dreadful Dead

The notion that men react to loss intellectually is not new. Nor is it inherently unappealing. One of Tolstoy's most moving characters, Prince Andrew, in *War and Peace,* reacts to the death of his wife in childbirth with what can be described as an intellectualized depression. In his complex articulation of rather simple psychology, Tolstoy describes not a conscious grieving process, in which one feels loss, sadness, and anger, but rather, a change in Prince Andrew's personality. From a heroic, idealistic man he turns into a selfish cynic. He logically and thoughtfully expounds the view that education and medicine are bad for the poor. Medicine is generally bad, he explains — it doesn't really cure anybody, only kills, or at best only prolongs everybody's sufferings.

When he discusses these ideas with his friend Pierre, there is no mention of the obvious connection to the loss he has suffered. And strangely, as he argues his position he becomes more lively and engaged. "His glance [becomes] more animated as his conclusions become hopeless," we are told. Yet the reader feels the poignancy of the underlying loss. And so does the prince's friend, Pierre, who responds with, "Oh, that is dreadful, dreadful!...I don't understand how you can live with such ideas."

It is precisely because of the absence of simple, straightforward emotions that we end up feeling for the intellectualized, emotionally absent man. Of course, it is not that Prince Andrew is actually not feeling the loss — the truth is almost the opposite. He is so devastated by it that he must mount a powerful, all-consuming defense against his feelings. He'd rather change his deeply held convictions about life than allow his emotional pain to take the lead. In that respect, to the extent that women can tolerate more painful emotions, they are psychologically stronger than men. The latter, fearful of psychic pain, turn their sufferings into philosophies or activities. Or sometimes into a big joke.

In the movie *Life Is Beautiful* Italian filmmaker Roberto Benigni did all that by approaching the emotionally unapproachable — the Holocaust — with the psychology and art of the tragicomic. In the movie, in order to protect his young son from the horrors of the concentration camp, the Chaplinesque protagonist, a funny, naive waiter, pretends that the camp, indeed the entire war, is a huge cops-and-robbers kind of game for children. In one of the most dramatic moments of the movie, his son breaks down. He is ready to quit the game and wants to go home. The father, using "reverse psychology," acquiesces. He starts walking out of the barracks, disparaging the game and devaluing the prize they'd get for "winning" (actually, surviving). It's a huge gamble: not only can he be shot by the guards, but what if it doesn't work and the child still wants to leave? To our relief, of course, it does work, and they stay (alive).

It might take a genius to pull off this kind of movie. But I also think it probably takes a man to think of such a scheme in the first place. In addition, it's hard to imagine a woman acting in such a "dissociated" way — Benigni is also the actor. Interestingly, the father ends up saving the child, but not himself. The mother, on the other hand — who acts on pure emotions, choosing to join the two of them on the train to the concentration camp — survives.

The Holocaust aside, in many ways this movie is about a father-son relationship: feelings remain unspoken, if not denied, and are then metamorphosed into actions, fantasies, and ideas. But the audience, very much like the Tolstoy reader encountering Prince Andrew's dark intellectualizations, cannot help but feel with great poignancy everything these men are working so hard at not feeling. Perhaps the opposite, "female," art form in this sense is the opera or the Hollywood tearjerker — these are so emotional that many men can only react to them with cynicism and distance.

Now clearly, we don't always empathize with "unfeeling" men. Some men are so dedicated to expunging emotions from their psychological repertoire that they drive us into boredom and irritability. Men who have experienced severe loss very early in life can be particularly susceptible to that syndrome: their emotions die with the (literal or figurative) death of their parent, which has the double "benefit" for them of not feeling the loss while remaining loyal or close to the dead parent.

Such men in a sense have been through a psychological Holocaust. Emotionally speaking, they have seen the worst. Therefore, they don't have much to lose and their emotional philosophy is that less is more. They question everything and laugh about anything. They have no sacred cows. In psychotherapy, as in marriage, such men can be frustrating because their feelings are inaccessible — and you just can't get water out of stone. But they can also be incredibly moving because they are so well developed intellectually that they know they are suffering from their inability to feel.

In describing these men, I do not mean to imply that this is a uniform reaction to the death of a parent at a young age — many variables are involved in shaping any human reaction. Nor do I think that the death of a parent is the only kind of early loss or trauma that can set in motion such a "character defense." The patient I will describe next is a case in point.

The Man Who Refused to Feel Abused

This patient stands out in my mind, among other reasons, for the way in which he entered therapy. His reason for seeking therapy seemed to *me* to be abnormally sane — but then again, what do I know, I am a psychologist. In the first session, the patient, a British investment banker with an avowed interest in philosophy, explained that he had come to see me out of curiosity about psychoanalysis. "You see," he said, "my passion, to the extent that I have any, is philosophy. When I was in university — or college, as it is called here — I embraced Marxism, especially its theory of cultural determinism. Now, as I'm approaching middle age, it's time to explore psychoanalysis. But I am rather skeptical about it, I must say, for precisely the same reasons that I liked Marxism as a young man — I do not believe in free will."

When I then asked the patient — let's call him John — whether there was anything troubling or painful in his life that might lead him to seek treatment, he smiled and answered in the negative. But then, with what appeared to be considerable pleasure, he added, "Naturally, *you* might say that *unconsciously* something is bothering me. My rebuttal to that is that I am not sure I'm willing to grant you the existence of the unconscious. But perhaps you can instruct me in that regard, and we can go on to have a lively intellectual debate."

When, in response, I asked the patient why he wouldn't just read some books about psychoanalysis, he cleverly answered that he was "well aware that psychoanalytic therapy is not merely an intellectual process and that emotional faculties are thought to be at play, so that one cannot fully appreciate the theory without undergoing treatment oneself."

This presentation completely confused me. At first I thought, oh great, a patient who is interested in the theory and practice of psychotherapy — we have a lot in common. But then — despite being a therapist I haven't quite lost my mind, at least not as of yet — I realized that there was something wrong with this picture. Nobody in their right mind, I thought, invests the kind of money, time, and emotional commitment required by psychotherapy merely out of intellectual curiosity.

I was also amused by the patient's appreciation for the absurd — his playful intonation revealed a touch of irony about his own presentation. And finally, I felt frustrated and irritated because he seemed to make a mockery out of the entire situation, me included. Now isn't it amazing how many feelings an "unfeeling" man can induce in his dialogue partner?

In some ways, this session was fairly representative of John's entire therapy. In his quest to remain emotionless he employed a variety of creative techniques: from questioning why I asked why to questioning why I didn't shine my shoes; from claiming he was bored in the session to claiming he was so relaxed he was falling asleep; from suggesting I serve coffee and doughnuts in the waiting room to wondering if I could connect some kind of electrodes to his head which would monitor his thoughts and spare him the need to talk, and so on and so forth.

When I suggested that these ideas were ploys, designed alternately to entertain, divert, or put me on the spot — all for the purpose of avoiding his feelings — he would claim, rightly so, that he was just doing his job as a patient, saying what's on his mind. And when I told him that this was a very clever way of destroying the therapy while appearing to comply with it, he would smile triumphantly and launch into something like, "Well, there you go again, Dr. Gratch. This is one of those epistemological tautologies which have crippled psychoanalytic theory from its very inception. I'm sure you know more about that than me and yet . . ."

As I told the patient, in such sessions I didn't know whether to laugh or to cry. The problem was, John was so good at baiting me with his intellectual puzzles that even though I knew better, I couldn't always resist him. So from time to time I allowed myself to engage in philosophical battles with him. But after a while I began to feel I was emotionally corrupted by this, and that I was betraying John's real therapeutic agenda.

As it turned out, there was nothing philosophical, amusing, or even complex about John's therapeutic agenda: his problem was that he was unable to love. Yes, he was married, and yes, he had two children, and yes, he cared for them. But secretly he viewed his wife primarily as a sex object and his children as a duty. He had never been in love, had married young out of physical desire, and did not really miss his wife or children on his frequent, often long business trips. And if you add to the mix John's cultural background — the stiff upper lip of an upper-middle-class British suburb — you end up with a picture of an emotionally absent man — his brilliance, success, and humor notwithstanding.

Most of us can relate to the pain of unrequited love: the longing, rejection, and jealousy, to name just a few of the feelings it arouses. And it seems self-evident that it's far more painful to be the one who is rejected than the one who rejects. But in some sense, the opposite is true. Because, in a way, rejecting someone who loves us brings into question our very ability to love. Losing a loved one is sad and, depending on the circumstances, can be devastating. But losing the capacity to love is to be destined to emotional barrenness as well as to lose hope that one can ever be loved. From that vantage point, women who "love too much" are more touching, while men who love too little are more tragic.

This is how I saw John. While he experienced himself as a kind, if aloof, man, I felt the unspoken desperation that was just under the surface. But what was this desperation all about? Why did John need to turn the hope of love into the emotional neutrality of nothingness? There was no death or other obvious loss in his early childhood. There was, however, a loss of trust, not only in people, but also in the very rules of reality.

By the way, as I hope you appreciate more fully by now, before John and I got to discuss that childhood experience, we had to cross the Rubicon of **Shame (boys don't cry).** And in John's case it was a double whammy. He felt ashamed of his shame because he knew, and in fact insisted, that he had nothing to be ashamed of — except that everybody who has such an experience is tormented by shame. What I'm alluding to here is childhood sexual abuse.

From about age five to eleven John was periodically molested by his older sister's boyfriend (and later husband). When he finally told me about it, even after he acknowledged "irrational feelings of shame," John refused to describe it as abuse. And when I made the mistake of using that word, he corrected and admonished me. This was not only because John liked to think of himself as an independent thinker, but also because his memories of the "so-called abuse" — we finally settled on that term — were not unpleasant. For one thing, he remembered "not disliking the attention, and perhaps even feeling special or powerful — almost as if I had something he really wanted which I could provide or withhold at will." In exploring this with me John was not interested in the legal or moral aspects of the "so-called abuse" but rather the psychological: "If I did not hate it, if I may have possibly even enjoyed it, why should we consider it abuse?" he would ask.

As absurd as this might sound, John's question is often at the core of what makes childhood sexual abuse so terrible, and so terribly confusing for a child. While sometimes, as in the case of rape or other violent abuse, the child's experience is that of sheer horror, in most cases the emotional picture is more complex. The child might be very attached to the abusive adult and he might get pleasure — if not sexually, emotionally — from some aspect of the interaction. When that is the case, the child invariably says to himself, "It's not that bad," or "At least I'm getting something out of it," or "Maybe I made it all up."

With these notions, the child intuitively seeks to protect the adult in order to preserve the possibility of love and coherence in his world. But try as he may, he cannot shake the knowledge that it's all wrong; that he is being used and manipulated, that he is made to feel shameful and guilty, that the secret relationship is alienating him from his family and friends, that it makes him question his masculinity and sexuality, and that he is becoming fearful or sickly. And even when this knowledge is repressed or ejected out of consciousness ("dissociated"), which is often the case, the child is no longer able to trust love or the rules of reality. He adopts a skeptical, icy disposition and rejects emotional attachments.

Much more can and has been said about the psychological consequences of sexual abuse. But in terms of **Emotional Absence (I don't know what I feel)** John's case illustrates not only the defense of not feeling — which helped him make a virtue out of necessity — but also the paradoxical power of emotions over intellect. John's attempt to enlist his intellect to avoid feelings had backfired, as the very feelings he was trying to oppress rose and took control of his intellect. Take his initial interactions with me, illuminated by what we now know about his history. He tells me he is interested in psychoanalysis — this would make me like him and make him feel special. He challenges me to an intellectual duel in my area of expertise — this would tempt me to dominate him. But he also informs me that he knows psychotherapy is not simply an intellectual process — which would remind me that I am wrong to engage with him intellectually in the first place.

Can you sense here that what appears to be an autonomous intellectual sequence is actually driven by the emotional dynamics of seduction, domination, and reversal of power? Not that John, the child, had seduced his abuser (although this is not as far-fetched as it may sound). But he did "seduce" me, setting our relationship on a trajectory that re-created his emotional experience with the abuser. And as could be expected, as our relationship progressed, John traveled through much of the emotional landscape of this early experience. Unfortunately, before he made it to the all-important underground Volcano of Rage, John's bank offered him a once-in-a-lifetime opportunity in London. "Perhaps I will discuss your observations regarding the so-called abuse with one of your English colleagues," he said as he bade farewell to me in the last session.

The Surgeon as a Metaphor

Everything else being equal, in choosing a surgeon would you opt for a supportive, kind, and empathic individual or a machine-like, emotionless technician? I hope none of us will have to make this choice, but personally, as much as I would lean toward the former, I would probably go with the latter. The reason, I suspect, is obvious: I'd rather be cut by a person who can treat my body as a soulless object of scientific study than by one who is "in touch with his feelings" about matters such as blood and pain.

While I don't believe that some professions or occupations are inherently more male or female, symbolically, at least in terms of emotional absence, the character defense of the stereotypical male surgeon is a textbook on emotional self-management in men. The surgeon — as a metaphor — is someone who is motivated by the desire to save, heal, and cure. In that respect he is like any metaphorical physician. But his particular art requires the kind of competent fixing which is best served by a paucity of strong emotions. The problem is, it's not really possible to have no feelings about cutting chests, penetrating brains, or holding life in one's hands. Unless, of course, you have no feelings at all, which is in fact the surgeon's prototypical solution to this dilemma.

In this respect, the male surgeon's dissociation of feelings is not all that different from my patient John's. Perhaps less philosophical than John — after all, he needs to actually fix things — he dryly absorbs and dispatches facts, information, statistics, techniques, and procedures. And the existence of emotions can be inferred only indirectly, as when we analyze his curt manner with us or his black humor with his colleagues.

Now this mechanical attitude toward feelings and information is not only evident in most men, but is also the chief cause of many misunderstandings and fights between men and women. In *Men Are from Mars, Women Are from Venus,* John Gray shows that when it comes to emotions, men and women speak two different languages. As he puts it, women use words to express feelings, while men use them to transmit information. While neither Gray (I assume) nor I think that this distinction is always true or without shades of gray, it nevertheless appears to be at the heart of many communication problems in relationships. John Gray lists several examples of how men misinterpret common complaints by women. For instance, when a woman says, "No one listens to me anymore," the man is likely to respond with, "But I am listening to you right now." As Gray explains, in this type of exchange the man translates the woman's words too literally, as if they are intended to convey information and facts rather than feelings.

One of my own favorite examples is a personal one. It took me years to understand what my wife actually meant when she would say, "Do you want to take the garbage out?" I would take it literally as if she asked me if I wanted to do it, to which I would instinctively answer, "No!" — why would I *want* to? Eventually I came to understand that posing her request (or command) as a question was not a factual, literal question but rather an expression of her respect for my emotional autonomy.

To an extent, men's literalism protects them from the emotional upheaval associated with crisis and trauma. At the same time, however, it takes away some of their capacity for joy. It's as if their emotional absence flattens their psychology into a two-dimensional one. I'm reminded of this apparent flatness every day when commuting to my New York office by train. Rows of men in dark or gray suits, briefcases and newspapers in hand, pour in measured steps onto the platforms, blending with uniformity into a monotony of color, pace, and speech, punctuated here and there by women and, on a lucky day, a few other visual nonconformists.

British psychoanalyst Christopher Bollas coined the term "normotic (as opposed to neurotic) personality" to describe the character of individuals who have an abnormal drive to be normal. Such people, says Bollas, live to conform to the objective, material standards set by society — for example, the accumulation of "things" such as knowledge, money, friends, wife, children, cars — without actually experiencing the subjective feelings, thoughts, or conflicts which give personal meaning to such achievements or relationships.

Bollas does not speak specifically of men, and clearly, women too can suffer from "normotic illness." But for men, the chief symptom of this disease is the flattening of emotions. The stereotype is that when women ask, "Do you love me?" men answer, "I'm here, aren't I?" One male patient, hardly amused, tells the story of how in the middle of a car-ride conversation in which his best friend complained that his wife was emotionally needy, his own girlfriend called on the cell phone to say hi and to ask if he loved her. "She takes away my ability to respond," he explained.

For some men, this kind of difficulty is just a matter of Shame — boys don't say such things, especially on command. But for others it's more about stoicism, neutrality, and boredom. For many, this deadening of the subjective is a subtle form of depression, characterized by the chronic, if unarticulated, philosophy that life is a chore. It is the state of mind that leads to falling asleep in front of the TV, or for that matter, in front of the steering wheel. It can last for years and it is often the path taken to the so-called mid-life crisis. From that standpoint, the mid-lifer's falling in love with a young woman (or with a sports car) can be seen as an ill-fated attempt to rejuvenate the self from its long, somnolent disengagement.

But even when there is no depression to speak of, men's emotional absence can get them, as well as others around them, into trouble. The basic laws of physics, such as the conservation of matter, seem to apply here: the emotions are not actually absent — they don't just dissipate or disappear. Nor are their intensity or quantity reduced. Rather, they take on a different shape — sometimes unintended, often unexpected.

Men are notorious for having delayed and displaced emotional reactions. For example, after his wife gave birth to their first child, one patient began having unwelcome, intrusive thoughts about punching pregnant women in the stomach. Translation: the patient had been angered by his wife's withdrawal and preoccupation during pregnancy, but in order to take care of her — which he had faithfully done for nine months — he unconsciously delayed his anger and displaced it onto suitable substitutes.

Turning off the emotion of fear and assuming the "fight" rather than "flight" reaction to a dangerous situation is the stuff that male heroes are made of. But it is also the path of dead soldiers, dead Everest climbers, and, less dramatically, failed business entrepreneurs. Whether you fly an airplane, ride a horse, or ride the stock market, you need to have a small but healthy measure of anxiety, to be used as data for evaluating the level of risk you are facing. If you drive eighty miles an hour without an inkling of anxiety — either about safety or about getting a ticket — why shouldn't you go even faster?

Interpersonally, emotional absence gets men into trouble not only because the people in their lives are frustrated with their lack of feelings, but also because if you are numb to your own feelings, you can't really anticipate or empathize with other people's. The man who minimizes his own emotional reaction to a cold or the flu is likely to ignore his wife's or children's need for TLC when they are sick. The father who won't let himself feel fear or sadness is the one who yells at his child to stop crying instead of listening to his pain. The emotionally absent husband who is attempting to feel young again by falling in love outside his marriage is still emotionally absent, even in relation to his new love object — he fails to anticipate and empathize with the pain and destruction she is ultimately likely to feel. And the man who doesn't miss his children or partner when he is away for business is not going to viscerally sense the potential impact of his absence on them.

This lack of empathy — for self and others — might be one of the reasons men seem unable to utter the words "I'm sorry." And it might be the reason that when they finally do utter them, they do so without conviction, kind of like an old dog's new trick. "I don't want you to say you're sorry," the spouse or girlfriend might respond to such an apology. "I want you to understand."

Lack of empathy or a general obliviousness to emotional pain also makes it easier to rationalize and intellectualize misconduct. If you commit white-collar crimes or violate campaign finance laws, you can build a rationale that these are victimless crimes and that you must do what everyone else does to survive in this dog-eat-dog world. But this is more of a rationalization than a rationale — a way of intellectualizing away feelings of guilt, which, had you allowed yourself to feel them in the first place, could have kept you out of trouble.

The same is true in interpersonal misconduct. Many men rationalize having an extramarital affair by convincing themselves that they are not really betraying their spouse. Not feeling the wife's pain makes it easier for them to sell themselves such diverse and creative lines as "It's only sex — not love," "We only kissed," "We didn't kiss," "We didn't have intercourse," "It's just a blow job," "My wife doesn't like sex," and "Alcohol made me do it."

More subtly, unmarried men on the dating circuit often praise themselves for being honest in telling a prospective date that they are only interested in a casual relationship. While this may be a good enough rationale to liberate them from the obligations of consensual morality, it can also be a way of rationalizing their guilt over their intention to sexually use their date.

When properly calibrated, men's emotional absence is a good thing — which is why it's there in the first place. One of the most dramatic illustrations of this I saw was in a patient whose youngest child, a four-year-old daughter — to whom he was incredibly devoted — was diagnosed with a significant developmental disorder. This man, who had been adopted as a baby at the age of six months, was truly a man of few words — and emotions. Even when going through the highly emotional process of searching for his biological parents, he showed little by way of emotions.

His search, which was as dramatic as any fiction could be, revealed that his natural mother was from European royalty; that his natural father was an Asian prince; that his father was married to another woman and had three children when impregnating his mother; that the father might have raped the mother; that the mother was forced to relinquish the baby by her family; that the mother subsequently became severely depressed and psychotic; that the mother and father both died at a young age; and that the patient had prominent close blood relatives.

Throughout the ups and downs of his long search, this patient maintained a curious, almost merry, investigative attitude, searching not only for his origins but also for his emotions. But for a long time he was only able to experience his feelings vicariously, through me, his wife, or even more so through other adult adoptees in a support group.

At some point during this process the patient's daughter was diagnosed with Pervasive Developmental Disorder. This kind of diagnosis, which could mean a serious impairment in a child's future functioning, would send many parents into a state of extreme worry and fear. And understandable as they may be, such emotional reactions can be harmful to the child's development. But this was not something my patient had to worry about. He was so calm and underreactive in nature that the bad news did not interfere with his love and devotion for his child. In a way, he didn't really care whether his daughter would read or not, have friends or not, and be independent or not (of course he cared, but he didn't feel much about it). He was going to enjoy her, be there for her, and do whatever was necessary for her without feeling miserable about it. He was the perfect parent for his child.

As this case shows, our weaknesses are also our strengths — and vice versa, which is useful to keep in mind when evaluating oneself and/or others. In a performance evaluation on the job, for example, one might get high marks for "follow-through" and low marks for "setting priorities." The problem is that these are two sides of the same character — the person might be someone who is inclined to focus on details rather than on the bigger picture. Perhaps he can choose to see the forest or the trees, but can he be so perfect as to be able to see both? Similarly, in a dating situation we might give our date high marks for appearance and low marks for intellect (or vice versa) — and then may not want to take the bad with the good. But we may not have a choice because our date is probably someone who has worked on developing the former at the expense of the latter.

From a psychological standpoint, this "package deal" proposition is always true about our defenses — they are our best allies as well as our most dangerous enemies, all at once. This is true even when one's defense is out of whack. My patient John, the man with the "so-called abuse," is a case in point, as his inability to feel was highly conducive to his career. An international investment banker, he had developed a reputation on Wall Street as an uncanny reader of turbulent financial markets — thanks, in large measure, to his ability to think coolly and clearly under stress and to generally stay above the fray.

The Ambivalent Cord

In all likelihood, men's emotional absence is part and parcel of their emotional hardware — their genetic, evolutionary predisposition. In addition, as philosopher Myriam Miedzian explains, boys were traditionally raised to be soldiers, that is, to kill, not to empathize. Yet, from an internal psychological perspective, men's reluctance to feel has more to do with the capacity to love than the capacity to kill. As discussed by, among others, psychoanalyst Karen Horney, what men fear most is losing themselves in a relationship with a woman. Therefore, the more their partner needs them, the more space from her they need.[1]

Along these lines, some men cannot respond emotionally to

any woman who wants them. When pursued, they become cold, hardened, and harsh. Tolstoy described Prince Andrew, one of his most beloved male characters, in such terms, saying he treated his sister with "extreme logic, as if punishing someone for those secret illogical emotions that stirred within [himself]." It is indeed their *own* feelings of dependency in relation to women that men struggle to deny by feeling nothing and by pushing women away. One patient was so fearful of losing his independence in a relationship that in his mind he transformed any woman interested in him into a needy, pathetic caricature. At one point I said to him, "I'm amazed by the kinds of mental gymnastics you perform in order to avoid losing yourself inside a woman." Interestingly, the patient's response to my comment —"You don't understand, I'm actually trying to make my way into one"— points to an important paradox which is at the heart of men's emotional absence: their fear of losing themselves in a woman is actually a wish.

In the case of this patient, in his rebuttal to my observation he consciously meant to say that he knew he was too picky and that he was trying to find a way to love one of these women. His less than conscious idea of love, however, was that of a passionate forgetting of one's fundamental separateness and selfish desires. No wonder he was so afraid of what he wanted. As you might expect, the developmental origins of this conflict lies in the early relationship of boys with their mothers. I will discuss this later in the book, but as a preview, consider a slip of the tongue made once by this very patient when talking about the time he left home for college: "It was time to cut the ambivalent — I mean the umbilical — cord!"

Some time during my first year in graduate school, I had a conversation with my mother about the developmental theory of separation and individuation, which has to do with how the child carves out a path of psychic separateness from his mother. "From the mother's point of view," said my mother, "the child comes from inside of her and will always remain part of her." At the time, I was eager to dismiss this statement as a mother's reluctance to let go. But now that I have children myself, I can see what she meant — and I'm not even the mother. Nevertheless, precisely because this is the mother's emotional reality, the child must create his own, separate emotional reality. This, of course, is equally true of boys and girls, and in some sense it is an easier job for a boy, because by virtue of his gender he is already different from his mother, in a very physical, basic way. Yet this difference also represents a loss, a "vagina envy" of sorts, and it gives rise to the desire to return to a state of undifferentiated merger. This is where emotional absence enters the picture, its mission being to eject this dangerous wish out of consciousness so as to guard against its fulfillment and preserve the process of separation.

So in this respect, men are afraid of the love within them. But to make things more complicated, they are also afraid of their own hate, which is another important developmental element underpinning emotional absence. Several important British psychoanalysts have traced the development of this "schizoid" defense, the separation of emotions from intellect, to a time in infancy when in order not to feel angry or hateful toward a loving but also frustrating mother — a duality inherent in all parenting — the baby splits his internal image of the mother into "the good breast" and the "bad breast." There are some rather complicated psychoanalytic theories about what happens next, but the bottom line is that the developing child is afraid of biting the hand that feeds him.

This too is true for both males and females. But men's emotional absence offers them the tool or the means of distancing themselves from the angry, hateful feelings. The price of this distancing, however, is a general withdrawal, aloofness, and isolation, along with the sense of being a cold, even bad person, a person who is too hateful to love. It is in fact the case that many men with commitment difficulties are afraid of intimacy because of their own anger and destructiveness. They are afraid, and many times with good reason, that once they commit to someone, all their rage — about the fact that this person, like all others, is not a good enough emotional provider — will destroy their love and will also provoke retaliation.

Of course, this withdrawal is usually not that dramatic and total. It often shows itself, for instance, in an observational rather than participant attitude toward other people and the self. In that sense, every man is a bit of an observer, perhaps a writer—but more of a journalist than a novelist. Let me illustrate. One of my patients, who actually was a journalist, once brought to a session a "documentation of a crisis" to which he had been a witness the night before. Late that night his girlfriend had returned to their apartment drunk, and in a fit of unprovoked anger had begun throwing and smashing dishes and glasses on the kitchen floor. After trying unsuccessfully to calm her down, the patient withdrew and sat down at his desk to document everything she was saying and doing, so that he could "bring it [to me] for analysis the next day." As we talked about it, it became clear that the real reason the patient became a documentarian — an observer rather than a participant — was that it provided him with a way of controlling his own anger about his girlfriend's drunken fit.

The same patient would remove himself not only from his girlfriend's but also from his own crises. For example, when he once called me to request an extra session, rather than saying, "I need to see you," or "I'm going through a hard time," he said, "I'd like to have an additional session this week so that you can take a 'snapshot' of a psychologically important moment." This patient's reactions may seem rather singular, but the fact is, men do this kind of thing all the time. When they say to a woman, "Calm down," or "You are overreacting," or "I'll think about it," or "What are you getting so excited about?" they are in effect trying to transform themselves from emotional participants in a contemporary drama into its dispassionate historians.

Men's tendency to live in the world of ideas and to use such ideas to intellectualize their feelings can be mocked for its silly refusal to recognize emotional reality. But it can also be celebrated for its contribution to cerebral life. One patient very much wanted to be in a relationship but was so phobic of commitment that, as he jokingly put it, he was afraid to say hi to a woman in the hallway because he would then have to marry her. Now while for years he had stayed away from women who were emotionally available for a relationship, eventually he was able to "trick" himself into a relationship. He did so by telling himself and his cooperative female prospect to "just not consider what we do together a relationship." This became an ongoing joke between the two of them as they proceeded to develop a loving "nonrelationship," putting themselves on the fast track to engagement and marriage.

This act of subjugating emotional reality to *ideas* about emotional reality may seem silly or immature. But sometimes it works. I used this technique a few years ago when buying a new car. My wife wanted to buy a station wagon — for all the practical reasons people with kids buy them. But to me, symbolizing the suburban defeat of creative freedom, a station wagon was an "over my dead body" kind of issue. So employing all my intellectual firepower, I convinced myself that a minivan was less suburban than a wagon — "It's more like a sport utility vehicle." So we bought a minivan, and I've been very happy with it ever since — never mind that soon thereafter it became the new universal symbol of suburban life. (Predictably enough, now that the station wagon is vanishing, I secretly wonder what it would be like to have one.)

As this example shows, sometimes men not only impose ideas over emotions, but also ideational reality over actual reality. Now while at the extreme end of this tendency there is psychosis, one does not need to be crazy to occasionally or momentarily not see reality. One patient told me in his first session that he was coming to see me because of pressure from his fiancée. He further told me that because of this pressure he had been lying to his fiancée for the past six months, telling her he was already in counseling. And to support that lie he had "made up a regular Monday evening appointment with a counselor," which had the added advantage of having an excuse to have an evening away from her. When I asked him why he had done all this, he slipped and said, "I thought counseling would help...," as though he actually was in counseling. So this man, not really knowing why he had made up that lie, momentarily convinced himself that it wasn't a lie. Now not being psychotic, the patient immediately caught and corrected himself. But it's easy to see why he slipped away from reality for a second — after all, he eventually did pursue counseling, and probably had intended to do it all along.

Virtual Intimacy

If one way to find out what emotional absence is all about is to explore theories of psychological development, another way is to check out the Internet. The Internet is not only a new medium, but also a new interpersonal space with its own unique psychology. In combining the live communications feature of talking on the phone with the unilateral, reflective mode of writing a letter, the Internet is a place of meeting between minds without bodies. It is a place which requires no physical or psychological exposure, demands no consistency or commitment, yet offers the hope of endless possibilities, only one of which is the option of reality. It is a vast emotional playground where one can play without the risk of consequences.

For example, if you are shopping the chat rooms for discussion groups or for Internet pals, you can remain as anonymous as you'd like to. You are thus in the unusual position of calibrating the proportions of your observational versus participative behaviors. You can experience yourself as the unseen voyeur who is protected in his own private space or as the polar opposite — the exhibitionist who is risking everything by letting a stranger into his inner sanctum. Or anywhere on the continuum between the two. To borrow a metaphor from psychoanalyst Henry Guntrip, this interpersonal space is like the one between two porcupines coming together to warm up. If they're too close to each other, they're hurt, but if they are too far apart, they're cold. So they keep moving back and forth, looking for that intermediate place where it's not too painful and not too cold.[2]

Given this description, it should be self-evident that no emotionally absent man worthy of this label could resist the temptation of "surfing the Net." And I suspect that this schizoid nature of the Internet habitat is one of the reasons it is populated by more men than women. So what can the Internet teach us about the emotional absence of its inhabitants? Anecdotally speaking, the male patients in my practice seem to use the Internet in the way one might use group therapy or a prostitute — as a natural laboratory, an emotionally protected arena where one can experiment with new, emotionally risky behaviors.

So for example, if a man is unsure about his sexual orientation but is fearful of exploring actual homosexual sex, he might go virtual first. Or if he is frustrated with the lack of sex in his marriage but is afraid of sexually transmitted diseases, he might take on an Internet lover — with the added "advantage" that he can more easily rationalize his guilt away. Other men simply find it easier to open up or "talk" about their secrets and fantasies online.

And then there are those who come dangerously close to living online. One man came to therapy at the age of thirty, after separating from his wife of seven years. He was a lanky, wiry man with a drawn baby face, wild, frizzy hair, and thick black glasses. Casually and carelessly dressed, he was a computer scientist as you may have guessed. Cerebrally inclined, extremely kind, and dryly funny, he was also mathematically and musically gifted. As a teenager, he had been a real computer whiz, but rather than becoming a "hacker," he became an Internet vigilante — he would illegally penetrate the computer systems of large companies, and then call the next day and instruct them on how to improve their security. And he was so good at this that already in his freshman year of college, technology conglomerates were competing to employ him. But at that time, and for years to come, he was more interested in academic research than in the material world.

In his first few sessions with me, the patient chose to talk about career issues. But given the recent breakdown of his marriage and his anxious avoidance of the subject, I encouraged him to shift his focus. So at last he began to tell me the story of his marriage. It turned out that the patient and his wife had never had much by way of a sexual relationship, and that what little sex they had was inhibited and tentative. For his part, the patient felt uncomfortable with his body, as he did with the physical world at large. And even though he wanted to have more sex, he was too kind to upset his wife about it. As for her, she was generally inhibited about her sexuality. She came from an old-fashioned, tightly knit, strict Catholic family of Italian descent. She had married the patient at the age of nineteen, having had no previous sexual experience and not even a conversation about sex with anyone.

When she met "Don," the patient, she immediately fell in love with him — or at least with the idea of him and with his mind. She saw him as someone who would take her away from her small, uneducated world and open her horizons to the excitement of technology, art, and science. Perhaps it was a way for her to separate from her somewhat suffocating family. As for Don, his interest in her was more passive. But he was enamored of her straightforward, naive youthfulness and was taken by her admiration for him. And so, in the first few years of their relationship, the two were very much in love, but perhaps more like a brother and sister than lovers. Nonetheless, when she announced that she wanted to separate, the patient was shocked.

Her only explanation was that she had married too young, and that she needed to find out who she was first. The patient was too smart to accept this explanation as is, but was afraid to confront her. He didn't want to hear that he was unattractive, too skinny or clumsy, or that he was not sexually aggressive enough. And he was afraid of the humiliation that would come with asking and finding out whether she was having an affair. So fairly characteristically, Don accepted the situation, packed his computer, and moved out. He then immersed himself in his research and tried to forget about his troubles. But he was also forgetting to eat, and was showing other signs of depression. Eventually, when his mother commented that he was becoming skinnier than ever, he decided to seek help.

As we discussed all this in therapy, about a year after the separation, Don became more and more interested in finding out why his wife had left him. But he was still not going to ask. Calling her was too humiliating, and he was still afraid of what it would be like talking to her. On the other hand, he didn't mind using the Internet. During their years together, Don had introduced his wife to the World Wide Web, and she had became quite involved in a couple of "chat rooms," or discussion groups. Now he decided to take advantage of that.

Knowing the mechanics and security procedures of the Internet server used by his wife, he was able to open an alias account for himself and to enter various chat rooms where she could be found. In doing so, Don took great care to "develop his character" as he put it. As he proudly told me, he made sure to use syntax and vocabulary distinctly different from his own, and to make certain spelling mistakes that he would have never made as himself. And to boot, he also changed his gender. So when joining a chat room, he would introduce himself as one Pamela Hoggan, a professor of comparative literature, with interests in early Renaissance art, the Bloomsbury group, and Gertrude Stein. The latter was a hook for his wife: while he himself knew little about Gertrude Stein, he knew that his wife had been reading her work a year or two earlier.

And it worked. He found his wife, she responded to one of his messages, and they began to have a "conversation" about Gertrude Stein, literature, and life in New York. At some point, "Pamela" would leave the conversation, to give Don a chance to read more about Gertrude Stein. She would then return and strike up conversations with others in the chat room. This went on for a few days, at which point — to increase his credibility as much as to play with the system — Don entered his real self, simultaneously with Pamela — into the chat room. He exchanged some polite words with his wife as Don, then jumped back into his Pamela character, resuming her "voice" and continuing her conversation with his unsuspecting wife.

After jumping back and forth, Don exited, and the other two continued their chat alone. Patiently waiting for a strategic moment, Pamela finally found an opening to ask the wife about "other, or personal interests." The wife said she had recently separated from her husband. Pamela, heart racing with suspense, jumped at the opportunity and asked why. The wife suggested they go into a "private room" and so they did. There, in the privacy of intimate virtuality, Don learned that in the last year of his marriage his wife had fallen in love and had had a relationship with a woman! As the wife explained, she was not too sure about her sexual identity, but felt that she must explore it further. Pamela was completely understanding. "What happened to the relationship with the woman?" he asked. "It didn't work out — we were different people," replied the wife.

As Don later told me, at that moment he felt a surge of longing and sexual passion for his wife. So he turned to Pamela for help. "Why not explore it more with me?" Pamela seductively addressed the wife. "I myself am not sure about my orientation, and I'd like to explore it, especially with someone like you. And we can start by getting to know each other here." To Don's amazement, the wife agreed, and they then started a virtual relationship, which over several days progressed from stroking and caressing scenarios to passionate sexual imaginings, complete with mutual (and actual) orgasms. But a week or so later, Pamela vanished from the Internet with no trace or explanation.

As Don and I discussed in therapy, in going undercover on the Internet, he was able to find the *information* he wanted to have (i.e., why his wife had left), while avoiding some of the pain he would feel if he had confronted her directly. In that sense he protected himself from the emotional consequences of loving his wife: rejection, betrayal, and jealousy. But he also protected himself from the consequences of hating her: in the virtual seduction of his wife he had deceived and penetrated her, got his way with her, and left her hanging, just as she had done to him. And while his conscious feelings throughout their virtual intimacy ranged from sexual passion to detached amusement, he clearly got back at her with a mountain of hostility — without knowing it and with no fear of retaliation.

The "How To" Manual for Getting Water out of Stone

There *is* no manual because you can't make anyone, let alone men, feel anything they won't let themselves feel. Nevertheless, there are some things you can do to be more or less inviting of emotions. The first important principle is to strike while the iron is hot. One analyst recommends that with certain types of highly emotional people, the therapist should strike while the iron is *cold*, which makes sense if you want someone to hear you out. But when you want someone to feel, helping them to hear you is less critical than helping yourself to hear them. With men, what you need to do is listen, and listen carefully, especially on the rare occasion when they do feel something.

This often means that you need to listen to, encourage, and indulge surface emotions first, even if you're searching for deeper feelings. With my patient Don, above, the unconscious hostility which he demonstrated in his Internet intimacy with his wife was also evident in relation to me in our very first session. "I looked you up, you know," he said, and went on to inform me about my research interests, publications, address, and the best driving route from my office to my house. "The Internet is an amazing thing," he said, and I more than agreed. But I did not disclose — at that time — my feelings of being violated. Nor did I interpret to him his controlling hostility. Why? Because from his conscious viewpoint, checking me out was a playful, collegial act of kindness — it wasn't even a consumer asserting his rights. So it was too early to challenge his feelings.

The same was true of the anger and hatred he expressed in the virtual violation of his wife. While he knew that deceiving her into an online affair was wrong, he felt no conscious anger or hatred toward her. So in analyzing it, I focused first on the more obvious feelings of shame, humiliation, and rejection. And I encouraged the expression of such conscious feelings whenever possible, by listening to them, asking follow-up questions, and validating them. And I let the sleeping dogs of his penetrative rage lie — for the time being.

In this case the surface feelings were relatively easy to hear and empathize with, but many times they are not. Nonetheless, if you want a man to feel, you have to take what you can get — you must welcome all feelings, negative as well as positive. For one thing, negative feelings are often followed by positive feelings. And more important, the capacity for feeling is indivisible, so we must take the evil with the good. But even when the good is nowhere to be seen, if you want an emotional man, accepting and surviving negative feelings is critical. When a man has an angry outburst, his partner naturally has the impulse to want to make it go away. However, from the viewpoint of facilitating emotions, it is better for the partner to adopt the detached, almost amused attitude of "Go ahead, vent your anger, it's not going to kill me." It's a different matter, of course, when such anger becomes abusive.

For many women responding to positive feelings from men is just as difficult as coping with negative ones. It may be easy for a woman to express her love and to request that her man be more expressive of his. "You never say I love you," "You never buy me flowers," and "You don't seem to care about me anymore" are common complaints of women. But what happens when men *are* more expressive of their love? Many women seem to jump at the opportunity to overreciprocate and reexpress their love to such an extent that they suffocate and shut up the man in the process. Other women see it as a sign of weakness and a reason to stay away.

Clinically, "Strike while the iron is hot" can be interpreted to mean that an emotional crisis, or for that matter any crisis, is also an opportunity. And among other things, it is an opportunity because the clinician can leverage the crisis to facilitate change. "Things are not working as they are," the crisis says to us, "and I'm here to make sure you'll make the necessary changes." For men, the crisis is often failure of the defense of emotional absence — for whatever reason, they are no longer able to avoid powerful feelings. So in this context, the job of the therapist is not to patch up the guy and send him back into his former state of obliviousness, but rather, to help him tolerate a wider range of emotions. And this is true for the nontherapist as well. After all, life is full of crises. And while a crisis in our partner may generate in us fear and even judgment, we must rise to the occasion and respond instead with strength, supporting the emotional chaos of today, not the failing Band-Aid of yesterday.

Now what to do if the iron is never hot, if a man's emotional absence really gets in the way of intimacy, and if there isn't even a crisis to liven things up? And what to do if after accepting and exploring the surface feelings we want to go deeper? Here are some techniques I've developed with patients, all of which are based on the same principle: If you can't beat the enemy, join him.

Winning with Logic

One patient came to therapy at the insistence of his wife because of various irresponsible behaviors. He acknowledged that he was impatient but argued that impatience was inborn and that, therefore, there was nothing he could do about it. He was thus impatient with the whole idea of therapy. Assuming a dispassionate, logical attitude, I said, "Who knows, maybe impatience *is* innate — at this point the research is still inconclusive. But let me ask you this. If you were an experimental psychologist, the kind who runs mice in mazes, and you wanted to induce impatience in a mouse, what would you do?"

The patient liked this scientific task. He thought for a moment and came up with the idea of "placing food in front of the mouse behind a glass partition, to tease and deprive it." I concurred that this might induce impatience and went on to offer another possible approach, giving the mouse food every time he pressed a lever — to spoil him. The patient agreed that that too might induce impatience. I then went on to generalize that either deprivation or overgratification can give rise to impatience. At that moment the patient, who grew up as an only child and without a father, jumped with amazement. "That's exactly what my mother did — both. She first spoiled me to death when I was really little, but then when she started working, she made me do all the housework — cleaning, cooking, everything, every fucking day — I had no childhood from that time on!"

"I guess from that time on it was kind of like the food behind the glass partition," I couldn't resist saying.

Winning with Action

Because they are socialized to "bring home the bacon," men tend to act on their emotions in the external world, rather than experience them internally. So, for instance, when one of my patients was fired from his job, he proceeded to fire me. Consciously, this was motivated by practical, financial considerations. But when he came back three months later, still unemployed, we figured out that he was so angry when he was fired that he had to *do* something about it. And what he did was to kick the dog — transforming himself from powerless to powerful by means of a displaced, retaliatory action.

By its very nature psychotherapy is not action-oriented. Indeed, the therapist's legitimate repertoire includes little by way of action — going over the time, wearing an unusual tie, or talking too much are pretty much it. But what he or she can do to reach men is to simulate action, or at least use the language or body language of action. For example, a forty-year-old man married to a woman of the same age was undecided whether he wanted to have a child. "I am obviously ambivalent, and we really need to analyze it so that I can make a decision," he said. "Listen," I replied — with a tone of impatient contempt — "I am a psychologist, so I would love to analyze this for the next seven years, which is probably what it would take. But there is no time for analysis. You ran out of time for that. It's time to act, one way or another." That helped him to get in touch with his panic.

Another patient was also unable to make a decision, in his case about a career change. He was a Swedish career diplomat, working permanently with the Swedish consulate in New York. Initially, the idea of foreign service had been exciting, but after several years he began to hate the travel, the political pressures, the long hours, and, eventually, the job itself. But he had no other skills, his English was limited and heavily accented, and his wife and kids were firmly American. So while New York offered no obvious alternatives, going back to Sweden was also out.

Now the more frustrated and helpless he felt, the more he focused on these admittedly constricting, external circumstances — as if he could change them. But as I told him, the only thing he could change was his internal life, his feelings about the situation. The problem was that this did not involve action, so the patient didn't know how to change it, nor did he really want to. He preferred to be a prisoner of the external reality rather than a liberator of the internal world. Until I presented to him the paradigm of Nelson Mandela, an actual prisoner turned president. The point here was not to offer a ray of hope, but to speculate on the internal freedom Nelson Mandela must have achieved in order to emerge from twenty-eight years of imprisonment without bitterness or hatred so that he could become a leader rather than a victim or a victimizer. The point was to demonstrate to the patient that internal freedom is actually a necessary condition for external freedom. But this example only appealed to the patient because its outcome involved a bottom-line change in the world of actions. Nonetheless, I was still able to point to the fact that during his imprisonment, there was no way for Nelson Mandela to expect that his twenty-eight years of external nonaction would culminate in such a dramatic reversal.

Detective in the Dark

Men's emotional absence often leaves them in the dark not only about what they may feel, but also about their emotional memory. In telling a personally moving story from their childhood (or from last week) they may become suddenly casual at the peak moment, as if it were just a blip in their past. To help them out — or to help yourself to connect with them — you must become a detective of the mind, searching for the missing emotion. In that role, you can proceed carefully with logical deductions or better yet, play dumb, rather like Detective Colombo. Actually, to avoid being manipulative it's best just to *be* dumb and simply stumble upon the solution. This is hard to do, but occasionally I have succeeded.

One patient was a complete emotional mystery. Nice and outgoing in general, he was never able to say anything personal about himself. This was obviously a problem in therapy as many of our sessions were punctuated by long silences and vague recollections of nothing special.

One day the patient reported that he had had an unpleasant taxi ride on the way to therapy. The cabby apparently had gone on a tirade about "spics and kikes" and others whom he wouldn't let in his cab. The patient was wondering why he'd stayed in the taxi or didn't confront the cabby even though he felt uncomfortable with what he'd said. Slightly bored, I was thinking hard about what to do with this tidbit. Straining to connect it to anything else, I finally blurted out, "I don't know why, but this makes me think of the affair you had with your boss last year." Consciously, I really didn't know why it made me think of the affair, and I only figured it out when the patient reacted with his own left-field *emotional* association — when he was five or six years old, the patient had walked in on his father having sex with the neighbor's teenage daughter. The patient had guarded that secret, occasionally forgetting about it altogether, never speaking of it with anyone. He now began sobbing as this forcefully entered his consciousness. As we were discussing this, the connection to the taxi ride — as well as other situations, such as not confronting his best friend about his heavy drinking — became more evident. The patient was forever colluding with other people's inappropriate behaviors.

Naturally, men's emotional secrets are not limited to the past or to third parties. In fact, they are often about you, in the here and now. When this is the case, you might be better off with the more intellectual bent of the Sherlock Holmes approach. Here, you might be looking for a symbolic, "off-site" expression of feelings toward you.

One patient's wife, an experienced patient in her own right, had told him that when I was on vacation he seemed to miss me and to be angry that I was not there for him. In telling me this, the patient smiled and went on to inform me — without even a hint of defensiveness — that he had had no such feelings whatsoever. I smiled too, privately, or not so privately, making fun of my own work. The truth is, the more experienced I become as a therapist, the less I make such interpretations to my patients. Not because they are not true, but because on some level they are almost always true, which makes them kind of irritatingly pat — and useless. What is often more important than the fact that he feels abandoned by the therapist is how the patient processes this fact and what he does with it.

For this patient, like most men, such emotions were hidden behind mounds of intellectual symbolism. "To change the subject," the patient went on, as I was listening for clues that he was possibly doing anything but that, "I sat next to a psychologist on a train ride to D.C., so I had three hours to ask him all the questions about your profession that would be inappropriate to ask you." "What did you ask him?" I further perked up my ears. "Well, many questions, as you can imagine. For example, were his own sexual fantasies influenced by his patients' fantasies? Or when does he see his children if he works both early morning and late evening hours?"

I now smiled again and told the patient he apparently hadn't really changed the subject and that it seemed his wife was right after all. "Elementary, my dear Watson," Holmes would have said when his sidekick asked for an explanation. In my absence, the patient latched on to an off-site substitute with whom he could be intimate (do my fantasies stay with you?) as well as angrily devaluing (you are an absent father!).

As I shared this formulation with the patient, he was intellectually intrigued. He still had no feelings to speak of, but I trusted that these would come with time — on their own volition. Perhaps on my next year's vacation.

The Devil Is in the Details

One patient seemed almost too happy merely three weeks after the painful breakup of his ten-year marriage. He was excited about business, excited about the new BMW he was planning to buy, and excited about starting to date again. And best of all, he had just made a reservation for a Christmas skiing vacation in the Canadian Rockies. I knew that he and his wife were avid skiers, but they usually went to Vermont or Colorado, so I asked him why he was going to Canada. He went on to say, with no apparent emotion, that before they were married he and his wife had had a great skiing vacation in the highest, remote Canadian town of Kimberley, and that they vowed that one day they'd be back.

I then asked where he was going to stay. He looked at me somewhat perplexed, and said, "In a hotel, of course." "What kind of hotel?" I asked, not fully knowing why. "I actually got a nice large suite in case I meet a girl I want to take with me." He smiled. "What girl would you spend this kind of money on?" I asked, thinking that Christmas was right around the corner and that there wasn't much time to meet a girl.

"You know what's funny," he replied casually, as if speaking off the cuff on an unrelated matter, "the other day I spoke to Linda [his wife] on the phone and told her about my vacation plan — I thought maybe she'd come with me. She always wanted to go back there, you know." Having said that, the patient began to let his mind go, imagining being with Linda after a long day of skiing and a dip in the hot tub. "She would open her body to me, like she always did, all the way, like nobody else has ever done for me. And I would fuck her hard and long until I'm all emptied out inside her, my whole body shivering with animal love…" This may sound pornographic, but it didn't at the time, because as the patient was elaborating on his fantasy, his raw desire turned into deep longings, and his happy, casual manner was terminated by raw sobbing.

So not atypically, this man's feelings about the past were tucked inside a small detail of a plan for the future — in this case, hotel reservations for vacation. And again not atypically, the devil was also in the...sex.

Forfeit the Home Field Advantage

I personally hate sports metaphors, but in dealing with men, you can't completely avoid them. This particular technique, self-evident as it may be, is really a summary of all of the above. How to help men to ask for help when they don't feel they need it? By playing in their ballpark. Example: A patient left a message requesting an extra session because "my wife thinks that I'm out of my mind and that I need to see you." In the session he insisted that this, in fact, was the only reason he asked for an extra session. "If that's true," I said, "then you *are* out of your mind. But since in my professional judgment you are rather sane, there must be a better reason. Do you know what it is?" "I think I do," he conceded and went on to discuss it.

Now the reason I was able to directly and successfully confront this man about his feelings was because I first joined him in his mind game — if only in order to emerge from it and pull him with me. But therein lies the danger of playing around with emotional absence — you may not come out on the other side.

A Word of Caution about Joining the Enemy

In applying these techniques one must never go too deep into the territory of emotional absence. Whether you are a therapist, a girlfriend, a spouse, or a business partner, you must always remain intact in your ability to provide a model of emotionality. Otherwise, you and your man will end up in the land of alienation and despair.

A month before his wedding, a patient received a call from one of his best friends, telling him he had been having an affair with his fiancée. The friend apologized profusely and stated that their friendship was more important to him than any woman. The patient, who was very much in love with his fiancée, was distraught.

More than anything else, he was afraid he had lost his fiancée forever. But he graciously accepted the friend's apology and endorsed his sentiments about their friendship. That night the patient had a dream in which he was climbing up a big office building, stopping by for an interview or a chat with different men on each floor. The higher he went, the more powerful the men he met, but all of them, one way or another, ignored or rebuffed him. At the penthouse, however, a beautiful, sexy woman led him to a large room with a soft, sensuous bed in the center. She then lay on the bed and opened her arms and legs, inviting him to join her.

When the patient described the dream to me the next day, it was clear that the emotional "weight" of the dream was at the end — the relief and joy of "winning" the woman. This also corresponded to the patient's conscious concern about losing his fiancée. But because this man loved the intellectual aspect of dream analysis, and because of my own emotional absence, I tried to outsmart both of us by focusing on the less obvious meaning of the dream, the one having to do with being rebuffed by men, that is, the male friend who betrayed him, and by extrapolation, his father, who was a powerful yet emotionally distant man.

While this analysis was technically correct, the patient argued with it, saying he had no feelings about his male friend, and didn't see the connection to his father. What he didn't say, and what I only later realized, was the obvious. At that moment he had no interest in my analysis regardless of its truthfulness. At that moment he was struggling, albeit privately, with feelings of abandonment and betrayal in relation to his fiancée and nothing else.

So in joining this patient's tendency to intellectualize, my analysis missed the emotional boat altogether and landed us in a psychological desert. Interestingly, and not coincidentally, I had become like one of the men in his dream. I felt stupid and bad about this, but was then able to find the silver lining — or perhaps it was just my own intellectualizing defense. I was able to show the patient how his intellectual approach to life had invoked my own emotional absence. So he had not only re-created the dream in my office but also his father in me, which was further grist for the mill.

What's the bottom line on emotional absence? As I hope I have demonstrated, like shame, it is not really the enemy. If anything, when not overused, it can be a helpful defense. Nor are we really at war. So in dealing with these defenses, in therapy or in everyday life, our strategy is not to destroy them. Rather, it is to subtly invite them to relax. When we are successful at that, stone walls become permeable and men not only talk — they become poets.

Masculine Insecurity

...I'm tired of being on top

A Dangerous Influence

The first order of business in being a man is: Don't be a woman." This, in the words of psychiatrist and author Robert Stoller, is what men's gender identity is all about. In our society, Stoller says, men always keep women at some distance: they don't form close friendships with them; they are afraid of being trapped or enveloped by them; they criticize their emotionality; and they talk dirty about their anatomy. In addition, men are terrified of displaying their own feminine traits. Tenderness, hairlessness, roundness, high voice, caretaking, affection, and the uninhibited expression of emotions are all thought of as the enemies of maleness. And, of course, there is the ultimate fear of being sexually desired by another man. All this, Stoller suggests, and I concur, adds up to one inescapable observation: men apparently feel that women, and femininity itself, are a dangerous influence.

In trying to shed light on this phenomenon, Stoller, together with anthropologist Gilbert Herdt, has found and described a remote tribe from New Guinea whose entire social structure is based on the explicit and conscious notion that women are dangerous. According to Stoller, men in that Sambian tribe believe that women's menstrual and vaginal fluids are contaminating. They believe that through sexual intercourse women empty men of their male substance, semen, the essence of vitality and masculinity. Naturally enough, in order to protect themselves from these female dangers Sambian men impose a strict separation between the sexes. Even in the family hut, where married men live with their spouses and young children, there are separate female and male spaces and paths. And all contacts with women, most particularly sexual intercourse, are scrutinized and regulated.

In studying the Sambia, Stoller and Herdt concluded that this isolated, mountainous tribe needed to foster and support male aggression so that it could defend itself against the brutal enemies who surrounded it. Clearly, "feminine" vulnerability and attitudes would undermine this type of aggression. But amazingly enough, for that very reason femininity plays a critical role in the development of masculine aggression in Sambian culture.

For the first seven to ten years of life, Sambian boys spend no time with their fathers. In fact, they have no real contact with any men. In infancy they are considered to be an extension of the mother's body — so much so that they are not even named until nine months of age. And in the following, "formative" years, they continue to enjoy an intense and exclusive closeness with their mother.

But then, somewhere between the ages of seven and ten, all this comes to an abrupt and cruel end. The boy must leave the family hut and move into the men's clubhouse, the nerve center of the village warriorhood, where all boys reside until the age of eighteen. From this point on the boy is not allowed to talk with, touch, or even look at his mother. Instead, initiation into manhood begins: the boy is forced to perform oral sex on, and "receive semen" from, older adolescent boys. Since the Sambians believe that men do not produce semen internally, and must receive it from the outside, this sexual activity is viewed like breastfeeding, and is encouraged and engaged in on an ongoing, promiscuous basis — the more the better.

When the boy reaches puberty, he joins the ranks of the older boys. He begins to "give semen" and is no longer allowed to receive it. And interestingly, from age eighteen, at which point marriage (by arrangement) takes place, all homosexual activity ends. This course of development is strictly enforced and is followed by all boys.

Stoller's analysis of masculine development among the Sambians focuses on what he calls the boy's "symbiosis anxiety." Simply put, since the boy experiences himself as one with mother, the fear is that he will develop as a girl, not a boy. Hence, the complete removal of the mother and the introduction of severe, aggressive, and cruel male influence. Despite the trauma of the loss of his mother, the boy's ultimate desire is to become a man. And in any event, having lost his mother, he has no choice but to identify with his father, as represented by the older boys. He then grows to be like those boys and, eventually, like his father — aggressive, hostile, cruel, and heterosexual.

We can now see that without the fear of femininity there would be no need for masculinity. The psychological principle here is simple yet powerful: in trying to conquer a fear one is likely to go overboard. Demosthenes, we are told, became the greatest orator of ancient Greece because he had struggled to overcome a speech impediment. On a more contemporary note, a "control freak" is someone who is afraid of losing control, and a "neatness freak" is someone who is worried about his own messiness. And, of course, this dynamic also explains why successful actors are often shy people.

In terms of male development, while boys in our culture do not travel along the Sambian path of torture, their journey to adulthood nevertheless requires a similar developmental maneuvering. Political correctness aside, and notwithstanding the changes brought about by the women's movement, boys in our society still start out their lives with a symbiotic closeness to their mother and usually end up identifying with their father. Somewhere along the way, generally after the age of six or seven, they begin to distance themselves from their mother — and all other girls. Eventually, even in adulthood, they keep all women at some distance.

For the seven-year-old, this is a difficult time. On the one hand his mother provides unmatched love, warmth, and support. And he too loves her tenderly, even passionately. On the other hand, his father, his pals in the playground, his brothers, TV, books, competitive sports, all overwhelm him with messages like "Boys are tough," "Control your emotions," and "Don't play with girls." And on his own accord too, the boy admires and wants to have what he perceives as the strength and power of masculinity.

To make this even more complicated, while the boy can gently push his mother away, he cannot rid himself of the femininity she has already bestowed on him. Nor does he really want to. It's bad enough that he has to let go of his mother; why also destroy what she has already given him? Yet, the external and internal pressures of masculinity continue to make their demands.

The solution? What most boys eventually do is to relegate their mother's early influence to the private, silent, and unarticulated world of the unconscious. There it is camouflaged into their permanent character structure, where it becomes part of "the child within." This process, which psychologists refer to as "internalization," is critical because it renders useless boys' flight from the feminine: they can keep "outside" girls at a distance but not the one within. They have let in a Trojan horse, and they will have to cope with it for the rest of their lives.

Thus, how men cope with their repressed femininity becomes the epicenter of male development. To express or to suppress (my feelings, my femininity), that is the question. What I call masculine insecurity refers to this conflict and its various manifestations, the most obvious of which is men's incessant need to feel, and appear, sufficiently masculine at all times. Seen in that light, men's emotional absence is nothing but a protective antidote to their own feminine desires.

In daily life, as much as in couple therapy, one can sense this conflict in men's reactions when their spouse, girlfriend, or child cries. Whether they try to fix the problem, ignore the tears, or even comfort the person by grasping her hand, one can always detect a wince of discomfort and anxiety. Usually, it betrays the man's wish that these tears would just go away. Now, while sometimes this simply means that the man wants to protect the other person from emotional pain, more often than not it is a matter of self-protection. When a man sees a woman crying, it is as if he is looking at a mirror of his past, a picture of his own potential vulnerability. He panics in self-recognition and assumes the preventive poise of self-control.

This reaction, of course, is only one side of the conflict. The other side, the desire to be vulnerable, is just below the surface. Men often speak of their envy for women's capacity for crying, and in fact, one of the most frequent problems of male patients in psychotherapy is their inability to experience emotions as women do, spontaneously and expressively.

A dramatic version of this conflict occurred with one of my patients. As we explore his story it will be helpful to keep in mind the following theoretical "pointer." Freudian psychology views men as the primary, even superior sex: they are powerful, have better equipment, and they run the world. Women, according to this notion, are forever trying to be like men ("penis envy"). Stoller, on the other hand, considers the female gender to be primary: masculinity will not develop on its own without a defensive distancing from femininity and external male influence. Interestingly, Stoller (and others) have shown that the latter view resembles the biology of gender development in the fetus: without the addition of male hormones, the fetus will not develop male organs and will grow as a female.

Femininity Lost and Found

"Eli" entered psychotherapy ostensibly because of a strange phobia which interfered with his career. His career, he confessed, was all he really cared about, and in fact, he had been very successful at it. In only a few years he rose from being a bank teller in his small southern California hometown to become an auto executive in Detroit and, finally, a senior marketing executive in New York. By the time he came to see me, his forceful, persistent sales pitches, coupled with his exuberant, self-confident style, had won him national recognition in his industry.

The phobia he related in the first session was a fear of beer bottles, which concerned him, he said, because he had begun to avoid going out with clients so as not to feel the intense anxiety and dread that ensued when someone next to him would have a bottle of beer. Since he indicated that he had some history of excessive drinking, we first explored whether his phobia was simply based on a fear of a destructive relapse. But within a few sessions it became clear that it was more about the bottle than the beer, and that for Eli, a bottle was not just a bottle.

Eli came across as a caricature of maleness. He spent all his time at work because he loved the hunt. He loved accumulating wealth and he spent it almost exclusively on male toys — motorcycles, boats, and a couple of small airplanes. He was aggressive, outspoken, and brash. But he was also charming, and he had a knack for saying the most hostile things in the most endearing manner. "You know, Gratch, my wife is top of the line," he would say, which didn't sound so terrible except it appeared that he very much treated her like a product. "My wife says that I am a robot, that I don't have feelings for her, and she might be right! When I ask myself why I love her, I think of things like, she makes a great home, she takes care of me, and she is a great mother. One time we had a big fight and she was crying and I started laughing like I was enjoying it or something — I'm telling you, I'm like a machine. But I'm very happy with her, and we are planning to have another child next year.

"The only thing that bothers me is this beer bottle thing," he went on, and finally began to tell me how his phobia evolved. Briefly, while he had always been attracted to women and had never had sexual relationships with men, Eli had had sexual fantasies about being penetrated by men since his early twenties. And he had occasionally used beer bottles for anal stimulation while masturbating. But these fantasies, he said, didn't really bother him — he could have lived with them without ever feeling he needed to act on them.

The real problem had started a couple of years ago at a Christmas office party. While holding a bottle of beer near his mouth, he felt that the man he was talking to had figured out what he, Eli, had been doing with beer bottles. "The strange thing, Gratch, this man really did figure it out. It was like he read my mind, because he actually started making fun of me for what I do with these beer bottles. I swear, Gratch, it was weird. And since then, I can't go near any place where there are beer bottles because I worry that people will find out and think that I am gay."

During Eli's treatment we explored the question of his sexual orientation. But he was generally comfortable with his heterosexual lifestyle. What he was terrified of was not the possibility that he was gay, but rather, the idea that people would think of him as gay. In his mind, that meant being perceived as weak and unmanly. Similarly, what bothered him about his phobia was not his sexual fantasies, or what his wife or close friends would think about them, but rather, the fact that they interfered with his ability to mix with clients. Above all, he presented his phobia as a business problem.

After a few months of psychotherapy Eli's phobia was resolved. Like any psychological "symptom," it represented several unconscious factors. Yet, the therapeutic process that resolved it highlighted most vividly the concept of masculine insecurity. In particular, it demonstrated how we can use this concept to better understand, perhaps even gain entry into, the inner world of men.

When we reviewed his personal history in therapy, it became clear that Eli's sexual fantasies were related to his relationship with his father. As we saw earlier, boys must let go of their mother in order to identify with their father. But what happens if father is not available for identification? In the case of Eli, his father was a strict, physically abusive, and coldly detached man who demanded compliance, strength, and above all, no display of emotions. His mother, on the other hand (and to a lesser extent Eli's two older sisters), was overreactive, irrational, and hysterical. And needless to say, his mother was completely dominated by his father.

This left Eli, the child, in a terrible dilemma. The only way to preserve any emotional life was to model himself after the women in his family. But this, of course, posed an unthinkable threat to the kind of masculine identification mandated by his father. So what's a boy to do? Eli's solution (in the sense that his character or personality attempted to resolve this conflict over the years) was to become like his father on the outside, while secretly preserving feminine fantasies inside. For various reasons — one of which had to do with the way his father repeatedly forced him to submit to a rectal thermometer and "would jam the thermometer inside of me"— these fantasies took on a sexual form.

But as I explained to Eli, these were essentially nonsexual conflicts. While I voiced this idea repeatedly, Eli didn't really get it until, as if by some divine intervention, something out of the ordinary happened in therapy. On that day, Eli came to see me for an early morning session, just before an important presentation to the executive team of his company. At the end of this session Eli was shocked to learn that his notebook computer, which he had left in the waiting room, was gone. Both he and I were stunned and upset as we realized that the computer — which included Eli's entire presentation — had been stolen from my waiting room.

Then Eli panicked. Not so much because of the computer, and not even because of the presentation — once in the office, he said, he would be able to reproduce the presentation materials fairly quickly. He panicked because the lost presentation included some data that he could now access only through his boss, and he would therefore have to tell his boss that he had lost his computer. He first thought he could say he had left it on the train, coming into the city. But that would simply seem irresponsible. The alternative, in his mind, was to say that it was stolen from his therapist's office. And this is what he truly panicked about: he would now have to tell his boss that he was seeing a therapist. When I asked why he couldn't say "a doctor's office," Eli replied that his boss would know it was a therapist! This immediately reminded me of how his beer bottle phobia started: the man just knew what he did with those beer bottles!

As Eli and I followed that association, we saw a clear, nonsexual analogy to the beer bottle phobia. Eli's fear was that if the boss knew he was in psychotherapy, he would think of him as weak and unmanly. After all, in his therapy we discussed all those feminine fantasies and emotions. But what are we to make of Eli's feelings that, just like the man at the office party, his boss, too, could read his mind and know about its weak, feminine contents? What I suspected all along now became evident to both Eli and me: unconsciously, Eli *wanted* people to know about his female identification. He particularly wanted men to know about it. And he especially wanted men in positions of authority to know about it. Ultimately, what he has always wished for was that his father would see his femininity — his emotional vulnerability — and would accept and love him for it. In this way, the dynamics of Eli's phobia was an illustration of one of Freud's greatest theoretical formulations, that is, behind every fear there is a wish.

Once Eli and I stumbled upon this, we quickly hypothesized that the man at the party who read his mind was probably able to do so because Eli had made a gesture with the bottle, or held it in a manner that gave him away. And now, Eli could easily see himself telling his boss that he was at "the doctor's office" in such a shame-filled, hushed, or defensive tone that the boss would get the message that this was no ordinary doctor.

As we discussed this for a few minutes, there was a sense of crisis in the air. Another patient was waiting for me, and Eli had to leave for work. But just before he left, when Eli understood that he actually wanted to reveal his secrets to another man, he also realized that he didn't have to do it with his boss. Instead, he was able to find a way to tell his boss that he had lost his laptop at the doctor's office without projecting his feelings and thoughts into his words. He then went on to deliver a great presentation, and subsequently, his boss personally gave him a brand-new, top-of-the-line computer.

More important, this event crystallized for both Eli and me the therapeutic process that resolved ("cured") Eli's phobia. Once he realized that his sexual fantasies represented the wish to "cry on a man's shoulders," Eli no longer needed to experience it sexually. The bottle became a bottle, and he no longer had a secret he needed to keep himself from revealing by phobically avoiding the public place of revelation.

As with any patient, this "cure" was not as simple as my telling might lead you to believe. In the case of Eli there were many ups and downs, understandings and misunderstandings, diversions and resistances. And the "cure" wasn't a cure, for it resolved the phobia but not the complex emotional world that surrounded it. But in our quest to understand masculine insecurity, Eli's conflicts, and the manner in which they unfolded during therapy, bring into focus one of men's more universal struggles.

Notwithstanding the changes in our society regarding sex-role expectations, men are still driven to experience themselves and to act in a narrow masculine range. In ways that are not necessarily conscious and not merely a reflection of social pressures, men strive to be tough, strong, rational, and calm. Perhaps more than anything else, they feel compelled to become great providers. As we have seen, these "masculine" aspirations are based, in part, on man's need to deny his "feminine" vulnerability. They thus represent an important source of self-actualization and self-esteem for men. At the same time, they create a heavy burden of responsibility and place the male ego under the constant threat of failure. I say constant threat, because, being human, men inevitably fail (in something), because what goes up must come down, because the higher you soar, the lower you can sink. Therefore, underneath this burden lies the wish for passivity, vulnerability, emotionality, and irrationality — all those qualities, which, rightly or wrongly, are associated with traditional ideas of femininity.

These ideas of femininity, we can now speculate, represent men's unconscious memory, not of their mother, but of themselves as a young, girl-like boy, basking under the maternal influence of femininity. Indeed, research supports this view, showing that boys at a young age are just as emotionally vulnerable, if not more so, than girls. As any first-grade teacher can tell you, boys that age constantly fight to hold back their tears. Girls, on the other hand, appear to be calm and composed.

Unconsciously, then, men's desire to let go of their responsibilities represents the wish to return to that place and time with mother, where tears, including tears of joy, were still allowed. But like my patient Eli, most men experience this wish in the form of a fear, a fear which they usually cover over with a thick layer of masculine indifference.

Listening to Viagra

In announcing the megamerger of his company with another telecommunications giant, one CEO described the new partnership as "the Viagra of telecommunications." He thus expressed in new words an old idea about the politics of potency in corporate America. Whereas Sambian man had to be physically aggressive, Western man has developed a more sublimated form of combat. While he sometimes fights in the battlefield, more often he fights in the workplace. And although he might feel that the stakes are just as high — the preservation of masculinity — our man doesn't really fight. He performs. He maneuvers, chats, demands, confronts, works long hours, stays ahead of the curve, cranks up the data, stabs the competition in the back, and whatnot — all in order to successfully master the slippery steps of success. Corporate Man, in particular, lives and dies for, and by, his performance evaluation. (Of course, these days, this is true for many women as well.)

As we can see, the key word here is performance, which includes both the straightforward and hard-to-quarrel-with notion of accomplishment and the more complex and defensive idea of enactment, or being on stage. Political leaders like Ronald Reagan and Bill Clinton exemplify the latter. These are essentially performing personalities. They are so good at acting in a role, they don't even know they are acting. That's why they seem so genuine and are so popular despite the contradictions in their personal lives.

A different version of that personality — the ambitious, boastful, and aggressive businessman — was labeled by some analysts earlier in the century as the "phallic-narcissistic character." In the eighties, on the floor of the New York Stock Exchange, this character was resurrected. Or perhaps he never expired. And while medical and behavioral psychologists labeled him "type A" and documented his risk for long-term, battlefield-related diseases, feminist analysts diagnosed his behavior as "penis waving."

But regardless of his various transformations, the essential feature of this man is the drive to perform acrobatic acts of masculinity, preferably in the public domain. As we shall see in the next chapter, this performance is motivated to a great extent by the narcissistic need for recognition. But it is also the result of man's struggle to reject his femininity. "Look at me, I am a man," is what the corporate (or other workplace) warrior says. This fundamental connection between performance and masculinity is one of the reasons why impotence and its current antidote, Viagra, are such a powerful if overused metaphor for masculine insecurity.

Workplace conflicts resulting from masculine insecurity can be quite irrational, not to mention costly. One of my organizational clients, a Wall Street investment house, needed to replace the software system that was used by its stock traders. Now even though the new system was critical to the firm's trading operations and had no serious competitors in the software market, resistance to it among the traders was so fierce that it took close to ten years to start installing it.

In studying the situation, I learned that in the absence of clear direction from the company's chairman, the men responsible for installing the new system had clashed with the traders — the vast majority of whom were also men. At one point, during a heated meeting about the project, one of the senior traders announced that he would not use the new system because it required that he turn off his computer at night (which he was supposed to do anyway so that the cleaning woman would not execute stock trades on his terminal!). "We don't have the time to turn it on and off every day," he shouted.

This is mind-boggling even for Wall Street, a place where the male ego, in perfect analogy to male anatomy, rises and falls with performance, or more accurately, the perception of performance, that is, performance anxiety. While many women do extremely well on "the Street," the short-term volatility of the stock market is particularly suited to men whose masculine identity rests on the precarious balance between the joy of being on top and the fear of falling to the bottom, or between the fear of staying on the bottom and the thrill of climbing to the top. Now speaking of precarious balance, let's turn to male anatomy.

Impotence as a Metaphor

Performance and performance anxiety are intrinsic to men's masculine insecurity, which is why impotence is such a common problem. Among my many patients who came to treatment because of impotence, the one who comes to mind here is "Christopher," who at the height of his career as an entertainment lawyer had decided to become a movie producer himself. Admirably, at age forty-five he made that change, and successfully so.

He came to see me a few years later on account of what he called his "sexual problem." Already in the first session this patient struck me as a charming, warm, and eager-to-please man who was good at everything he did because he knew how to make people perform. This was true in his marriage as much as in his job. He not only helped his wife with her work as a Broadway actress, but also with her role as a mother. He had been especially helpful to her when she struggled with infertility and with difficult issues related to the adoption of their three children. And later on he was equally helpful to his grown son when he decided to search for his biological parents — he practically produced his reunion with them. Nonetheless, while enticing others to perform in their roles was the secret of his success, it was naturally his own performance that mattered to him most.

It was therefore hardly surprising that Christopher's impotence was triggered by what he perceived to be a professional failure when he ran into budget and schedule troubles with one of his movies. At that time, his anxiety about the movie took the form of feeling unsuccessful and inadequate. He then became obsessed with these thoughts and his self-doubts began to creep into his sexual life. At first he had only intermittent difficulties, but as he grew more and more concerned about his sexual performance, he became completely unable to "achieve" an erection. This is when he came to see me.

Initially, I was completely taken by Christopher's charm and generosity. Like everyone else in his life, I felt I wanted to perform for him — and I did pretty well. But underneath his kindness, he was an exacting, demanding man. So after a couple of sessions in which I "failed" to cure his impotence, I began to feel the pressure to perform. And before I knew it, just like the patient's penis, I crumbled under the pressure. I was seized by self-doubt and feelings of inadequacy and began to wonder whether I could help this man at all.

In truth, it is easy to feel inadequate in my line of work. The problems are enormously complicated. The patients are in pain and they desperately want help, but their resistance is equally strong. The pain "wants" to be there because it has meaning, on top of which, people are afraid of change and cling to the familiar. The therapeutic process is slow and the outcome is uncertain. And you cannot outmaneuver your opponent with a brilliant stroke of genius. As a therapist, you don't have the answers, and you must learn about the patient as he learns about himself. And since you deal with the "stuff of life" you never know enough.

However, when I began to doubt myself in this case, I knew that these feelings were induced by the patient. In pressuring me to perform, he was making me feel what he felt. And it was this kind of pressure that made his penis "fail." Therein lies an important paradox about impotence and its treatment: the more you worry about it, the worse it gets. Why is that? Why is it that when we feel pressured (evaluated, corrected, judged, scolded) we don't do well? Why do we become "nervous" rather than simply perform as we are expected to, indeed, as we expect of ourselves?

I once rode with a corporate executive and his driver to pick up an important business guest from the airport. We started the trip late because the executive was delayed in his office. When we were finally on the road, we were caught in rush-hour traffic. The executive asked the driver to get off the highway and try a local route. The driver complied, but not knowing the local roads as well, he made a mistake and we were lost. The executive lost his temper and started yelling at the driver to do better. The more he yelled at him, the more mistakes the driver made. We ended up being so late that the guest was nowhere to be found — he had taken a taxi. And the executive was furious and miserable.

Why did the driver act like my patient's penis? Obviously, because the executive acted like my patient. But what is the nature of this dynamic? The answer lies in the fact that the executive himself was late to start the trip. Not completely consciously, he was apparently ambivalent about picking up this "important" guest at the airport. He then made the driver feel what he felt, resistant and reluctant. And the driver complied and unconsciously acted on these feelings.

So did my patient's penis. It failed to perform because, unconsciously, its master didn't want it to perform. Without quite formulating it as a thought, Christopher was tired of being on top. Tired of having to please his wife, and the studio, and the cast. Tired of having to be aggressive and make a lot of money and take care of everybody. He was tired of being firm and he wanted to be soft. And this is what psychological impotence is all about. It can be a dislike for one's own aggression, a desire to be taken care of, an unconscious homosexual wish, or a simple retreat from performance pressures. But all these and other possible dynamics represent man's hidden desire to shed his masculine defenses and to find a feminine place of rest.

The problem is that men are so anxious about the symptom of impotence that they demand an immediate cure — from themselves, their doctor, their therapist, their penis. But the more they want it, the more their body must resist. The wise therapist, therefore, will ally himself with the autonomous penis, rather than with the demanding patient. In doing so, he will turn the tables on the patient, demanding of him to experience in feelings and thoughts what his body is displaying symptomatically. And the frustrated spouse, in this case, should probably do the same. "I don't care about your penis, I care about your feelings" is the message.

As I sometimes tell patients (in a futile attempt to explain how psychotherapy works), the paradoxical treatment of impotence is a good metaphor for the psychotherapeutic process as a whole: in order to make progress one must first renounce one's goals. You must first accept your impotence (which is not such a bad idea in itself, if the alternative is the depressive underside of overreaching), and then embrace all its intentions and meanings. Then, and only then, potency might return, seemingly on its own. But you can't cheat — you have to own the wish you are afraid of first. In that respect, psychotherapy is not about changing people, but rather, helping them to be more of who they are. The therapist's job, in this view, is to promote self-knowledge — nothing less, nothing more.

As for literal impotence, will the relatively new drug Viagra short-circuit its psychology and revamp its treatment? Will it altogether eliminate this classic symptom of masculine insecurity? Perhaps. There are already signs, however, that in many cases the unconscious resistance to potency will outsmart Viagra. As the great psychologist Howard Stern said, it will create a whole new set of problems because all those husbands who don't want to have sex with their wives will have to find other ways to avoid it.

Dating: The Masculine-Feminine Split

In dating, the woman's approach to the man's masculine insecurity can be, to use a word from Wall Street, a deal breaker. The practice of most therapists working with adults includes at least several women who answer to the following description. Smart, independent and successful, introspective, attractive and charming, reasonable, supportive and genuine. And yes, as you may have guessed, this "type" of woman is in therapy because she is seemingly unable to meet the right man and to complete her life vision with love, partnership, and/or children.

Now perhaps like other people in her life, this woman's therapist is often in the dark — at least initially — as to why this most appealing person has been unable to find love. But if the therapist and the patient can tolerate the darkness a bit longer, an amazingly coherent and repetitive pattern emerges. This woman usually has no trouble meeting men for the purpose of dating — the paucity of appropriate candidates notwithstanding. But it never works out. Typically, the woman first gets involved with a "nice," emotionally sensitive, and open man. But she soon discovers — or imagines (even as a therapist sometimes you just can't tell which it is) — that this man is too needy, "weak," or boring. He is perfectly nice, she thinks, but he has no pizzazz. Or he is not successful enough. She then breaks up with him, and like a general who fights the previous war, she now attempts to date a more assertive, independent, or ambitious man. But here she discovers — or imagines — that this man is not treating her so well. He is financially stable and he is responsible, she thinks, but he is also insensitive, selfish, and critical. So she breaks up with him too. Or if she's more masochistic, she hangs in there until he breaks up with her.

Sometimes, this pattern is obscured by variations on the main theme. The order of the type of men dated might be reversed, or there might be a string of one type, followed by a string of the other. But basically, from the perspective of this archetypical single woman, the world of men seems to be divided into wimps and bullies.

So what's going on here? You might wonder. Do men really come only in these two varieties, or is this intelligent, perceptive woman making it all up? As with all either-or questions with unacceptable answers, the answer lies in the question — it's a little bit of both. There are, in fact, men who are more or less aggressive, and there's truth to the saying that "nice guys finish last." But there is also the more balanced middle, where many successful *and* sensitive men reside in relative harmony. But this woman does not see the center, because she herself is not in it. Let me explain.

When you examine the personal history of such a woman, what stands out is that for some reason, she has been unable to comfortably identify with — admire, respect, look up to — her mother. The mother may have been (or may have been perceived by her as) crazy or incompetent or obese or just "weak"— to the point that, as a little girl, this woman had continuously vowed never to be like her. She therefore ended up with a character organized around the principle of "anything but my mother."

On the surface, therefore, this woman is more identified with her father — by default or by virtue of how he contrasted with the mother, the father was more worthy of identification. Yet, it is not quite possible to simply dismiss one's mother. So in fact, despite her valiant effort to erase her mother's influence, underneath it all this woman experiences herself as the mother she couldn't help but absorb. And her fear of being like her mother also bespeaks this deeper, less conscious layer of identification. In short, a large part of this woman's psychology is based on her desire to dismiss and reject the mother without and to deny and eject the mother within.

And this is the dynamic that controls her dating pattern. As much as she'd like to be treated well, the kind, sensitive man quickly becomes a threat to her tough, male-identified exterior. If she lets him in, she'll become just as mushy as he is, which is to say, just like her mother. So this kind of dating experience only reinforces the defensive element of her gender identification. The man she's dating may not be aggressive enough — perhaps in mirror image he had overidentified with his mother — but is he the pathetic loser she now makes him out to be? Maybe. But more likely, he is the projection of the intolerable mother inside of her from which she must flee. In other words, now that she had found and/or recreated her mother in her man, she must get away.

But strangely, as much as she now wants to be in the company of a "strong" man, the assertive, ambitious man is also a threat. Typically, this man does not want to be passively pursued. He wants to have at least the illusion of being in the driver's seat. And he doesn't want to date a competitor. So to get along with this man, she must allow him to take the initiative, and to receive his aggressive affection with passive receptivity. But that squarely places her where she had vowed never to be — by her mother's side. So she either fights this man for control, which as far as he is concerned is a nonstarter, or she yields and goes along with his agenda. But the latter option doesn't go that far either, because she ends up feeling abused or mistreated, and the longer this goes on, the more she experiences herself as irrational, weak, or masochistic. So with her worst nightmare coming true, she mobilizes a fight-or-flight response, either of which leads to the breakup of the relationship.[3]

The self-help literature is awash with suggestions and advice as to what this woman should do to improve her love life. The problem with much of this advice, as well as with the advice rendered by many a therapist, is that it usually involves specific behavioral tactics without an overall emotional strategy. "Don't call the guy — let him pursue you," is an example of such a tactical advice. But this tactic will not work, because the only guy who would call is the "wimp," who is attracted to the bully in her. "Why wait for a call?" another therapist might say. "You should call him!" Well, this also won't work because the bully is not going to sit at home and wait for her call — he'd be out with the women he can bully.

These tactics will not work unless and until this woman becomes emotionally receptive to a more balanced masculinity. "But how do you do that?" this woman might ask her therapist. "Beep," the therapist should say, "wrong question." While the need to do something to facilitate change is completely understandable — often enough it is driven by a ticking biological clock — this woman's desire to fix the problem is part and parcel of the defensive male identification that landed her in therapy in the first place. One of my female patients with this pattern was trying to *do* something about her problem for a long time. First she dated endlessly, back and forth, from wimp to bully and back again. Then, when we finally identified her pattern and traced it to her fear of becoming (a woman) like her mother, she embarked on a course of action to become more feminine. She structured time for herself to "work" on her feelings, took a course on "how to flirt," drew male-female diagrams with "pointers for forward steps," and scheduled "reciprocal feedback sessions" with friends to help her stay on top of her progress. The paradox, of course, was that all this activity was pretty "masculine." More precisely, it was a continuation of her defense against doing nothing and simply being, which she equated with incompetence, worthlessness, and emotional self-indulgence. Her mother, we should note, was an unsuccessful artist, who "did nothing" with her life. As the patient described it, she was a stay-at-home mother who served burned or undercooked dinners along with rambling, emotional expressions of anxiety and self-hate.

So tactics can be self-defeating, unless of course they are simply an expression of a coherent and authentic inner voice. This is another reason why, on their own, behavioral tactics are of limited usefulness — and why I don't like them. There is a dishonest element to them, one of games and manipulation, as if we are trying to mislead the other party as to our true intentions. Emotional strategy, by contrast, involves uncovering hitherto unknown parts of the self, developing a fuller and more balanced way of being, and replacing old patterns with new freedoms. This is quite a mouthful, I know, so I will say more about it in a moment. But first, let me return to...men.

As I said, the "wimp" and the "bully" do not reside merely in the imagination of the "male-identified" woman. They exist in reality as the two polar types on the continuum from femininity to masculinity and as the two faces of the conflict of masculine insecurity. Earlier we saw that at the heart of that conflict is the boy's ambivalent identification with his mother. But as in the case of my patient Eli, the boy's subsequent need to identify with his father further complements and complicates this ambivalence.

In devoting their lives to the pursuit of career success, men in Western societies continuously hone their aggressive, achievement-related skills, and more often than not, at the expense of such "softer" elements as sensitivity, acceptance, and play. In addition, long hours or business travel often absent them from their family. For a young boy, this kind of father — you might say a sketch, if not a caricature of a father — represents a particular kind of dilemma. If he seeks to become like him, as boys are naturally inclined to, he must discount his own feelings of rejection and treat himself with the same indifference or harshness with which his father has been treating him.

This defensive identification ("identification with the aggressor") is akin to the "Stockholm syndrome," in which the passengers of a hijacked airplane emerged from captivity justifying or sympathizing with the hijackers so that they did not have to feel the terror and powerlessness of their ordeal. In adulthood, this path leads to a repetition of the father's path, which usually involves succeeding in one's career but failing in one's relationships — with friends, spouse, or children. This, it appears, is a milder, Western version of what the Sambia men of New Guinea have to go through.

Or the boy can "choose" to feel the pain of being ignored or mistreated by his father and to reject him as a role model. But if he does this, he is likely to end up identifying with his mother and withdrawing from the world of men altogether. This is perhaps the path taken by the "wimpy" men dated and discarded by the "male-identified" woman. For this man, to enter into a committed relationship with a woman is to step into his father's domain, which is what he had vowed not to do. Paradoxically, this defensive identification with the mother is consistent with the repressed childhood wish to possess (in the sense of "have" or "be like") the father: this man does not want to marry a woman but a man. I'm not talking about homosexuality here, but rather, about the man who looks for the kind of masculine control and structure offered by the woman described above. But it doesn't work for him for the same reason it doesn't work for her — neither is really happy about being their mother's daughter.

In my experience, this type of ambivalent gender identification is one of the primary reasons single men and women do not meet the "right person." They are asking the opposite sex to complement their own skewed gender identification — an inherently unstable proposition. This may not be discussed much, and perhaps not even broached by therapists when it should be — I think because it gets confused with the political agenda of conservatism and religion. It is as if the words "feminine" and "masculine" are intrinsically sexist. Yet if you look a bit closer, it becomes evident that this issue has no political, religious, or moral implications.

As they grow up, boys need to be able to identify with their fathers. But they also need to maintain their early internalization of their mothers. And when they become men, they struggle to sustain and integrate both influences. Generally, however, men's feminine identification tends to reside, archeologically speaking, in a deeper level of their personality — it is usually associated with an earlier stage of development. While in need of expression, this feminine identification is also a threat to men's masculinity, which is why it's more likely to be openly expressed with a woman (or a man) who does not compete in the psychological arena of masculinity.

Relationships: The Masculine-Feminine Split

Even in long-term relationships or marriages, how the couple manages the man's masculine insecurity (and the woman's corresponding conflict) is critical. Much daily bickering as well as larger marital problems are the direct result of how male and female identifications are negotiated or distributed between the partners.

One patient, a complete skeptic about psychology, came to therapy only at the insistence of his wife. He frankly said to me, "Look, this is not going to change who I am, nor do I want it to. Work on some issues in my marriage? Okay. But don't ask me to start whining to you about my childhood. My parents were wonderful people. Plus, I don't operate on emotions. So I don't mind talking to you if it makes my wife happy, but honestly, I don't really need to be here. She is in her own therapy, which is good if it helps her, but the truth is, I don't really believe in therapy."

This patient's skepticism about therapy was only one manifestation of his reluctance to experience feelings in general. As he himself told me, he functioned in a logical, "rational" (is it rational to always function logically?) manner in all aspects of his life. Even in his sleep there was no play, fantasy, or poetry: on many nights he would lie in bed in a semi-awake state, solving business problems in his dreams.

His inability to fully experience emotions was a serious problem in his marriage because he was unable to relate to his wife's feelings. A retired police detective, he had started his own retail business and become quite successful at it. But every few years he would get into a disastrous business situation and end up using the family assets, including their house, as a collateral. While he understood why his wife might be "concerned" about these situations, he was completely unable to empathize with or relate to her feelings of insecurity, fear, and anger.

As a result of his refusal to be emotionally vulnerable, over the years the patient's wife took on more and more of the emotional role in the marriage. If she knew about a business deal in the making, she would become fearful, agitated, and anxious. The husband, in turn, would try to "manage" her "irrational roller coaster," as he put it. He would tell her to calm down, there was nothing to worry about, there was no risk in this transaction, he'd work it out, and so on. And naturally, in his attempt to manage her emotions he disclosed to her as little as possible about his business.

On her end, while accusing him of lying and concealing the nature of his business deals, the wife showed no real interest in the family finances. She knew little, if anything, about their income, expenses, savings, or investments. Consequently, every financial crisis came to her as a shock: "You promised this would never happen again!" she would cry.

And in between crises, the couple's ongoing dialogue consisted of her trying to pressure him to have feelings and him trying to convince her that she was emotionally overactive. In this kind of relationship (which naturally comes in varying degrees), there is an unhealthy, indeed an untenable, division of labor: the husband does the thinking, the wife does the feeling. The wife is hyperfeminine, the husband hypermasculine. But here's what's interesting. Clearly, the husband is wary of emotional vulnerability. So while he claims he wishes his wife were "a rational" partner, he is actually quite comfortable with her "hysteria" — because that's what's keeping him calm and logical. What he is truly afraid of — we saw this in the previous chapter — is the hysteria within, not without.

Likewise, while the wife says she would like to have a "feeling" partner, it suits her well that she does not, because that leaves the job of feeling to her — despite all the pain they bring her, she is obviously not uncomfortable with emotions. It is "thinking" or making business decisions or "male things" that she is uncomfortable with. (This, by the way, is a good example of the paradoxical similarity between psychological opposites. The husband who appears to be emotionally strong is quite weak, in the sense that he is terrified of his feelings, while the wife who appears so weak is rather strong in her tolerance for pain.)

So in this kind of masculine-feminine split, each spouse is uncomfortable with his or her own other-sex gender identification. Their relationship is structured in such a way that they unconsciously reinforce each other's cartoon-like gender role functioning. This is a problem not only because of the conflict regarding the expression of feelings, but also because this kind of polarization often shows up as a deep chasm of interests and values. In the case of this patient, he was only interested in football, boxing, mutual funds, and going out drinking with the guys. And his wife was only interested in soap operas, shopping, reading, and the movies — but no action movies, please. So other than the children, they had no mutual interests. They couldn't even go to the movies together.

These days, many marriages seem to be troubled by the opposite, or reversed, masculine-feminine split. For example, a couple on the verge of divorce came to see me for a desperate, last-minute attempt to keep the marriage together. They were desperate because after eight years together they were still very much in love, and yet they were convinced that they'd become completely incompatible. And although they had tried to work on it in the past several years, time only seemed to make it worse.

Here's how the wife described the problem: "We are just different people. Like, I always want to do things or go places and he doesn't. For him, the only vacation he likes is the beach. For me, that's boring. I'd like to go to Europe or the Far East or do things, and he just wants to hang out. But it's more than that. I like to plan things and he is completely passive. He never takes the initiative. Like, he never fixes anything in the house. I want to move to England, but he wants to stay here, near his family. I'm ambitious in terms of my career, and he is just happy coasting. Also, it kind of bothers me that he is not assertive enough at work. He lets his manager kind of abuse him and he doesn't stand up to him at all — it's like he has low self-esteem or something. When we first went out, I liked the fact that he was sensitive and patient and nonaggressive, but now I feel that we are too different, that we want different things out of life. And in the past year I started feeling that I am withdrawing from him — like I started spending a lot of time on the Internet."

And this is how the husband responded: "What she is saying is true. We want different things. I always wanted to work it out and I still want to, but I don't believe anymore it's possible. I have strong feelings for her, but she is always on the go, always pushing to do things. And she doesn't really listen. The other day I told her I felt she's been distant for quite a while. She is always on the computer. Maybe I can't give her the lifestyle she wants. It's true that I am not as ambitious as she is, and maybe it's a problem, but I am happy in my job. And I don't really want to go to all those places on vacation. And I do like to stay in the area where I grew up. You see, her family is all over the place; mine is all here, and I am very close to them. I also feel that she's changed ever since she got this management job. It's like she is more aggressive or bossy, although she was always like that to an extent. I used to like her assertiveness and decisiveness, but over the years it turned into insensitivity, or pushiness, or something like that. Or maybe I just see it differently now."

In this relationship, the very qualities that initially attracted the parties to each other had now become a repellent. The reason is that each partner felt trapped in the role assigned to them by the feminine-masculine split. The husband, overly identified with the female gender role, ended up feeling he was being bossed around by his wife. He was no longer willing to take it, but being out of touch with his (repressed or denied) male identification, he did not know how to change it within the relationship. Reluctantly, not realizing that he needed to change himself, he began to think about changing or replacing his partner.

The wife, on the other hand, felt tired of always being in the driver's seat. She now wanted to be "taken care of" by a strong man. She wanted someone else to worry about ambition, money, plans. But because she had no access to her female identification, she did not know how to fulfill this wish in the relationship. Not realizing that her husband represented a split-off part of herself (her denied femininity), she figured she'd replace him.

The plight of this couple was particularly painful and moving to witness because they really seemed to care about each other. But they were absolutely locked in the grip of masculine-feminine split. And while it was not evident to them, I thought it was quite likely that they would be in the same — or opposite, and therefore the same — place in their next relationships. As we saw in the equivalent dating pattern, the opposite place would be the more likely outcome, but sadly, it would be just as bad. In her next relationship, this woman actually said, she would consciously choose a different kind of man: strong, ambitious, aggressive. But as I told her, while she'd initially feel protected and taken care of by this man, with time she'd likely feel dominated, unheard, and oppressed. So in that relationship she would experience her female identification, while her new partner would play the role of, or represent, the masculine side of the split.

The man in the couple (by now her former husband) might go through the parallel experience of choosing a different kind of woman — one who is more sensitive and receptive. But with time, he'd be likely to feel she was too weak, submissive, and passive. His feminine qualities would disappear or, more accurately, be projected onto her. She, in turn, would receive these projections and act accordingly.

If this analysis is correct, the problem of the masculine-feminine split cannot be resolved by finding the "right" partner. Rather, one has to become the right partner him- or herself first. That is, one has to resolve or integrate the split within oneself in order to be able to recognize and team up with another "integrated person." It also follows that a couple who feels they are incompatible along the masculine-feminine dimension ought to attempt at working on the split before giving up on the marriage.

Unfortunately, for many couples this means telling the other partner how he or she needs to change. I say unfortunately, because, more often than not, this approach will only exacerbate the split. Consider a couple like the one above. If the wife keeps telling her husband that he is too passive and that he needs to be more assertive and ambitious, she only dominates him further with her agenda. So he is likely to feel, and appear to her to be even smaller — he doesn't even take the initiative when it comes to his own need for becoming more of "a man." And conversely, if the husband keeps asking the wife to be more sensitive, emotional, or supportive, he only perpetuates the notion that she is the powerful source of goods in the relationship. In effect, by giving her the power to affect his feelings, he further reinforces her aggressive, and his own submissive, role in the relationship.

So how should a couple work on healing or integrating the masculine-feminine split? This is a difficult question because the gender identifications responsible for this split are formed early in life and are deeply ingrained in our conscious, as well as unconscious, minds. What is needed here is a comprehensive emotional strategy, not some behavioral tricks.

The Case for Androgyny

"This boy in gym told me I was a girl in disguise," my seven-year-old son greeted me in near tears one day when I came home from work. He was clearly upset. Thinking on my feet, in a rare moment of composure and coherence for me, I said to him, "First of all, it's not true, but even if it were, I would still love you the same." While I felt good about my response, it didn't really seem to help my son. What did help was my follow-up suggestion that he get back at this boy by telling him that he, the boy, was a Barbie in disguise. Now that really perked up my son. He cracked up, and the next day reported proudly that he had successfully implemented my tactical advice. But I did hope that my initial response — the equivalent of a therapeutic emotional strategy — sank in so that my son could accept his own femininity.

But would I really love him the same if he were a girl in disguise? Here, a strange question calls for a strange answer. So consider the following passages from one of Virginia Woolf's most spirited novels, *Orlando*. As you read on, though, remember that the transformation she is talking about involves no sex change operation — those were not done back then.

> He stretched himself. He rose. He stood upright in complete nakedness before us, and while the trumpets pealed Truth! Truth! Truth! we have no choice left but confess — he was a woman.
>
> The sound of the trumpets died away and Orlando stood stark naked. No human being, since the world began, has ever looked more ravishing. His form combined in one the strength of a man and a woman's grace. As he stood there, the silver trumpets prolonged their note, as if reluctant to leave the lovely sight which their blast had called forth....
>
> Orlando had become a woman — there is no denying it. But in every other respect, Orlando remained precisely as he had been. The change of sex, though it altered their fortune, did nothing whatever to alter their identity.... The change seemed to have been accomplished painlessly and completely in such a way that Orlando herself showed no surprise at it. Many people, taking this into account, and holding that such a change of sex is against nature, have been at great pains to prove (1) that Orlando had always been a woman, (2) that Orlando is at this moment a man. Let biologists and psychologists determine. It is enough for us to state the simple fact; Orlando was a man till the age of

thirty; when he became a woman and has remained so ever since.

Clearly, in celebrating androgyny the narrator emphasizes the psychological continuity in Orlando's identity, irrespective of his sex change. Despite the external change, she tells us, inside, Orlando remains the same. This, in a sense, is our clue that the external androgynous form she is admiring is to a large extent a metaphor for its internal content. Indeed, "the strength of a man and a woman's grace" are not strictly physical traits. But before we abandon the physical, it's worth noting that the celebration of the external beauty of androgyny has a long-standing tradition in both classical and popular cultures. Michelangelo's David and even more so Donatello's sculpture of the same mythical male hero are vivid and beautiful examples of the male and female forms blended into perfection. Mick Jagger, David Bowie, Michael Jackson, and Prince — with beauty which is perhaps more questionable — are examples of androgynous men admired in popular adolescent culture.

It is hardly a coincidence that the advocates of androgyny as a physical ideal have always been individuals who were less concerned with the prescriptions of conventional morality — artists, writers and...teenagers. In challenging the rigid norms of their societies, such individuals — or at least the work and images they have created — were relatively free of homophobia and were not concerned about being the target of others' homophobic condemnation. But even mainstream ideas of male physical attractiveness involve "feminine attributes" such as a smooth skin and softly curved features. In fact, these days it seems that male attractiveness in our culture is embodied by the sensitive, boyish, and androgynous look of such Hollywood stars as Leonardo DiCaprio.

Now, Hollywood studio executives will be the first to tell you that the primary proponents and consumers of this ideal of beauty are teenage girls. It is also possibly relevant that the creator/admirer of Orlando was a woman. In other words, and going beyond the physical now, it's a sure bet that women would like men to be emotionally androgynous — strong and graceful, tough and sensitive, secure and vulnerable, and so on and so forth. But the question is, do men, especially straight men, want to be graceful, sensitive, and vulnerable? They surely don't act that way. But I say they do want to. Their symptoms, their acting-out, and their soul-searching in psychotherapy all say they want to.[4]

But, and this is a critical but, they can only obtain psychological androgyny if they seek it on their own initiative. In particular, they cannot be expected to attain it under the direct influence of a woman. We saw this in the femininity phobia of Sambian men as well as in the dynamics of the traditional form of the masculine-feminine split. But consider one more illustration, a domestic tale from a patient. "The other day," the patient began, "my wife found an injured pigeon. She carried it home to care for it — and I couldn't believe it, she had *tears* in her eyes! *Tears* for the darn pigeon! So I told her, for heavens sake, dear, what are you crying about? She got mad at me and walked away." This was Part One of the story.

In Part Two, the patient's teenage son later in the day accidentally stepped on or kicked the pigeon as it was limping in the backyard. When the patient got wind of this, he became really angry and yelled at his son for his carelessness and callousness — and, of course, for "upsetting your mother." The boy then complained to his mother, "Dad is out of control again," and she, in turn, sought the patient out and admonished him for being insensitive to their son.

When the patient related this domestic drama to me, it seemed he could either laugh or cry about the whole thing. Amazingly, as he was telling me the story a pigeon landed on the windowsill outside my office and started pecking on the glass pane! Now, while that had us both laughing — and I laughed again (to myself) when my next patient coincidentally related a dream from the previous night about pigeons — we also knew that somewhere in that story there was a serious matter to attend to.

In Part One, we then figured out, the patient was trying to distance himself from the threat of emotionality — so he criticized his wife's. But he also internalized her sensitivity, so in Part Two, when his son carelessly hurt the pigeon, he reacted emotionally. *Now,* of course, his masculinity was really on the line — he was having feelings for the pigeon! So as a last resort, rather than getting sad — or God forbid, tearful like his wife — he got angry. In short, he reasserted his masculinity by taking it out on his son. This, naturally, provoked his wife to come back and rebuke him for his insensitivity to their child, which brought this tale to its ironic conclusion with the following lesson for the patient: you cannot escape from a woman's influence by reacting to it. If your wife's tears get to you to the point that you must distance yourself, you are not going to feel so "masculine" after all — because underneath you are just as emotional. To summarize, you are better off *acting* like a woman — by staying with your feelings — than *reacting* to a woman.

But there is a lesson here for women as well. A woman's request, let alone demand, for emotional androgyny is likely to produce only its opposite. If you ask a man to express his feelings more, he might give you lip service by saying, "Of course I love you, honey," but he will actually feel *less*, and eventually even the lip service will be too hard for him to maintain. The more you ask him to be like a woman, the more he will insist on being a man. In the Greek myth, Hermaphroditus fights violently to ward off the desirous nymph who attaches herself to his body. And when the gods finally grant her wish to unite their bodies forever, let me tell you — he is not a happy camper! (Significantly, his misery-loves-company wish for revenge is that other men will "lose their half-maleness" as well.)

So men's emotional strategy — if they seek one — has to be pro-choice androgyny. Their mission, should they choose to accept it, is to integrate the two sides of the conflict of masculine insecurity. For most men this means accepting their repressed feminine desires, but for many — those who are "female-identified" — it means developing their arrested masculine desires. And women? What are they to do while their candidates or partners for love pursue their long-term strategic choice? First and foremost, women must recognize that how they deal with their own gender identification impacts on their partner's. When a woman is too feminine, her man is likely to be, or to become, too masculine. When she is too masculine, he's likely to be, or to become, too feminine. Once you realize this, it only follows that women's best chance for coping with men's masculine insecurity is to work on their own feminine-masculine integration.

Along these lines, women's emotional strategy — equally a free choice — is best described by the principle of "winning the loser's game." This principle, discussed in a classic investment book bearing that title, was inspired by another book, about... tennis. In that book, the author, Simon Ramo, explains that tennis is really two different games, one played by the pros and the other by the rest of us. As Stanley Angrist of the *Wall Street Journal* put it, "While a pro actually 'wins' his game, the winner in amateur contests is determined by the actions of the loser — who defeats himself." The implication is that unless you are a pro, you can only win if you play not to lose, that is, if you play against yourself, not against your opponent.

For women, coping with men's masculine insecurity is a loser's game — they can only win it by playing not to lose. And clearly, the prerequisite for this strategy is the capacity to ignore, which is to say, to accept as fact, the opponent's moves. So the first step for women is to stop trying to beat some femininity into their man and to accept his masculinity for what it is. Then, and only then, they can choose to work on their own integration of grace and strength, feeling and thought, passivity and activity.

I suppose we can say that women have their own "feminine insecurity" conflict — some women become too feminine as a defense against a forbidden wish to be, say, a corporate lawyer. These women fear that they will lose their femininity if they acknowledge the desire to compete in "the world of men." Other women go to the other extreme. Be that as it may, like men, women certainly identify with both parents, and therefore have the same potential for both conflict and integration of their gender identification.[5] But it is only when they choose the road of integration — as long and winding as it may be — that somewhere along the path they may notice that their man is on a parallel path. No, they did not inspire him, not even facilitate his choice. They simply focused on their own game and freed him to play his. But now, all of a sudden, they are getting along much better as a couple.

Paradoxically, then, recognizing gender differences and accepting the opposite sex for what it is is the only way for both genders to share the same emotional strategy, which, naturally enough, occupies the androgynous center between the two. But as I think I made clear, the key to this strategy is a parallel, not joint, path, the reason being that psychological integration of opposites cannot be achieved out of reactive necessity. It must be born out of free, proactive choice.

For the professional therapist, on the other hand, the emotional strategy of androgyny is not optional — it is what he is getting paid for. At least in my book, when it comes to masculine insecurity, the good enough therapist — male or female — must him- or herself be on the path of androgynous integration. This was driven home to me for the first time some years ago by a striking, heartbreaking dream of one of my patients.

This young man grew up in a family with two-dimensional, stick-figure gender representations. His mother was a beautiful woman, a housewife who "loved [him] to death" and suffocated him with physical attention and a babying emotionality. His father, a navy officer, when not gone halfway across the world treated him with a military hand, demanding obedience, precision, and logic.

Early in his therapy with me the patient had a dream in which, after struggling with uncooperative traffic and elevators, he made it to the therapy session just on time. But when I invited him into the office I turned out to be a woman. Horrified, he sat down on the floor and started crying with feelings of betrayal and despair.

Now why was the patient so devastated when I became a woman? The most obvious explanation was that he didn't want me to become overly attentive and emotional like his mother. He wanted me calm and objective. Fair enough. But the other way of understanding the dream, which is nothing if not complementary, is that he feared that like his father, I would betray him in my absence and coldness, leaving him stuck with his mother's feminine attentions. So clearly, the patient also didn't want me to be a military man. What he wanted — and deserved — was neither a female nor a male stick figure, but rather, a full-bodied, three-dimensional person, androgynously integrated.

While patients no doubt deserve this, it is not so easy to achieve, for a psychologist any more than for anyone else. For one thing, while Virginia Woolf's Orlando seems to altogether transcend gender — just as in living through several centuries he transcends time — I do not believe that the writer or the reader could ever transcend their gender. I could never be anything but a man to any of my patients, no matter how much they need to heal their masculine-feminine split. Nor could I personally achieve a full, balanced integration, as some others might. But I can work on it, and can commit to working on it, I hope, for the rest of my life.

This is what makes the job of the therapist emotionally and technically challenging: you must constantly work on your only instrument — yourself. For example, a few months after he started seeing me, one of my patients mentioned that he had gone to see his child's therapist to discuss something his child did in school. "I ended up talking about myself, about the same things we talk about," he said, "but I really opened up to her and became quite emotional — in a way that doesn't happen here, I think. And I wonder why. Maybe it's because you are a man, or maybe it's a personality thing. I don't know. And then I thought maybe I should see her — not that I'm prepared to switch right now — but I had that thought." When I asked him what made him feel more open with the other psychologist, he hedged only a bit before saying, "Maybe I felt you've been criticizing or judging me."

As you may have gathered by now, I am not particularly thin-skinned. But this immediately struck a painful chord. I didn't think I had been judging him, but as soon as he said it, I knew I hadn't been as sensitive and empathic as I could have been. And I realized at once that in analyzing his behaviors, I had, in fact, been critical — not intentionally, not consciously, but it was there. And it was done and I couldn't take it back. This realization was painful because it was such a basic failure — who needs a therapist who is insensitive and critical? It was also painful because I'd caused this person the kind of pain which I was supposed to help him heal. And it was painful because I hurt someone I liked. And last but not least, it was painful because I hated being criticized as much as he did.

Now such a moment — which in one form or another is a regular occurrence in the patient-therapist relationship — is full of emotional and intellectual tension for the therapist. First of all, who wants to feel this kind of pain? Even now as I write about it, I resist remembering it; I feel the urge to get away from it. Except that the work of the therapist does not allow that escape route — your job is to listen and to learn from this kind of pain. For one thing, feeling one's own pain is a prerequisite for empathizing with the patient — which I clearly needed to do. And you can't — at least I can't — fake it.

In addition, your own emotional reaction to the patient — if you know yourself well enough — can tell you something important about the patient. So in this case I needed to understand why I was being critical, and what better motivator than a bit of pain? But notwithstanding all this, the therapist doesn't really have time for the pain. He has to put his own pain aside and listen to the patient's. With this patient, I was lucky enough to quickly realize that I had felt judged by him from our very first session, and that I had unconsciously attempted to protect myself by evaluating or criticizing him. So while the patient was understandably and "correctly" concerned about my work with him, this entire psychological transaction was initiated by his own psychology.

Ultimately, this very analysis shifted the whole focus of the patient's therapy for the next six months, as we uncovered an incredibly rich history of performance and evaluation anxiety in his family. As for me, I not only survived the pain — I thrived on it. For the therapist, this kind of emotionally labor-intensive work can be the greatest reward of the job. Not only he is a witness or a facilitator of his patient's journey, but he also learns about himself as much as about the patient. And he grows with him. So one hopes, by the end of the work day, the therapist is not a selflessly spent, resentful soul who is tired of listening to people. Nor is he simply a businessman counting his money (not that these are such terrible things that are never a part of the therapist's, or anybody's, job).

So at the heart of any emotional strategy is the idea of life as a work in progress. And it is only when patients accept this notion — one which is particularly difficult for men — that their therapeutic journey begins to take root. At that point, they no longer need tactical advice — which even if you offer, they usually don't implement, and which fails even when they do. Instead, they develop their own tactics, consistent with who they are and with what they now know they really want. Following is a concrete example of successful tactics used by one of my female patients who turned this corner in her struggle to cope with the masculine-feminine split. The specific tactics are italicized.

The patient, who was always dating nice guys who "finished last" — they usually had no money or career to speak of — took a radical tactical step to implement the strategy of winning the loser's game. *She saved some money and quit her corporate executive position* without having another job or another employment plan. Consciously, she wanted to get away from what she felt was the "rigid, hierarchical, male-oriented" corporate environment and get in touch with her femininity. But on a deeper level, she attempted to rid herself of her duty-bound, aloof, and aggressive identification with her father and search for the emotionally free-floating, impressionable, and childlike images of her mother — who had died when the patient was a young teenager.

Now, in her place, I (as a woman[6]) would have never quit a job without at least a plan for another one. But it worked for her: within months she began to view those "nice guys" quite differently, and she met and married a nice guy who didn't, in fact, finish last. And eventually, she'd carved out for herself a part-time consulting position which, in her mind, was more consistent with her newly integrated gender identifications.[7]

My children, like all kids, do and say things with simplicity and truthfulness not yet complicated by the obstructive nature of mature psychological defenses. When my daughter was four and my son seven, they were finally able to play together and let us sleep in the early mornings. As my daughter was a Barbie fan and my son liked war games, in playing together they clearly had to bridge the gender gap. Incredibly, or perhaps ridiculously, they came up with a compromise game in which dressed-up Barbies, riding in jeeps and tanks, were fighting to liberate France from the Nazis.

Ideally, I'd like to believe that this type of play was more than a compromise, which is to say that my daughter actually enjoyed the battles and that my son really liked the dolls. To be perfectly honest, though, for defensive reasons which should be obvious by now, I'm much more comfortable with the former than with the latter part of this ideal.

Self-Involvement

...see me, hear me, touch me, feel me

The Czech writer Milan Kundera wrote: "All of man's life among his kind is nothing other than a battle to seize the ear of others." Wanting to be heard is surely no more male than female, but the notion that we spend our lives battling for an audience does seem to evoke — at least for me — men's inclination to assault others with their verbal agendas. In this context, to say that men don't talk is not only to misrepresent the truth — it's to reverse it. While some men hide behind a wall of silence, others are only too happy to expose themselves with a barrage of unstoppable utterances. These men are like the Alan Dershowitzes and Pat Buchanans of the male-dominated cable news shows, where host and guest engage in verbal combat for what appears to be the sole purpose of inserting their own self-important, intellectualized male egos into the audioreceptors of their opponent.

So it's not that men don't talk — it's that they don't listen. They do monologues, not dialogues. And while it's true that they don't talk about their emotional vulnerabilities in public, they show them to us, unaware all the same. Sadly, no matter how brilliant their ideas may be or how desperately they want to be heard, because of their presentation style no one really cares to listen to them for more than a couple of minutes — at most — or for reasons other than preparing a rebuttal.

Imposing and Exposing

In many families, dinnertime provides the setting or stage for the man at the head of the table to hold forth. He talks about the day's news or politics. He evaluates the food and his wife's appearance. He talks about his business conquests of the day. He interviews the children about their school performance. He interviews their mother about their behavior at home. He tells stories with important morals or, alternately, jokes with pointy punch lines.

Now throughout this performance, in which the man is the playwright, director, and lead actor, everyone around the table — with the occasional exception of the rebellious child or defiant spouse — anxiously pretends to pay attention to what's being said and to participate at a minimally acceptable level.

Fortunately, this family dinner is only a stereotype. Yet like all stereotypes, it's painfully familiar. What's it about? A poignant answer comes from a story told by a patient about his stepson. The child, a sixth-grader in a prestigious all-boys private school in Manhattan, was told in no uncertain terms by a taunting classmate that he had "penis envy." Not quite getting it, the patient's stepson looked up "penis envy" in the library's Internet-based encyclopedia, where to his great horror he discovered that this was something girls were supposed to have. Angry and hurt, he returned to the playground and confronted his tormentor. "You think I have penis envy? Well, what about this!?" he cried out, opening his pants and exposing himself.

The unfortunate result was that this exchange triggered in my patient's stepson a behavioral pattern of exhibitionism, which was even more traumatic for him than for the kids around him. Such masculine self-exposure is fundamentally not unlike the way in which men, to quote Shakespeare, strut and fret their hour upon the stage and then are heard no more. In other words, this child's exhibitionism was a truthful if crude demonstration of how men's self-involvement rises out of the conflict of masculine insecurity. It's not enough to comfort yourself with the knowledge that you are a man, you must also show it in public to all who care (and especially those who don't care) to see.

In a famous if dated University of California field study, researchers invited a large group of ten- to twelve-year-old boys and girls to play with a random selection of toys. In analyzing this study, psychoanalyst Erik Erikson observed that whereas girls tended to play with such interior spaces as the insides of a house, boys were much more likely to erect structures, buildings and towers. Erikson's conclusion regarding this sex difference, you may have guessed, was that boys' and girls' use of space during play paralleled the structure of their sex organs. To the extent that this is still true today, some sixty years later — the Donald Trumps of the world still seem to be predominantly male — it's easy to see why for many men this phallic preoccupation becomes an addictive defense. Since they associate emotional vulnerability with femininity, it's only logical that the compensatory mechanism they use to try to feel better about themselves involves the public display of uncontested evidence of masculinity.

This type of compensatory mechanism, which like an advertising campaign seeks to reverse a perception of a problem by displaying its opposite, is at the heart of narcissism — male or female. It is a common misperception that narcissism is a form of excessive self-love; the truth is, it's more about self-hate. In his self-centeredness, the narcissist does appear to love himself too much — "Look at me I'm so great" is what his every move seems to say — but this is all a rather brittle defense against less conscious feelings of self-loathing. Remember, Narcissus was in love with his image as reflected in the pool, not with his actual self.

Furthermore, as articulated by psychoanalyst Heinz Kohut, the narcissist can also be someone who consciously tells us he hates himself and that there's nothing good about him. At first this person seems to be the anti-narcissist, but if you scratch the surface of this self-devaluation, you find that the person is unhappy with himself because he is not as *great* as he really should be. A friend, a very successful man in his field, once asked me, "What's wrong with me that I'm not a President or a chief justice or something like that?" I see the same logic in female patients who might be quite attractive but who berate themselves for their appearance as if to say, "What's wrong with me that I am not a top model?"

So the best way to describe narcissism is as an attempt to regulate one's self-esteem. Of course, put this way, we are all narcissistic, and indeed we are. The second important element in narcissism is that of performance, both conscious and unconscious. The actor may perform on stage quite consciously in order to please his audience and gain their applause so that he can feel good about himself. But he can also forget about the audience, submerge himself in and identify with the character he is playing. This kind of performance, where the actor no longer knows he's performing, is akin to what theater professionals call Method acting.

Of course, even this type of actor might still hate himself, for being bad with money, for having sexual problems, or for failing to stand up to his producer. Until he accepts his limitations, his performance and the admiration it evokes in others will provide only a temporary relief, a distraction.

Now since the whole world is a stage, when it comes to narcissism at least, performance is not limited to the theater. It is also not limited to mental illness or health or to men or women. Nonetheless, there are differences in how male and female narcissism present themseves to the world. For one thing, as we saw in the second chapter, while women tend to hate themselves for failures in social relationships and physical appearance, men feel more inadequate when failing to perform, at their work as well as sexually. In other words, men's self-involvement is decidedly phallic.

Nervous Teeth

Now that we know more about narcissism, let's look at some more subtle forms of male self-involvement. One interesting feature of the self-involved man, and to some extent of every man, is that he is blind to his own self-involvement. Narcissus, the original self-involved man, was unaware that the beautiful boy returning his admiring gaze from the water was a mere reflection.

Likewise, because men are often unaware of their own psychological makeup, they think that their perception of other people is the objective reality as opposed to their own psychology projected onto others.

In this context I will always remember one of my professors in graduate school. A brilliant, authoritarian man, rather like a peacock he would habitually stretch his intellectual feathers for all to admire. Always seeming to need to demonstrate his brilliance, he would never fail to challenge his students' observations and contributions in class. As a result, all of his students were intimidated by him and many (myself included) were reduced in his presence to babbling idiots. My only defense at the time was the belief that this man, intelligent as he was, must have a distorted view of reality. Here was a professor in one of the best programs of its kind in the country, where surely there were at least a few bright students, acting as if everybody around him was pretty stupid — all the while not realizing, I speculated, that he had created this sea of stupidity to make himself feel better about his own intellect.

A more subtle example is that of a patient whose narcissistic blindness only emerged after a couple of years of therapy. The patient was married right out of law school to a woman whom he considered ideal; she was beautiful, hard-working, stable, and devoted. And in fact, she created a picture-perfect home for them. At first he liked the Martha Stewart ambience — the curtains, the table settings, the flowers, and the linens. But after a while he began to feel there was no place for him to put his feet up, to leave his clothes out, or to drop his newspaper. And he felt sexually constricted and bored — everything was just too pleasant and proper.

So about three years into the marriage, the patient started a very exciting extramarital affair. But since he was basically a straight-arrow type, he felt so guilty about it that he pretty soon confessed to his wife with the intention of ending the affair. His wife, however, would have none of it, and she immediately asked him to leave. He then moved in with the lover, who seemed to be a different type from his wife and with whom he had what appeared to be a completely different relationship. A downtown painter, the lover led a life filled with art and romance. Her East Village loft was haphazardly put together, with huge canvases of vaguely suggestive nudes lined up against or hung on the walls. In her relationship with the patient she was volatile, challenging, and possessive. And she introduced him to new kinds of intense sexual pleasure which he had never known were possible.

But eventually, after the patient broke up with the lover because he couldn't take the emotional roller coaster she subjected him to, and after he divorced his wife, he and I concluded that in one important respect the two women whom he loved were quite similar. The wife had an image of a marriage centered around her vision of the perfect home — an aesthetic idea, not a complex, imperfect reality. The lover had her own image of a relationship, one based on the aesthetics of sensuality and passion, and on a notion of the supremacy of art. So both women existed in the world of images and ideas, not reality, and both didn't see the patient for who he was. Both were equally oblivious to his emotional needs, especially when these didn't fit into or contradicted their own idealized worlds. In short, they were both rather narcissistic women who were unable to empathize with the patient.

But why did the patient fail to see that fact when he first became involved with these women? He and I pondered this question for a while, but the answer finally presented itself when, after he separated from both, the patient decided not to date anyone for a while. Being without a woman made him feel bad about himself, so by way of looking for a distraction he bought a cool sports car. And he felt so cool riding around town in this car that he bought another one. And then another one. Pretty soon he forgot all about his troubles with women and was the proud if not obsessive owner of six classic sports cars. He really loved these cars and got tremendous joy out of showing me their pictures as if they were his children or, more accurately, his girlfriends.

Now as soon as he and I realized that he was substituting the cars for the women he had loved and let go, we understood why he hadn't seen their narcissism earlier. Though he felt he had loved the women, his interest in them was little different from his interest in cars. The wife presented an ideal image of a home and the lover an ideal image of sex. The cars, I suppose, were a bit of both. So the patient was as much involved with image as the women were and equally in denial of the imperfect nature of reality — all in the service of regulating his self-esteem, of feeling better about himself. In short, he didn't see the women's narcissism because of his own.

In retrospect, this man's self-involvement should have been evident from the very beginning, except that he was so charming and good-natured that I didn't see it until later. In many men, however, self-involvement is not at all evident, even when they have little charm to hide behind. What comes to mind is a patient who was a senior partner in an accounting firm and who in fact did have a rather dry presentation. Underneath, though, he was torn by powerful emotions. Married for over twenty years and a father of three teenagers, the patient came to therapy because he "fell in love" with a young woman in his office.

Actually, "falling in love" doesn't quite capture the situation. He was so obsessed with this woman that he could not talk about anything else in the sessions. "Nothing happened between us, mind you," he said and went on to describe his preoccupation with her. "We look at each other so gently and intensely, and I can feel her entering the room without even looking. And I think about her and fantasize about her all the time. I just can't stop thinking about her. My wife asks me what's wrong — of course I don't tell her. And at work too, I sit in front of my terminal, daydreaming about her for hours — literally. I think people are beginning to notice that I am not functioning. Except that when she is around me, I come to life — I feel so alive with her, as if I've been dead for years. Of course, she is very, very pretty."

At first I could not help this man at all, because he was not interested in anything other than his obsession — how passionately he enjoyed it, and how he needed it to go away right now. I initially went along with this because I wanted to understand what he was experiencing. But after a few sessions I realized that, like him, I was hijacked by his obsession. If I knew nothing about the rest of his life — who he was and what his psychological resources were — how could I help him to combat this "love"?

So I gradually started steering him in other directions. He told me that he had felt some stress recently — nothing dramatic. At home, his oldest son had just been notified about his college applications. He was turned down from his top choices and was only accepted by his "safety school," an okay but unexciting state college. His younger son, a sophomore, was getting only B's and C's and was talking about not going to college at all. At work, his department was being reviewed by management consultants for possible improvement in productivity. While there was no reason to think there was a problem in his department, and his job was in any event secure, he was concerned that the review might come up with something negative.

This kind of stress seemed relatively minor, certainly insufficient to trigger his obsession. But against all odds, I hypothesized that it was actually quite serious, at least in one respect — his self-esteem was on the line. In terms of work, it was reasonable to assume that if fault was found in the performance of his department, he would take it as a reflection on himself. So I extended that logic to the home front, hypothesizing that he also took his children's academic "failure" as a reflection on him. So perhaps he was feeling he was no good, a failure. But to such an extent that he would engage in an obsession threatening his marriage and his work? That seemed unlikely. Until he told me more about the woman he was obsessed with, and about himself.

Their "relationship" had started when she was assigned to him for training. He was her mentor and she was learning some rather complicated things from him. At some point he encouraged her to make a presentation to the partners. She didn't feel ready for it, but she went along and it went extremely well. It was after the presentation that she began to look at him with awe and admiration. "It was as if she felt I had bestowed my powers on her," he told me. "I made her look good and she made me feel like I was the greatest thing." This confirmed my hypothesis that the patient's obsession was a "feel good" device that appealed to his diminishing sense of self-esteem. But why was he so vulnerable to relatively minor threats to his sense of self? This became poignantly clear when he told me about his family of origin.

His parents were both immigrants and in some ways typical. They were hard-working and strict, and they expected a great deal of their children, especially when it came to academic performance. When the patient was eleven years old, his sixteen-year-old brother invented a piece of software that might (and in fact did) play a major role in the development of cable TV. From that day on everything changed in the life of the family. The parents first shopped for an investor, exposing the brother and the family as a whole to a good deal of media attention. Then they immersed themselves completely in their older son's college application process. Finally, while the patient's brother was in college — at Stanford — they decided to open a business with him in California. Convinced that this was their ticket to the American dream, they cashed in their pension funds, moved the family to California, and invested all they had in the business. And as if this were not enough to make my patient feel disregarded and to make him envious, while in college his brother met and later married a teen-idol movie star.

This history explained (1) why the patient had low self-esteem — he felt undervalued by his parents in comparison to his brother; (2) why academic and work performance were such sensitive issues for him — ditto; (3) why his son's failure to get into a better college was in fact a big deal for him — this "failure" reminded him of a painful period in his life, when he felt abandoned by parents who had stopped functioning as his parents in order to pursue his brother's brilliance; and (4) why desiring a pretty girl was the best avenue to remedying his low self-esteem — it was an unconscious attempt to compete with, or become like, his revered brother.

This history also demonstrates how narcissism is self-generating. The parents, feeling that their child is their best chance to remedy their own low self-regard, demand and expect top performance.

The child, feeling unaccepted as he is, represses those feelings and tries to deliver for his parents. But unconscious feelings of low self-regard persist, and as an adult he tries to remedy them by starting a new narcissistic cycle with his own child. This cycle also illustrates another hallmark of narcissism — the vicarious nature of its joys and sorrows. In the case of my patient, his parents lived vicariously through their children. And taking a page from their book, the patient lived vicariously through his children, as well as through his department and even through the young woman he was obsessed with. It was because *she* was beautiful and young that *he* felt alive. It was because *she* admired him, that *he* felt good about himself. So good, in fact, that he didn't want to lose her — physically and even more important, as a presence in his mind. Hence the obsession.

Clearly, there is a cultural aspect to narcissism. In the case of this patient it probably has to do with the immigrant's dogged pursuit of the American dream. I suspect children of many immigrants can relate to my patient's story — or his brother's. Or both, since each story is the flip side of the other. And of course, one can say that the aspirations of immigrants merely highlight the values of the society into which they attempt to assimilate. Indeed, the pursuit of the American dream can be a narcissistic pursuit — a preoccupation with the attainment of external indications of success as a means of achieving feelings of internal self-worth — for anyone.

Much has been said about the ill effects of our society's narcissism on women — for example, the definitions of physical attractiveness based on models, in spite of women's experience of being objectified and their propensity for eating disorders. Less has been said about its consequences for men. Obviously, the cultural pressures on men are less about physical appearance and more about the appearance of success. Although the style or manner of the pressure applied on men varies within subcultures or even regionally, the message is always the same, and more often than not the messenger is the father. For instance, in New York it's the cut-throat style of investment banking, with the father laying down the law as in, "You'd better get straight A's if you want to get somewhere in life" (*If you want to get my respect, you bum,* is what the child actually hears). In Hollywood, it's a warm and fuzzy message such as, "You are so wonderful, you'll have no trouble getting an A" (*I guess I'm not so wonderful if I don't* is what the child hears here).

In the last couple of decades the latter approach has gained tremendous popularity in various corners, from management training seminars to child-rearing guidebooks. In my experience, "positive feedback," or praising of children, and to a lesser extent of adults, can be just as if not more detrimental than negative feedback. For a child, both are equally evaluative, giving him the message that he is being observed and evaluated, that his performance is important for *the parent* (as opposed to for himself), and that his value depends on his ability to perform.

But whereas the Wall Street approach is straightforward so that at least the child knows what's expected, the Hollywood approach is more manipulative — the child hears words of love but feels something much more conditional. And he doesn't even get the chance to feel angry or scared — he just feels compelled to perform. For example, does Barbara Walters care about the feelings of her interviewees when she sensitively and lovingly asks them to bare their souls on national TV, or does she care about their ability to deliver a dramatically moving performance for her audience? It's probably both, but which is the bottom line?[8]

Clearly, as times are changing, the pressure to succeed — an unfortunate component of many a father-son dynamic — becomes a more common element in father-daughter and mother-daughter relationships as well. Nonetheless, the ancient dynamic of Abraham and Isaac — the father who's willing to sacrifice his son on the altar of some idea, expectation, or test — is still fundamentally a male thing. For better or worse, girls are still less likely to pay the price (and reap the benefit) of their fathers' obsession with a grand design — their intellectualized, idealized notion of what power and achievement can do for them, and if not for them, by way of projection for their children. On another biblical note, this father-son dynamic was captured by the prophet Jeremiah, who said, "The fathers ate unripe grapes and the children's teeth are set on edge."[9]

In psychology, as in life, narcissism tends to have a bad name. Yet many influential analysts have pointed out its positive contributions — such as jobs involving high-visibility and high-performance situations in which it might be a requirement. Psychoanalyst Heinz Kohut, for example, advanced a whole theory about how narcissism develops in everybody from early childhood onward. The implication, with which I agree, is that self-involvement is only pathological when extreme. A healthy dose of self-love — even as a defense against unconscious self-hate — is a good thing in that it motivates us to take care of ourselves and inspires us to improve our performance in whatever we do.

Of course, the $64 million question is, where's the thin line between healthy and excessive narcissism? While it's hard to pinpoint, I think we know it when we — or more likely other people — cross it. As a general principle, if our expectations of ourselves or of others — including our children — are only slightly above our or their potential, our narcissism keeps us in good shape. But if our expectations are much above potential, we are likely to inflict unproductive pain on others as well as on ourselves. Finally, if our expectations are at or below potential, we are not doing anyone a favor either. The other guiding principle, of course, is that to the extent possible, our capacity for love should be altogether independent of such performance expectations.

Pointy Ears (the Abusive-Boss Syndrome)

One way to look at men's self-involvement is that it's an asset on the job but a liability at home or in intimate relationships. The rationale behind such a hypothesis is that at work, looking good is good politics, and that the appearance of self-confidence inspires confidence in others. And in fact, many professionally successful people boast this kind of exuberant, outgoing, self-assured, and totally self-involved personality. In the area of interpersonal relationships, on the other hand, you not only need to emotionally care for others, but also to lower your guard and disclose such feelings as self-doubt, insecurity, and fear of rejection. The self-involved man, however, might be too invested in divorcing such feelings from consciousness by looking good to be willing to open up in that manner. And he might be equally too invested in the good image of his significant others — since they reflect on him — to allow them to be open with their own inadequacies.

While there's truth to this hypothesis, ultimately there's no way to split and partition a man's psyche into a working machine and a lover. A man who is frustrated with his wife or girlfriend will take it out on his work — and vice versa. So at work too, a man's self-involvement can become a real problem. Most typically, it's first a problem for everyone else around him — unless and until his company mandates him to seek counseling or therapy, which happily is not unusual these days.

One such patient of mine, a man in his mid-thirties, was a systems manager in a pharmaceutical company. He was referred to me by his human resources director because of three different complaints by subordinates that he had been verbally abusive toward them. When in response to my inquiry the patient, "Mark," described the incidents in question, it turned out that all three involved women. And it also turned out that all three involved women who he felt "didn't listen" to him, "didn't get it," or "didn't do what they were supposed to." In talking about this, the patient acknowledged that his behavior was abusive and inappropriate, but he insisted that he was "maddeningly provoked by these women's blind incompetence." And he denied that his behavior had anything to do with their gender; although he later explained that at the time he was afraid of "some sort of legal ramifications regarding sexual harassment."

In the first session, I noticed that Mark was fixing his gaze on me in a particularly intense manner. He seemed to maintain eye contact at all times as if to supervise or control the movement of my eyes. This made me feel uncomfortably tense, so I finally asked him about it. "You know," I said, "I can't quite pinpoint what it is, but there's a way in which you're looking at me that seems kind of tense or anxious. Do you know what I'm talking about?" For a fraction of a second Mark looked taken aback by my question, as if caught off guard. But then, an amazing transformation took place: he leaned back on the couch, relaxing not only his gaze, but his entire body. Then, resuming his original body and eye posture, he answered, "I'm always like that — practically all the time. And I know exactly what you are talking about!"

Here he paused, and fixing his gaze on me even more rigidly, he added, "I think it has to do with my ear." "Your ear?" I asked, suddenly finding myself struggling with an irresistible urge to look away from his eyes, toward his ears. "My right ear," he said, turning his head sideways for a second or two, quickly showing it to me. It was too fast for me to really take a look, and in a way it only intensified my curiosity, as well as his hovering, hawk-like efforts to control my gaze. Nonetheless, I was able to see that there was some malformation in his ear — it was pointy and contorted.

"You see, I was born with an ear deformity — having to do with a rare genetic aberration. My whole childhood, my mother was always taking me to doctors. From about the age of six to eleven or twelve, I had an endless series of plastic surgeries which, by the way, only made it look worse. And I had to wear these gauze bandages and dressings on my ear or head for weeks at a time, always feeling everyone was staring at me! So I guess over the years I've developed a way of staring as a means of preventing people from looking at me — at my ear. It's basically a way of hiding.

"Anyway, I don't know how we got on this subject, except that you asked. But I don't know that it has anything to do with what's going on at work."

"Maybe it does, and maybe it doesn't," I said. "Were your parents helpful in dealing with all this as a child?"

"My parents split when I was about five and my father was

kind of in his own world — I didn't see him much afterwards. My mother always told me how wonderful I looked, and how my ear looked perfectly fine, and how it would look even better after all the surgeries. But she was very emotional. She was always looking at me and crying, and I would just think, 'God damn it, stop this drama.' Of course I didn't tell her that. And I guess I never told her that kids were looking at me or anything — for Christ's sake, *she* was always looking at me, as if *she* was in pain. And we had terrible fights and she would end up crying. So to answer your question, no, my father was nice enough but useless — he wasn't really there — and my mother, she didn't help much, she was such a basket case herself. She was so fucking incompetent! And she was so fucking controlling — she was always right and it was always her agenda and her way."

By now Mark worked up quite a rage and seemed to be gearing up for more. But he suddenly stopped himself and sighed. "I thought I put this anger with my mother behind me years ago, but I guess I didn't. She still annoys the hell out of me, the old lady — but I thought I came to terms with who she was. I guess I didn't."

At this point I told the patient the joke about the two psychoanalysts getting together for lunch. "I had dinner with my mother the other day," says one analyst to the other, "and I made a terrible slip of the tongue. I wanted to ask my mother to pass the salt but instead I said, 'You fucking bitch, you ruined my life.'" As this joke illustrates, mothers do get a bum rap in psychoanalytic theory. Nonetheless, the mother-child relationship is as powerful as any. And for this patient, as the father was apparently absent, it was particularly powerful. The sad thing was that this mother was obviously not a bad person. In fact, in working to fix his ear and in telling him he looked wonderful, she was clearly well-intentioned. She just took to an extreme what all parents do to unintentionally harm their children — she tried to protect him from pain.

But ultimately, she did this — as all parents do to some degree — to protect not him, but herself. She obviously couldn't tolerate her own pain regarding the physical imperfection of her son. In that respect, her failure was that she didn't *see* her son — all she saw was his deformed ear. As a result, he felt not that his ear was slightly and irrelevantly odd, which could have been his psychic truth, but rather that he himself was deformed, which unfortunately became his psychic truth.

Now having analyzed this with Mark, it became instantly self-evident why "blind incompetence" on the part of female subordinates would set him off. As he put it, "It was this kind of female modus operandi that made me feel like the 'elephant man' in the first place." Of course, the patient's own blind incompetence — which is always at the core of men's self-involvement — consisted in not seeing these women for who they were, human beings with limitations and imperfections. Just as his mother couldn't tolerate the pain evoked by the sight of his malformed ear, he couldn't tolerate the feelings evoked by his subordinates' mistakes. And just as his mother made him feel worse, by projecting her own psychic malformation onto his ear, he made them feel worse by projecting his damaged sense of self onto their imperfections.

This patient's ear, where much of this dynamic started, will always stay in my mind as a pointy reminder of the self-defeating nature of narcissistic self-love. Had the patient not tried to control his image by controlling my gaze, I doubt I would ever have paid more than passing attention to its pointedness or otherwise imperfect shape. But in his ear involvement, the patient practically forced me to focus on it, or to focus on not focusing on it, which is obviously the same thing. I suspect we all have had variations of this experience with other people; for example, with men who call attention to their imperfect height (if they didn't self-consciously mention it, you wouldn't notice they were short) or imperfect hair (if they didn't make a self-deprecating joke about it you wouldn't notice it was thinning).

This patient's mother, you might say, had too much empathy for him — she completely identified with the pain of having a damaged organ. One can also easily imagine the opposite kind of maternal response, that is, having too little empathy and being completely insensitive to the child's feelings about his ear

("There's nothing wrong with your ear and I don't want to hear about it"). The truth is both reactions are equally unempathic — clearly, the patient's mother failed to empathize with his need to feel he was okay even if his ear was not. When extreme and sustained, either kind of empathic failures — ignoring a child's feelings or catering to them — can facilitate a narcissistic development. When a child feels his emotions are not seen, he feels he doesn't matter. Since this is too painful to contemplate, he retreats into fantasies of specialness, which are often grandiose and vengeful. On the other end of the continuum, when a child feels that his emotions are always seen and responded to, there's little reason for him to give up on his naturally egocentric notion that the world revolves around him.

To be fair, my pointy-eared patient was not all that narcissistic — he was actually a modest, caring person. Nor did he have a consistent pattern of abusing his subordinates. In fact, he was generally considered a great supervisor to work for. And he responded extremely well to our brief therapeutic relationship. He took responsibility for his actions, and to the best of my knowledge has had no further incidents of this kind. Nonetheless, his story captures the central dynamics involved in what I believe is a rather pervasive phenomenon in corporate America, one which I've come to think of as "The Abusive Boss Syndrome."

Over the years I've seen several such "abusive bosses." But I've also seen their "victims," who always find it helpful to try to understand their boss's psychology. One such patient was a young man who had just come out of business school and was working for a "hot" multimedia Internet company in New York City's Silicon Alley. Initially, the patient did well because he instinctively knew that he had to make his boss feel like a genius. But after a while, this strategy backfired because he failed to be concerned with his own image, so that his admiration for the boss was interpreted by the latter as an admission of weakness. And in fact, the abuse started when the patient one day nervously admitted to not knowing something — which he probably could have known, but which had absolutely no bottom-line implications.

The boss made a nasty, condescending joke, the opening salvo in a sadomasochistic cycle which the patient didn't know how to stop, and which gradually made him feel miserable about his whole life.

Interestingly, this patient was in a position to quit his job. He had some savings, and he had a set of highly desirable technology-related skills which could land him a comparable job practically within a day. But he was "not a quitter," and he was determined to try to understand and master his situation with his boss. So together, he and I developed a series of diagnostic questions and options which he eventually was able to act on to resolve the problem.

First, you need to rule out other types of abusive bosses. While none are mutually exclusive, in addition to self-involvement, other psychological or behavioral factors such as impulse control disorders, "temper," depression, alcoholism, and self-destructiveness could be at work. But in the absence of such indications, and if the boss is a driven, performance-oriented man who is demanding perfection of others as much as of himself, and if he appears to be self-confident to the point of arrogance, and if he admires power, intelligence, or beauty, chances are you are dealing with a self-involved man who is latching on to a sign of weakness in a subordinate as a means of projecting his own passive, self-doubting, performance-resistant self onto someone else, so that he doesn't have to experience it in himself.

If this is the case, the remaining diagnostic questions are more about yourself than about the boss. Are you capable of looking up to someone without being overly deferential, as in, "You are great, and I'm great too"? If not, you'd probably be better off looking for another job. Dealing with this kind of boss is not unlike dealing with the neighborhood bully who zooms in and picks on the child he can get a reaction from. If you say something to the boss about your feelings (e.g., "It makes me feel uncomfortable when..." or "It makes me insecure when you...") he knows you're hurting, which is no good, because he knows he can use you to make himself feel better about himself. If you are too intimidated to say anything — after all, he's the boss — that's no good either, because he easily senses your vulnerability, and again, he got to you. Even if you pretend to ignore him, it's no good — he knows you are pretending.

But if you realize that the insecurity you are feeling in relation to your boss is a deposit from him, that is, that the purpose of his abuse is to make you feel what he feels inside, you can simply return the deposit to its owner. This obviously involves some sort of confrontation, which requires two more diagnostic questions before proceeding. Can you afford to lose the job? If not, confrontation might be too big a risk — although the risk of being miserable in a job for a long time might be worse and is likely sooner or later to lead to job action against you anyway.

Now what if you can afford to lose the job but don't want to? Say it's really good for your career. In this case you need to assess whether or not your boss is equally abusive to all his subordinates. If he is, it's probably a losing battle — his behavior is consistent regardless of the personality or style of the other party. If he isn't, there's your evidence that he can behave himself when he wants to. In most cases, the self-involved boss is selectively abusive, which means *there is* something you can do about it.

So now you are ready to *confront your boss*. What a joke — how many of us would actually do that!? It's difficult enough to find the guts to say to a bully, "If you come near me again I'll break your legs," but it's even more challenging to find the equivalent words in a professional or workplace setting. So the next question is, are you tough enough inside to do this? The problem is, you can't fake it. The boss's entire character structure is built around his overdeveloped capacity to sniff out vulnerability in others — so that he can (by now you should be able to complete this sentence on your own) make himself feel better about himself. So merely saying the right words to him is not going to work — you have to say it with conviction, which means you must internally know that you won't take any further abuse from him. If you don't know that, you need to get some help — from a friend, a coworker, or a therapist — before you confront him.

Help that will put you in touch with your value and power as an employee in your company and, better yet, as a human being.

So assuming you now *are* ready to confront your boss, what is it that you say? Well, your job is to remind him that he is confusing you with his insides, that you are not mush, and that you won't take it from him. If you do that, he will move on and pick on someone else. In fact, if you do that, you're quite likely to gain his respect and therefore to join his narcissistic orbit, that is, his illusional world of greatness where no one, including you, can do any wrong.

This narcissistic orbit, you should know, can be stable in the sense that you can be a member planet for a long time. But it always remains illusional — even if we are great, sooner or later we realize there is someone greater than we are. So this is a fundamentally precarious orbit, which brings about the last question you should ask yourself, if not before then after the confrontation: Is this a club I really want to belong to?

Regarding the words to use when confronting an abusive boss, the irony is that when you have this inner toughness, they are relatively easy to come by. They can consist of a sentence as simple as "I don't appreciate the way you are talking to me," or "Did anybody ever tell you you are a bully?" or they can be as complex as "I don't understand what makes you think you can talk to me in this way. So I made a mistake, so what, I'll fix it. But I plan to make more mistakes, just like you or anybody else. I am not a child, and certainly not your child. I love my work, and I would love to continue to work for you, but not under these terms."

Or, if you are a psychologist, you might want to say, "Stop bullying me. I am not going to be the recipient of your feminine projections. Have you thought about accepting the girl within you, rather then dumping her on others so that you can beat up on her?" But then, unless he is in therapy — and even if he is — your boss might simply dismiss you as a nut.

Now all this is not a call for arms. As appealing as the mantra "I will take no abuse" might be, going to battle with one's boss is generally a losing proposition. This, by the way, was the conclusion reached by my patient. He ended up handing his boss a letter of resignation explaining that he would like to work in a more humane environment. Perhaps predictably, the boss asked him to stay and promised to treat him differently. But the patient declined. The lesson in this is that most people have more power in relation to their boss (and employer) than they think. There are exceptions, of course — some of us would "confront" a tough boss not to stop abuse but rather as a means of avoiding taking responsibility for our own poor performance. In my mind, not respecting the legitimate power differential between oneself and one's boss is just as self-involved and destructive as the assaults of the abusive boss.

It's safe to say that abusive bosses are everywhere. But while it may be a complete coincidence that the two managers described above were in high-tech areas, in my experience technology brings out the narcissist in all of us. How? Well, it promises speed, efficiency, and ease of operation — nothing short of a revolutionary performance. And as it usually delivers this kind of miraculously empowering results, we come to depend on it with expectations of perfection. But sooner or later — and often enough at the most inopportune moment — there's a glitch, and the "system is down." To which we react with intense narcissistic rage, as if the rug were pulled out from under our grandiose feet.

And no matter how advanced high tech gets, there will always be a glitch. As a contractor I know said — explaining how people who spend $100,000 on renovating their kitchen can end up unhappy with it — "Wood bends." So no computer and no computer programmer could ever transcend the material nature of reality with all its imperfections and limitations.

Little Finger, Big Toe (the Anti-Narcissist)

So far, I've discussed cases in which self-involvement in men is pretty much what it appears to be (except that in the man's inner world it is the opposite of what he would like you to think it is). But not all men conform to this stereotype — some are more subtle in their narcissism and some camouflage it altogether. The latter, of course, are the most dangerous ones because their anti-narcissistic presentation lulls you — and themselves — into complacency. Let me explain.

I was once caught in a terrible traffic jam on my way to work. To my great dismay, I was unable to reach my first patient and ended up missing the entire session. Amazingly enough, this had never happened before, but what made it particularly bad was the fact that this was only the second session with a new patient. So as I was dialing the patient's phone number later in the day, all kinds of scenarios flashed through my mind. Did he wait in the lobby of my building for forty-five minutes? What did he do there all this time? What was he thinking? Was he pissed off? Disgusted? Would he ever come back? What an awful way to start a therapeutic (or any) relationship!

Well, fantasies are great because reality can be even stranger. When he answered the phone the patient was incredibly gracious. "I was okay," he said, "I actually used the time to review some memos which I had to go over for work today." And in response to my rather factual apology and explanation, he added, "It sounds like it was more stressful for you than for me." "I guess so," I said. "I'll see you the same time next week." We hung up, with me feeling amused, relieved, and happy. It was only months later as I was getting to know this patient that I realized that in that brief telephone conversation he had attempted (and nearly succeeded) to destroy me as his therapist. This is how.

First, by being not at all upset about my no-show he indicated he had absolutely no emotional expectations of me — not even ones regarding basic responsibility. (Guess what — it turned out his parents were completely irresponsible when he was a child.) So while on the surface he was "taking care" of my needs by reassuring me, in another sense he was saying I didn't matter to him at all — it was actually good for him that I didn't show up. (Guess what — when at age eleven his mother "out of the blue" sent him and his brother to live with her mother, he was relieved.)

Second, by being so attuned to my emotional state, the patient put my psychology in the foreground while his receded to the background. This tactic actually took many forms in his interactions with me: he would comment on the furniture and paintings in my office, suggest that I shine my shoes more often, ask that I choose the topic of discussion for the session, and dutifully offer to pay for missed sessions (even though as I had previously told him, that was my cancellation policy in the first place). This "transference" to the therapist, as is often the case, was consistent with the patient's way of relating to other people in his life. Financially, he took care of his mother. Emotionally, he took care of his girlfriends. And in both ways, he took care of friends, associates, and even strangers.

This is the interpersonal life of the anti-narcissist, not to be confused with the more female notion of "codependency." While there's some overlap in these two concepts, there are also differences. The main similarity is that men and women who retreat to an "enabling" position by casting everyone else in their lives in the role of the star performer both kill with kindness. That is, in devoting their lives to caring for others they develop the "moral superiority of the masochist," or the belief that everyone else sucks. In short, they are professional martyrs whose secret joy is making others feel indebted and guilty and bad. So under their incredible acts of kindness there are incredible feelings of rage.

But the male version of this, which I call the anti-narcissist, has its own hidden, often unconscious, and ultimately self-involved agenda. In the case of many of my male patients, this agenda involves a secret sexual life — literally or figuratively. These patients often stand out in my mind long after I stop seeing them: they are unusually warm, charming, giving, and talented. They are incredibly devoted to a partner who, in one form or another, is glamorous — in appearance, success, aptitude, or whatever. And the dynamics of their relationship are such that the man is totally comfortable playing the supportive-actor role — an apt metaphor if I may say so myself, because as they describe it in therapy, there is always a sense of a well-coordinated performance in their public appearance. They look good and they look as though they are good to each other — and in certain respects they are. But perhaps too good to be true, or to be wholly true.

In all these cases, at some point during the relationship something with the spouse or girlfriend would go wrong — an affair, drinking, depression, marijuana, or other difficulties which inevitably damaged the relationship and devastated the patient. But the patient would remain loyal, either emotionally denying the problem or accepting it and assuming the helping position. And this state of affairs would last for years, prompting many of the couples' acquaintances to wonder why or how the man is "putting up with all this."

To be anti-cynical for once, love and unshaken belief in the notion of commitment was in these cases the principal reason. But there was also a less conscious component which sustained not the relationships but the dynamics of what appeared to be the man's selfless devotion. In one such case, the patient came to see me in a deep, suicidal depression after his wife of nineteen years revealed to him that she had been having an affair with another man for the past five years, and that she previously had another serious, long-term affair. In discussing this with me, the patient acknowledged that in the back of his mind he always suspected that "something was going on" — at one point a friend practically told him he had seen his wife in a compromising position with her boss. And now, what troubled the patient most was the fact that he had not confronted his wife years earlier so that they could either have gotten help or ended the marriage then, when he was "young enough to start over."

As I told the patient, this, in part, was the depression talking. In reality he was not too old to start over, as he in fact did, a couple of years later. Still, it was obviously important to explore why he didn't confront his wife over the years. When we did that, the patient disclosed that he himself had had a few "dallies" over the years. While he clearly stated that it was wrong of him to have had these, he insisted that his affairs were different than his wife's — they were "purely sexual" and "episodic," and they never threatened his commitment to the marriage. As we were discussing this, however, it became clear why the patient had never confronted his wife: he felt that he couldn't do it without disclosing his own infidelities, which he wasn't prepared to do. So more or less consciously, this patient chose to close his eyes to the fact that his wife was practically leading a double life.

In this case, the patient's narcissistic difficulty in empathizing with others was evident in his inability to see that from his *wife's point of view,* his affairs could be deemed to be just as devastating as hers. But the less obvious, anti-narcissist element of his self-involvement was to be found in the dynamic through which his "meaningless" secrets were reinforcing or colluding with his wife's behavior. And in that way, the patient was an active participant in the process which was destroying his marriage and possibly his life.

Another man came to see me for advice about his wife's drinking. "I think she has a problem," he said. "She drinks every day and she gets moody. I don't bug her about it, but I know she won't get help on her own. Don't get me wrong, Doc, she is a wonderful woman and I'll do anything for her. Maybe she doesn't really have a problem. Maybe she's just feeling down and I need to support her and be there for her."

In this case, by the end of the initial consultation I strongly suspected that the patient's wife had been suffering from both alcoholism and depression for years. It was also clear that the patient was extremely devoted to the notion of taking care of her. But by the end of the second session it emerged that (1) caring for his wife's depression was a relief for the patient from worrying about his own sexuality — he occasionally had sexual fantasies about men, and (2) there was an unspoken agreement between husband and wife — you don't bug me about drinking and I won't pry into your sexual fantasies.

And in a third case, the man was impressively supportive and accepting of his wife's sexual difficulties. As a child, she had been sexually abused by her father and therefore had fears and conflict about being penetrated. As a result, the patient and his wife had little by way of a sexual relationship — they were intimate about once a year. Here, too, the patient's helpfulness was partially a way of hiding his own sexual secrets, which did not come out until well into his third year of therapy — he was unable to become aroused unless fantasizing about dominating prostitutes or other such "whorish" women. The patient felt quite bad about having such fantasies while making love to his wife, so while he very much wanted to have sex with her, on a less conscious level he was relieved not to have to deal with the guilt he felt over his fantasies.

The common denominator in the sexual secrets of these three anti-narcissists was that they emotionally removed or separated the man from his woman. In other words, they were the opposite of devotion, the outer or conscious raison d'être of the anti-narcissist. Now as we'll see in the final chapter, it is common for men to experience such nonsexual sentiments sexually. But regardless of how it shows (or actually hides) itself, the self-involvement of the anti-narcissist is always there, operating covertly to counteract the anti-narcissist's apparent disposition of extreme helpfulness and consideration.

It is hardly a coincidence that in this chapter I've borrowed heavily from the world of the theater — after all, men's self-involvement is all about performance. To continue with that metaphor, if the narcissist is an actor, the anti-narcissist is the audience. But as Aristotle first theorized, the spectator's enjoyment of the tragic drama, his *catharsis,* consisted of identifying with the emotions portrayed by the actor. In other words, the anti-narcissist is a closeted narcissist, who, given the right circumstances, will come out of the closet and be who he really wants to be.

What are the right circumstances? Usually, being pushed into the limelight by an even bigger or more skilled anti-narcissist. Arguably, the therapist is the prototypical anti-narcissist. I, for one, certainly identify with my patients. I am moved, inspired, amazed, saddened, and horrified by their experiences. My work certainly involves living vicariously. As one of my patients once put it, "You have the greatest job — it's like you're watching a soap opera and get to see what happens next the following week." From that comment you might gather that this patient's self-involvement was not all that hidden — he must have fancied himself George Clooney or some other actor. Nonetheless he was right in the sense that the drama of his life as well as that of many of my other patients was emotionally cathartic for me. But he was wrong in one important respect: in watching *ER* one can hardly break through the TV screen and join the action, whereas working with patients on very intimate emotional matters constantly tests your capacity to maintain boundaries. That's one of the reasons why some therapists will never say anything about themselves to their patients. It's the easiest way — though not always the best — to avoid the temptation of violating the therapeutic boundaries. This temptation would be hard for anyone, but if I'm right that many therapists are essentially anti-narcissists, their deepest unconscious desire would be precisely to violate these boundaries so that they can reverse the therapist-patient's role and be taken care of by the patient.

Unfortunately, when the therapist is not conscious of this desire he (or she) might act out on it with considerable damage to his patients. Therapists who are gurus of sorts, therapists who get involved with their patients outside the office, therapists who offer their lives as a model for their patients, and therapists who have additional business relationships with their patients are all common examples. But fundamentally, no therapist is exempt from the risk of at least some such violations, even if minor in nature — except for the one who never speaks or who has no personality.

In my own work, such violations occur with patients who are so anti-narcissistically gifted that they catch me off guard. One such patient was a European diplomat who, by virtue of his training and soft, charming personality, was extremely skillful in getting people to talk. Early on he figured out that I had children and would occasionally ask me how the kids were, to which I would say fine and move on. (As a therapist I am personally not so rigid with my boundaries that I will not disclose certain information if asked; but as I tell patients, I usually don't answer questions until we discuss what's behind them — so they have to be pretty persistent to actually find out things about me.)

One day when this patient asked me about the kids, I smiled. It was an early morning session, and just before I left home my daughter had said something incredibly funny — the kind of amazing thing which all kids say once in a while and which confirms their parents' suspicion ("narcissistic projections") that they are geniuses. So I related my daughter's brilliant utterance to my patient and he seemed to genuinely and graciously enjoy it. But soon after the exchange I began to feel troubled by it. In addition to the fact that there was a narcissistic bragging in it, I felt that when I quoted it to the patient I basically forgot that I was his therapist. This may not seem like such a bad thing — and in a certain respect it wasn't, because who wants a therapist who's always conscious of his role to the point that he is not human and therefore paradoxically not a good enough therapist?

But it was a bad thing, analogously akin to a parent who mentally forgets he has a child. Not that I think of my patients as children, but the analogy is that unless they have serious narcissistic issues, at least in their minds most parents don't ever stop being a parent. So in terms of my patient, in the back of my mind I was wondering whether I would hear any echoes of my forgetful violation with him in the next session.

Sure enough, in the next session the patient reported a brief daydream he had on the weekend while on the playground with his son. In this daydream he ran into me and my son in that playground and our children wandered away from us, playing together. After a couple of minutes my son came back crying, saying that his son pushed him down on the gravel. The patient scolded his son and asked him to say he was sorry but also felt some satisfaction that his son was stronger and more assertive than mine.

As the patient put it, "I don't need a therapist to tell me that this daydream suggests I don't feel I have equal power in relation to you and that in my daydream I give myself more power through my son." But notwithstanding his considerable intellectual and emotional insights, the patient did need a therapist to make the obvious connection to the previous session. He was clearly angry with my self-involvement and wanted to push me back to where I belonged.

In this case, being aware of my own self-involvement allowed me not only to understand why the patient was angry and thereby to validate his feeling, but also to study the mechanism by which he always put other people on center stage. "You turned me into your wife," I said to him — and he immediately understood. His wife was an interior decorator who became somewhat of a TV personality. Initially, the patient encouraged her to pursue her glamorous interests, but with time he became increasingly angry that her public commitments had pushed him to the sidelines. So ironically, my (modulated and monitored) self-involvement helped the patient see how he played an active role in creating the dynamics he wanted to change.

There is another, more Freudian way of understanding the anti-narcissist's self-involvement. In my description above, it's almost implied that the anti-narcissist is feminine in the sense that like the traditional wife he is the caring facilitator of someone else's performance. But the residual Freudians among us would say that I am confusing *caring* with *voyeurism,* and that the latter, like aggression and sadism, is actually associated with masculinity. And that in fact Freud discussed how such *active* or "masculine" instincts can undergo a reversal and become *passive* or "feminine," so that sadism can become masochism and, more to the point, that the anti-narcissist is a voyeur who can therefore flip into an exhibitionist.

In reaching to my own experience as a therapist, it's hard to deny that there is an intense voyeuristic quality in my interest in the material presented by patients. So I can see that discussing my daughter with my patient was a reversal into exhibitionism. Of course, the more voyeuristic someone is, the more he eventually feels compelled to expose himself — if only to confirm to himself that he actually exists. On theoretical grounds, however, the Freudian distinction between the active and passive instincts and the association of the former with masculinity and the latter with femininity is problematic. In fact, it has been greatly criticized, particularly by women analysts. In terms of our discussion, for instance, while Freud considered exhibitionism passive and feminine, actual sexual exhibition is practically exclusively male. While at this moment I'm disinclined to and probably unable to resolve this issue, I mention it as a reminder against oversimplification in the exploration of sex differences.

I suppose most patients would naturally guard against the overtly self-involved, boundary-breaking, exhibitionistic therapist. But clearly, they should also beware of the boundary-erecting, selfless observer who in his eternal frustration might turn into his own opposite. Likewise, therapists — most of whom err on the side of self-denial — should be careful not to become a flat caricature of the objective, personless, and desire-free analyst. One of my patients, at the time a Ph.D. candidate in clinical psychology, expressed doubts about his ability as a psychologist in training. "Unlike you, I may not be cut out for this," he said. "I don't feel I care enough about my patients; maybe I'm too selfish to listen to other people all day long." "Well," I replied, "perhaps you should try to be even more selfish with your patients — I can't imagine doing this kind of work for someone else's benefit."

In working with anti-narcissistic patients it's often difficult to demonstrate to them that they are actually narcissists in disguise. Their conscious experience of the world is that they are controlled by others' whims, needs, and schedules. This is where dream interpretation comes in handy. For instance, one patient, the New York correspondent of a West Coast newspaper, related a dream in which he was getting a pedicure during which the pedicurist damaged his big toenail. The patient mentioned this dream in passing, saying it was one of those dreams that have no significance. But when I pressed him for associations, something intriguing began to come to the foreground. A couple of days before the dream, he said, while working on a New York story about Korean immigrants, he was interviewing a manicurist, who afterward offered him a manicure, during which she hurt his fingernail.

The patient then told me that he was annoyed by this, and also annoyed by the story, which was assigned to him by his editor. "It was just not that interesting a story to work on," he said. "As for the toenail," he resumed telling his associations, "the only thing that comes to mind is that a couple of years ago, the newspaper sent me to cover the World Economic Forum in Davos, Switzerland. In my one morning off I went skiing and I fell and hurt my toe. Of course they had an emergency hospital there for all the world's leaders, and the doctors had nothing to do. So I ended up being operated on by the President's surgeon! That was quite a treatment."

So this is what the dream did: in displacing the annoyance of the little finger — the insignificance of the journalist as a recorder of others' lives — with the memory of the big toe — where the patient got to play President — it showed us that the patient wanted to come out of his anti-narcissistic closet. He wanted to be part of the action rather than cover it. To put the icing on the cake of this interpretation, the patient had another thought about the toe. "It's obviously more phallic than the finger." He smiled.

As evident in this case, almost by definition self-involvement has a physical or bodily dimension. Since our society sanctions and cherishes it more in women, this is more evident in women's concern and preoccupation with their appearance. But even if more subtle in most men, their self-involvement is never without this dimension — symbolically if not literally. The reason is simple: the empathic failures that promote self-involvement (in both genders) occur very early in life, starting at a time when our sense of well-being is experienced primarily through the gratification of bodily needs. When these needs are not adequately met, our bodies become painfully overvalued and like a messenger end up announcing to the world our overly entitled desire for compensation.

Beauty and the Beast

Once upon a time, there lived a prince who was spoiled and selfish. On a winter night, he turned away an old woman who had asked for shelter. The woman, who was really a powerful enchantress, changed the prince into a hideous Beast and cast a spell on all who dwelt in his castle. She left behind an enchanted mirror and a rose that would bloom until his twenty-first year. If the prince had never been loved by the time the last rose petal fell, he was doomed to remain a beast forever.

In my office sit many such male beasts. Well beyond their twenty-first year they nevertheless are still waiting to be loved unconditionally by a perfect blond. Of course, in reality these men are not at all hideous. They might be a bit short or thin or balding. Or they might be extremely good-looking, for that matter. But because they feel beastly they are convinced they can only be cured by the unconditional love of a beauty.

Unfortunately, unlike the fairy tale, no Belle ever shows up. The reason is that since they can only fall in love with appearance, the person under the blond mask does not feel loved by them and therefore can never love them. So they are doomed to live in a constant state of punishment — by a taste of their own medicine. They live and die for beauty.

Of course, these men are perfectly capable of metamorphosing themselves back into a prince. They do that in the course of dating when attempting to date a nice, decent woman whom they end up judging and dismissing as the beast incarnate. As we saw in the second chapter, this metamorphosis involves the projection of feelings of shame onto the other person. There is, in fact, an intimate connection between narcissism and shame: grandiosity is essentially a flight from the experience of shame. The other thing we saw in that chapter as well as in this one is that for men, looking good is not necessarily the same as being good-looking. More likely, it's having a woman who's good-looking, and a good-looking job. Let's remember that as we take a good look at several forms of transformational beasts.

One patient, a married man in his late thirties and the father of two small children, came to therapy because he was unhappy in his work as well as in his marriage. He was a periodontist, working as a partner in a group practice he had bought into several years earlier. He was making good money but was tortured by the constant feeling that he wasn't as successful as he could have been. His partner, he said, was not ambitious and was reluctant to upgrade equipment and to keep up with progressive treatment techniques. Also, the office was in an old, unattractive building in a low-middle-class area, and most of his patients couldn't afford the more sophisticated and lucrative treatments he was trying to push.

At home, a similar picture emerged. He and his wife had a close relationship with a rather open dialogue. She was a dental hygienist and an aspiring opera singer. She didn't make a lot of money but she loved working with people and enjoyed her work. His children, like all kids, added both joy and stress to his life. But what really bothered him was a nagging sense that his wife was just not the right person for him. She didn't have exactly the same sense of humor and she didn't share his interest in traveling. He was also not as attracted to her as to some of the women he would see in the street or in the office.

"A prince," I said to myself upon hearing this, preparing to look for signs of beasthood. But I didn't have to look very hard — it was all over the place in the previous chapter of his work and love life. Before buying into his practice, the patient had worked as a salaried periodontist in Rockefeller Center in a technologically sophisticated, progressive group with a wealthy patient population and beautiful offices. But the patient was quite miserable there. Not only did his boss make it clear to him that he would never become a partner, but he was also an arrogant, hostile prick who dominated and manipulated the patient with his sarcastic humor and infantalizing put-downs. Nevertheless, the patient stayed in this job for more than ten years.

He finally couldn't take it anymore, so he quit without having another job and began to look for an opportunity to buy into a practice — which eventually led him to where he was today. Quitting that job also corresponded with an important event in his personal life — the breakup of his first marriage. From his description now it seemed that his first wife was everything his second wasn't — she had a great sense of humor, she was a successful lawyer, and he was passionately attracted to her without reservation or ambivalence. Except for three things — details, details — her sense of humor was hostile toward him (he didn't care), she had cheated on him (he suspected but managed to deny it), and she ultimately left him for another man (he was devastated by that).

So in his attempt to regulate his self-esteem, this patient went from being treated like an unlovable beast to becoming a spoiled prince. With the first job and wife he tried to feel good about himself by choosing a successful and beautiful environment — but that only highlighted his feelings of inadequacy. With the second job and wife he tried to do it by choosing a lesser environment so that he could feel better about himself by comparison — which also backfired. So in fact, in both chapters of his life the patient did the same thing — he projected a part of himself onto the environment in a doomed effort to find an external solution to an internal problem. If you conclude from this that the patient's ideal environment would have been somewhere in between the two extremes, you may or may not be right, but you still don't get the point. The point is that for this patient — as it is to varying degrees for everyone — the attractiveness of the environment was all in the eyes of the self-involved beholder.

This patient needed to downgrade *and* upgrade *himself*, not his environment. He needed to integrate the prince and the beast inside of him into a realistic sense of a good enough self-worth before he could see who his wife and job actually were — free of his narcissistic projections. Then and only then could he figure out if they were environmentally correct for him. In this case, after a long therapeutic process, the patient did figure it out. When he began to accept his limitations and enjoy his celebrations, the chips fell down as follows: the job was out and externally upgraded and the wife was in, internally upgraded.

As we saw in the second chapter many women are familiar with the way in which men critically project their own sense of inadequacy onto them. As in the case of the patient above, these men's attempts to feel better about themselves by "downgrading" their spouses or girlfriends only backfire, because they end up feeling downgraded by reflection. What I've found clinically interesting over the years is that these downgraded men compensate for their low self-esteem at nighttime, with heroic dreams. One such critical husband was lowered from a helicopter to save his wife from a fire in her office building, while another conducted an amazing emergency surgery to save his child from choking.

Of course such dreams have individualized meanings as well. For example, one man who was harshly critical of his wife's emotional vulnerability had a dream in which he was able to fly. But he flew, mind you, in order to escape from a disgusting pig who was chasing him and digging his pink, phallic (the patient's, not my description) nose into his back. The patient related the dream to a traumatic childhood experience in which another boy repeatedly induced him to perform oral sex on him. So the dream showed how the patient's character attempted to cope with the terrible shame he felt about this humiliating childhood experience. To escape feminization, the patient had to be capable of flying, that is, he had to develop a fantastical, grandiose sense of masculinity. And this defensive masculinity was the same place from which he rejected his own feminine vulnerability and projected it onto his wife.

In the second chapter I discussed "the checklist," men's tendency to project shame onto women in dating situations. Clearly, that discussion could be repeated here, in examining the transformation of undesirable, internal parts of the self into external environments. I'll spare you the repetition, but I'd like to mention a related transformational syndrome which I personally find particularly heartbreaking to work with. In this syndrome, the man is genuinely looking to fall in love and commit to a lifelong partnership. But time and again, after he falls in love with a woman who seems to be absolutely right, he begins to have doubts. Something about the woman bothers him — it can be something small like big thighs or something...small like lack of interest in music.

But whatever it is, though it didn't really bother him at first, now that he is focused on it, it gets bigger and bigger in his mind until, in the words of one patient, "it eats away at whatever is good in the relationship."

I find this painful to watch because typically the patient goes through this experience at least twice, each time genuinely believing — and often even convincing his skeptical therapist — that he has found true happiness. His disappointment in his own capacity to love, when his Belle is once again transformed into a beast, is anything if not poignant. Of course, there is always an illusional element to falling in love, the illusion being that feeling loved by the *other person* — who's temporarily imbued with unparalleled specialness by our own idealizing love for her — will keep us feeling good about *ourselves* forever.

But when the person's entire sense of self is invested in the illusion, no matter how genuine or intelligent he is, when it dissipates there's no there there, and love is gone as swiftly as it came. Now the most painful experience of this syndrome comes — as is often the case in psychotherapy and in life — just before the healing phase, when the patient realizes that there was nothing wrong with any of the women he (thought he) loved — he probably could have been happy with all of them. This is painful not only because of the loss of love and opportunities, but also because of the realistic sense of internal damage that the person is left with — *he's* the one with the problem, not them. The silver lining, though, is that it's precisely this painful realization that can launch this man on a therapeutic trajectory at the end of which he may come to see that beasts and beauties are for the birds — or for fairy tales.

Fake It till You Make It

As we've seen, the problem of narcissism develops early in life and is intimately entangled with our very sense of self. So it should come as no surprise that dealing with men's self-involvement is a huge challenge, which can take years — in or out of therapy. In fact, there are volumes upon volumes of psychological literature on this topic, most of which offer little hope for a short-term fix. So if you're looking for quick answers in this chapter, you'll be disappointed.

Nonetheless, now that I've reduced your expectations — there's always something to be learned from average politicians — let me offer a road map if not a prescription for coping with self-involvement. The first step is to empathize with the poor little bastard. I'm being sarcastic because this is not an easy thing to do — genuinely. It's a little hard to empathize with someone who doesn't think you exist, isn't it? Though it's certainly easier for a therapist than for a spouse or a friend. After all, as a therapist you shouldn't expect recognition and attention from your patients — at least not consciously. However, as we've determined before, therapists are human and they do expect such things. Nonetheless, many of them are still capable of empathizing with the self-involved. The secret is not in their training, but rather in their conscious willingness to put their own emotional needs aside and to put themselves in the patient's emotional shoes.

A girlfriend or a spouse can do that too — at least temporarily. "But you're getting paid for it," I can hear you say. Well, your reward will come too — only a bit later. To make it easier in the meantime, think about it this way — your self-involved man has suffered from his parents' narcissism even more than you are suffering from his. So you are actually in a really good position to empathize with his sense of emotional deprivation. *See him, hear him, touch him, feel him,* and console yourself with the thought that you are modeling for him how to love.

And when you feel resentful and angry about his blindness to your emotional existence, try the following hypothetical experiment which I've developed for myself as a means of dealing with my anger at my insignificance in the narcissistic streets of New York City. Like many people, I used to get really mad when a taxi driver would cut me off, when a fellow subway rider would block my way to get a seat, or when a fellow movie fan would cut into the line ahead of me. But then I began to document — with a degree of self-repulsion — that in virtually every such situation I myself was fully capable of doing, and at some point in time had probably done, the same thing. In fact, I was probably angry at least in part because this fellow New Yorker had beat me to the punch with *his* sense of entitlement. When I realized that, I took myself out of this narcissistic competition and I subsequently found myself less angry and more amused by the mean streets of The City.

Because it relies on the fact that one way or another we are all self-involved, this method can be easily applied to the egregious behaviors of the self-involved man. A version of this is one of my favorite techniques in couples therapy — to point out to the wife or girlfriend (or sometimes the man) that as she is criticizing the man for being critical of her she is doing to him precisely what she's accusing him of doing to her. "But what I'm saying is true," she replies. "And he feels the same way," I retort. This is a winning technique which never fails to bring the couple closer together, as they realize that they don't come from different planets after all, and that there are no victims and victimizers in their relationship.

Now back to phase one, empathizing with the self-involved man — we're still there. There is life after this phase — actually there're two more phases — but if you're already frustrated, maybe this relationship (or this chapter) is not for you. In real life this phase is as long as the extent of the man's self-involvement. In my experience, when a spouse is not willing to engage in the anti-narcissistic behavior required by this phase, the couple ends up separating. This, of course, is not the woman's "fault" — clearly, if the woman is self-involved the man should relegate himself to the same anti-narcissistic phase. It's really nobody's fault. But it is, I believe, a leading cause of divorce as well as of many other interpersonal conflicts. I think of it not as the battle of the sexes, but as the clash of narcissism — two otherwise loving or lovely people are apparently unwilling to take turns in getting their needs met.

Phase two is the beginning of your reward for all the patience you have shown — not that it doesn't require additional patience. Here you need to define, confront, or educate the man about his self-involvement. The reward is, that in doing so, you get to express a bit of your anger, but only a bit, because you still want your patient — I mean your partner — to hear you. A personal example comes to mind.

Once while we were driving out of town, my wife interrupted me in mid-sentence and said with some anger, "Do you think this is the first time you're telling me this?" "Don't you ever repeat yourself?" I responded with indignation. "It's about your narcissism," she explained, and I got it and apologized. What I understood, even if reluctantly, was that I've probably shared with her this tidbit of my thoughts at least twice before, but that I didn't remember that I did because at the time she didn't exist for me other than as an audience — she could have been anyone.

If you think this is bad on my part, consider the fact that it took me years to be able to see my own narcissism and to acknowledge it to myself and to my wife so instantaneously. But it was my wife who helped me get there by holding a defining and educating mirror to me. Now in case you wonder, my wife is a psychologist, too, so she might have an unfair advantage in that regard. Except that once again, you don't need training to tell someone — or even to show them how — they are self-involved. True, my wife and I use the language of psychology — even when we fight. But our fights are hardly unique and the translation, I believe, is easy enough. She said "narcissism," but a plethora of other terms would do the job — it shouldn't be that difficult to explain why repeating oneself endlessly is offensively self-centered.

Now lest I commit the same sin right here and now, let's move on to phase three. Once the self-involved man is more aware of his narcissism, it's time to confront his hostility and reap some more rewards, still in the form of expressed anger, as well as pay the price for the battles that will ensue. I already discussed in the second chapter how you must resist the critical projections that come your way from a beast who's trying to become a prince —

at your expense. But here I'm suggesting that you take this a step further — the self-involved man needs to know that what you dish out to others is what you get back. So in this phase, you don't *feel* but rather *deal* the pain. Remember, the narcissist only understands the language of his own pain. So he must feel the same kind of pain you're feeling in order to begin to empathize with you. So in criticizing him, make sure to hit him where it hurts. (But do try to remember you love him.)

I do the same with patients — and I say this not in jest, but rather after careful consideration. In the movie *Analyze This*, there's a scene in which the therapist, frustrated and bored with his patient, fantasizes telling her something like: "Look at yourself. You are so pathetic. Why don't you just stop whining and get a life!" As most of my patients know, the difference between me and that therapist is that I don't fantasize about saying such things — I say them. Of course, not in these words — because I never feel such words — and never disrespectfully. But I am tough on my patients and I often say hurtful (though, I believe, loving) things, especially to self-involved men. I once even told a patient, "I'm sick and tired of hearing about your psychological problems!" — though admittedly it wasn't as outrageous as it sounds when taken out of context. The patient was expressing feelings of shame over being "someone who has psychological problems," so my comment was actually empathic in that it implies that he didn't have to feel ashamed of his problems. But it also implied that his problems were no more special than anybody else's, and that it was time to grow up — which I've told other patients when appropriate.

With many self-involved patients I've discussed openly and aggressively their superficial interests in appearance, fame, and status. And I've uttered to patients such harsh statements as "I don't think you care about other people's feelings," "Nobody is good enough for you," and "What makes you think you're so great?!" The truth is this is a high-risk strategy, because it challenges the person's core defense — the grandiose fantasy of being special. The risk is that the self-involved man will respond to such confrontations with an avalanche of rage or will simply terminate the relationship. But then again, this is why this kind of confrontation comes at phase three — after long periods of empathizing with and defining the person's need to feel special.

And there are other things you can do to soften the blow. For one thing, you should always acknowledge the ways in which the person *is* special. For example, one of my patients, a physician and a senior researcher in his field, was in Europe for a medical conference. On his way back, when he arrived at the airport he was informed that his flight was overbooked and that he couldn't get on it. He was so offended that after a brief argument with the flight attendant at the gate, he challenged her with "And what if I just walk through and board the plane?" "You'll be arrested, sir," she answered. "I don't think so, I have a ticket," he responded, and proceeded to walk past her onto the plane.

Well, he ended up spending the night in a Parisian jail. But he survived and lived to tell me about it a few days later. Now contrary to what this story suggests, under normal circumstances, this man would not strike most people as arrogant or smug. In fact, he was a warm, likable person, and he did not tell me about this incident without berating himself for his "stupid sense of entitlement." (As a physician he had access to a psychiatric diagnostic manual and at some point had diagnosed himself as having a Narcissistic Personality Disorder.)

"What's stupid about it," I said, "is that if you really wanted to get on this plane you could have said that you were a doctor and that you needed to get back to the hospital — which happened to be the truth. But you didn't want special treatment that you were possibly entitled to. You wanted special treatment for just breathing, or uttering a wish. A lot of people would say that what you do for a living is pretty important — but not you. You want to be important for nothing!"

In response, the patient had an impressive rationale as to why he didn't use the physician/hospital card: "I've always told myself that I will not use being a doctor in that way — it's a matter of principle." I didn't argue with him over this point, but he didn't argue with me either when I said, "This sounds more like a rationalization than a rationale — you just wanted to feel special."

If you are not outrageously narcissistic yourself, chances are that you can confront the hostility inherent in a man's self-involvement with a degree of empathy and interest that will reduce your own anger and keep to a minimum the cycle of reciprocal recriminations which typically ends in a narcissistic explosion. It is important, however, to be direct and punchy with the self-involved man, because paradoxically, it speaks to his sense of himself as a hero — it makes him feel good that he "can take it."

Once when I was a teenager and disappointed in love, a parent of a friend of mine, who happened to be a psychiatrist, comforted me with a challenging rather than an empathic comment. In discussing my loss, he said that I should mourn it in the same way that one would mourn the death of a wife, to which I responded by saying that mourning the loss of the dead is easier because at least you don't feel rejected. "Why should it be easy for you?" he challenged me, and I was more comforted by that than by his suggestion that I mourn the loss.

Generally, if the self-involved man responds somewhat favorably to the confrontations of phases two and three — even if it's a delayed, begrudging response — there's hope. Ultimately, of course, it's up to him to deprogram and reprogram himself, and most men eventually will — after all, as we saw, the self-involved man wants to be liked and is genuinely eager to please. Unfortunately, some narcissistic people, even when they experience the boomerang effect of the pain they inflict on others, cannot find within themselves the capacity to care. But even they might eventually respond, only for a different reason. Since they are prone to feelings of shame, they will gradually realize, at least, that the appearance of narcissism is not cool. So they'll become narcissistically motivated to change it — for appearance's sake. Or at the very least, they'll become committed to changing the appearance of narcissism — which sometimes is not a bad place to start. As the saying goes, fake it till you make it.

In reality, I should note, these three phases don't really exist separately from each other. But their overlap is such that in dealing with the self-involved man, it's best to have more of the first phase earlier and more of the second and third phases later. I should also admit here that the therapist does have an important advantage over anyone else in implementing these phases. By definition, the patient is in psychotherapy for purely narcissistic reasons — for himself. So when the therapist confronts him with his lack of regard for him — the therapist — the patient usually understands that the therapist is not talking out of his own need to be regarded, but rather is offering a more or less objective observation.

Unfortunately, many therapists don't offer such critical observations at all, and the result is the all too familiar narcissist who with the help of therapy becomes even more narcissistic, offering his obsessive analysis of his own narcissism to anyone who will listen. Perhaps it's obvious that everybody goes into therapy with the expectation that they will get something out of it. But what the self-involved man should get out of it — as well as out of any relationship — is the revelation that there is more happiness in giving than in getting. Once again, the man has something to learn from traditional forms of femininity.

Aggression

...I'll show you who's boss

Remembrance of Things Past

One fall weekend morning, as we were feeding the ducks in the brook near our home, I asked my daughter, who was four at the time, "Which one is the boy and which one is the girl?" Since we had covered this territory before, if anything, I expected her to say that the green-headed duck was the boy and the gray was the girl. But instead she said, "The one who is chasing is the boy." And in fact, a green-headed boy duck was chasing a gray-headed girl duck. "How do you know the one who's chasing is the boy?" I then asked, once again expecting her to say, "Because he has a green head." But instead she said, "Because boys are the bullies."

Where did she learn this? Certainly not at home, I thought, before realizing that her older brother rather enjoyed bossing her around. But she could easily have learned it on the playground or from Disney movies. Or maybe it was "biological knowledge," unfolding along with her very personality, marching to the drumbeat of her feminine DNA. These kinds of questions about the reality and perception of aggression in boys and men have stimulated an enormous amount of research and controversy over the years. My own clinical experience confirms my daughter's observation that, at least superficially, men are more often bullies than women. Of course, it's quite likely that her observation merely reflected her father's bias (I would hope, not so much his behavior).

As for the research, my own reading of it is that there's plenty of evidence that as a group, men are biologically more predisposed to aggression than women. Many people, including many psychologists, prefer to deny that biology has any role in male aggression, fearing that if it does, the implication is that there's nothing we can do to control violence — most of which is in fact committed by men. But when defined as a tendency rather than as an actual behavior, even authors such as Terrence Real and Myriam Miedzian, who emphasize social factors in gender differences, concede that biology plays a role in male aggression.[10]

The most interesting biological theories are those that compare us humans to our nearest ape relatives, the orangutan, chimpanzee, and gorilla. As noted by authors Richard Wrangham and Dale Peterson, the males in these species use such brute force as rape, battery, and infanticide to dominate females for the purpose of increased reproductive success. The comparison of such animal violence to human aggression is clearly disturbing. But is it disturbing because we are different from or because we are similar to these *other* apes? (In 1984 scientists determined that we are actually part of the ape family!) Perhaps both. That most human violence is carried out by men goes without saying, and that rape and battery, if not infanticide, are violent behaviors men share with their ape relatives is also undeniable. But even when we consider psychological rather than physical aggression — as I will do in this chapter — it's hard to deny that it has some roots in the history of our biological evolution.

It's hard to deny it precisely because the system which produces male aggression — in Wrangham and Peterson's language "patriotism" — is actually unique in the animal kingdom. In fact, as feminists might be heartened to contemplate, in many species it is the female, not the male, who does the fighting. But as pointed out by Wrangham and Peterson, in the animal systems in which females are the soldiers, the action is fundamentally defensive, the goal being to defend the motherland from external intrusion. In the chimpanzee-human system, on the other hand, male warriors go beyond defense and often perpetrate unprovoked aggression.

In fact, in the world of primates, chimpanzees and humans are unique in that they are the only ones who regularly and deliberately kill adults of their own kind.

Of course, it's hard to think of ourselves as apes. Unlike *them*, we have language, art, culture, spirituality — and of course, real intelligence. But if you consider that our forefathers were apes for about three to twenty-two million years before they became humans about two million years ago, and that art — in the form of cave paintings and bone carvings — only entered our history about thirty-five thousand years ago, it's actually surprising that we are not more ape-like than we are. From that standpoint, the desire to deny our past, while understandable — who wants to think of himself as an ape? — is not only foolish, but dangerous. As I often tell patients who want to think that their childhood has nothing to do with who they are today, home is where we come from. These patients, who may come from "dysfunctional" families, want so much to separate themselves from them that they dismiss the intellectual proposition that causation of anything begins in its past. Sadly, as one often sees in the interpersonal life of such people, those who are unwilling to remember the past are doomed to repeat it. It is the woman who doesn't remember missing her absent father, not the one who remembers it, who ends up longing for unavailable men.

And so it is with those who in their unwillingness to tolerate any ugliness in man deny scientific theories of evolution, but end up burning books or repeating some other such menacingly apish behaviors. The scientists who research evolutionary theories, on the other hand, are probably rather gentle, sensitive, and in that sense more human, creatures. So in my mind, while men are sociobiologically predisposed to aggression, that very awareness — rather than its denial — is the key to curbing, sublimating, and coping with it. It is the paradox of any forward movement that one cannot separate from the past without having an ongoing dialogue with it — we must say good-bye before we say hello.[11]

But having said that, let's say good-bye for now to all this monkey business — I'm sure it will find its way back to our consciousness soon. While our roots are there, it's ultimately not physical aggression that is uniquely human, but rather the more sophisticated psychological and interpersonal forms of battery. In fact, whatever its evolutionary origins, men's aggression, much like self-involvement, is a direct outcome of the conflict of masculine insecurity. Rejecting mother's feminine influence is not enough — most men also seek to reverse the balance of power with her. As he grows up, the boy gradually attempts to relinquish his vulnerable, dependent relation to his mother and to substitute its opposite — the desire to be the boss. Sometimes as a teenager the boy actually starts challenging his mother, but at other times he transfers and displaces this into a desire to dominate all women or, more often, women on whom he becomes emotionally dependent. Or anyone else who would receive this mother transference.

The Battered Therapist

We are probably all familiar with the kind of couple in which the man appears to somehow mistreat the woman. And in fact, explosive men and wounded women do populate therapeutic couches and armchairs wherever they're to be found. This dynamic, by the way, must be distinguished from the related yet qualitatively different problem of domestic violence. While both share some psychological similarities and may in fact overlap, the latter involves a concern for physical safety and other consequences which require special considerations and place it outside the subject matter of this book. Of course, women, too, are perfectly capable of using and abusing men, but the mode of their aggression is usually quite different from men's.

One of my patients, "Len," came to see me at his wife's insistence after a fight in which he had lost his temper and thrown a book at her. In the first session he reluctantly stated that he realized he had a problem. He also explained that he had had a worse episode the previous Thanksgiving while he and his family were staying for the holiday at his parents' house in New Jersey. He had a yelling match with his mother and he ended up hitting her on the head with a hanger. After that, his parents decided that he was no longer welcome to stay overnight in their house. The patient's reaction was relief — he hadn't wanted to spend the holidays with them in the first place, and only did it out of obligation. After he told me that, the patient and I agreed that the outcome of the explosion revealed something about what had motivated it: the desire to get away from his parents without having to express it in words.

For two or three years, Len's therapy proceeded predictably and uneventfully. We spoke repeatedly about his difficulties in separating from his parents, but this often felt like an empty intellectual exercise. One day, out of the blue, the patient responded to one of my admittedly less-than-sensitive observations with an explosion of a kind I had never experienced before. He stood up, approached me with a menacing hand gesture, and started screaming at the top of his lungs. Then, his voice and body trembling with violent rage, he opened the door to my office and launched an onslaught of accusations about my incompetence for the entire world to hear. Finally, he stormed out, leaving me speechless and stunned. Simply put, I had never, and I don't think I ever will again, heard anyone screaming so loudly.

In the next session Len was appropriately apologetic. I, on the other hand, informed him that I felt too fearful to work effectively with this type of self-expression. The patient cleverly countered that he was finally allowing himself to show me his problem, and that my job was to accept it so that we could work on it in "the here and now." I agreed with him that ideally I should be able to welcome his problems into our personal interaction, and that in fact, this is how therapy works best. But I told him that I couldn't ignore my fear, and that therefore, if this happened again, I would terminate the treatment.

This seemed to work, and for a while we were back on track. But then, a new problem emerged. The patient began to show up late for sessions. First five, then ten, then twenty minutes late. We discussed what this could mean, including the possibility that he didn't really want to come to therapy anymore. But this, once again, seemed like an empty intellectual analysis from a Psychology 101 textbook. In addition, Len insisted that he was late for everything in his life, and he would get understandably frustrated about using whatever time he did have in the session to discuss his lateness. So eventually I gave up on this line of inquiry and laid off. His tardiness, however, didn't let up. Rather, it gradually escalated to the point that he would come five minutes before the end of the session, and sometimes not at all. And on the rare occasions in which he did come on time, he would sit down silently, sometimes not talking for long stretches of time.

Then came the second explosion. I don't remember what triggered it, but once again, the patient yelled and stormed out. Except that this time he returned a few minutes later. And as I was silently contemplating whether and how I should terminate the treatment, he sat down and started speaking.

"I was walking around the block and thinking about what I did. I then realized why I did it. I told you at the very beginning of this goddamned — quote unquote — process that it was my wife's idea that I get therapy. And I told you later, by being late, by not showing up, and by not talking, that I still didn't want to be here. But you did nothing. So just like with my parents, I had to blow up so that you'd finally get rid of me. All because I was afraid to leave on my own."

When he said that, I couldn't believe that I hadn't seen this myself — it was so obvious. But I then realized why my powers of observation had left me: ever since the first explosion, somewhere in the back of my mind I always expected a repeat performance, and like a battered spouse I was intimidated by the patient's rage and was thinking on eggshells. And this, of course, is the chief objective of this type of male domination: to catch the "opponent" off guard and to intimidate her into submission.

Another universal objective of male aggression, illustrated dramatically and somewhat simplistically by this patient's case, is that of psychological separation. Had the patient been able to say, "I don't really want to continue the therapy," or "I don't want to depend on you any more, Mom," there would have been no need for him to explode. But when one is more attuned to the losses than to the gains of separation, being thrown out is less painful than taking active leave.

Meanwhile, as you may have guessed, I am still seeing this patient. But literally no session goes by without a discussion of his wish to get rid of me and his fear that he won't be able to get along without me. And we both take comfort in the therapeutic fact that, emotionally speaking, I have become his mother and that he is finally working on separating from her. Among other things, this shows that you don't have to be a woman in order to become the target of men's desire to dominate women. If anything, in exercising their aggression many men feel they must win a doubleheader — so they turn a man into a woman and then proceed to treat him accordingly.

Responding in Kind

Sometimes, coping well with men means that we must meet aggression with aggression. In a confrontation, however, we must choose our weapons with care. Ideally, they should be (1) clearly superior, but (2) preferably conventional rather than nuclear. With my explosive patient, yelling back would have been a losing proposition — my voice couldn't match his decibels. Terminating the treatment could have been a winning strategy, except that it's more like a nuclear than a conventional weapon, which is why I didn't use it. But in not using it, was I a wimp? Was I inviting more aggression from the patient? Time will tell.

One thing I've learned from this and similar patients goes against the grain of what you are taught in graduate school. Mental health professionals (as well as law enforcement officials, teachers, and foreign policy experts) are routinely taught that when you are dealing with individuals who test the limits, you must specifically and explicitly inform them of the limits of acceptable behavior and the consequences of crossing the line. But, as any parent or teacher who has ever used the words "The next time you do this, I will..." knows, limit testers are so gifted in their art that they will walk the line and draw you into an obsessive dialogue about the definition and redefinition of the limits, all in the service of gradually grinding your authority into nothingness.

For example, with my explosive patient, how would I set the limits on the volume or length of his outbursts? What would I do if he just raised his voice and stopped on the verge of menace? Unfortunately, these kinds of questions are only too familiar to the many women who have partners with a "temper."

The answer, I therefore suggest, is almost the opposite of what is taught in graduate school — do not tell the person what your red line is. Rather, work on developing your own internal conviction as to what is truly unacceptable to you. Then, inform the aggressor of the *principle* guiding your limits, but let him wonder about the specifics. And be prepared to act when your principle has been violated. Of course, it will be easy to act because you will now have no doubts as to what's unacceptable.

Clearly, this is easier said than done. When I told my explosive patient that I was not going to terminate his treatment after all, he sighed and said, "You're beginning to lose credibility, just like my wife. She's been saying she'll leave me the next time it happens, for the past fifteen years!" "I suppose that's true," I said, "but I don't think I have the same tolerance level as she does. So let's hope you don't test me again. Unless, of course, you want to end the therapy, in which case let's skip the yelling."

So in dealing with men's aggression one must recognize their chimpanzee-like behavior and respond in kind. When responding with tears or their equivalent to her husband's or boyfriend's hostile criticism regarding, say, her appearance, a woman only invites further abuse. Initially the tears seem to soften the man's heart — he typically responds lovingly and regretfully to the tearful woman — as they offer tangible proof of his power. But precisely for that reason, they ultimately reward and reinforce his behavior, setting the couple off to a dizzying roundabout of emotional S & M. Therefore, rather than submit, the best strategy for a woman in this situation is to find a way to tell her man to "get lost" or "get a life" — but ideally, not before developing her own internal conviction regarding what's unacceptable behavior.

At the same time, it is also important to realize that unlike sheer violence, men's aggression is also a psychological defense intended to ward off their own feminine powerlessness. According to this hypothesis, the more powerless a man might feel, the more aggressive he will act.[12] So if you want to decrease his aggression you must increase his sense of power, which is something many women do rather well. Even if in jest, admiring and loving a man for his intellect, his work, his skills at basketball, his gentlemanly behavior — or whatever it is he perceives as masculine about himself other than his wish to dominate you — goes a long way to make him feel empowered. Granted, that's hard to do when you feel dominated by your partner, but that's when it's most needed. And it is easier when accompanied by the aggressive response of "Get lost" to his aggression — standing up to somebody makes it more, not less, likely that you will love him. After all, love comes from a place of liberation and equality, not victimhood.

Apollo and Daphne (Boy Germs)

One of my favorite sculptures is in Rome's Villa Borghese. Created by Italian Baroque artist Gianlorenzo Bernini, it captures and eternalizes a mythological moment in the history of the war — and love — between the sexes. The magnificent white stones show a young couple in a moment of triumph, despair, and transformation. As the youthful man reaches to hold his beloved, her skin turns into bark and her hair and arms into branches and leaves. Petrified in that moment is the figure of Apollo, the Greek god of music, poetry, medicine, and prophecy, chasing and catching the beautiful nymph Daphne, who would not return his love. While Cupid, the god of love, had struck Apollo with an arrow making him fall in love, he had struck Daphne with an arrow making her run away from love. So after a long chase, when Apollo finally catches up with her, the nymph prays to another god, her father, to destroy the body which Apollo has so desired. Her prayer is answered and she's turned into a laurel tree.

In *Metamorphoses,* the ancient Roman poet Ovid tells us more about the emotional duality underlying this love chase. On the one hand, Apollo clearly expresses gentle feelings of admiration and care. Concerned that Daphne might get hurt in the chase, he protectively calls out "*The ground is rough here. / Run a little slower, and I will run, I promise, a little slower.*" On the other hand, he doesn't stop the chase even though he is well aware that he has failed to convince her that he is not the enemy. In fact, one can sense his objectification of Daphne in his very admiration of her: "*He gazes at her lips, and knows that gazing is not enough. / He marvels at her fingers, her hands, her wrists, her arms, bare to the shoulder, / And what he does not see he thinks is better.*" Even his protective feelings toward her seem to focus on not damaging "those lovely legs" and other body parts, rather than on the person of Daphne.

Now why does Apollo chase Daphne? Does he really think it will make her love him? Well, men may not be thinking at all at such a time. Yet even if they do, they are often not at all conscious of the hostility inherent in their aim, whereas women are instantly aware of being targeted and objectified. Consciously, Apollo is looking not for conquest but rather for acceptance. I'm no shepherd, he tells Daphne and he tries to sell himself to her by mentioning his various godly qualifications: he's a healer, a fortune teller, and so on. In this manner, too, this god is rather (hu)manlike after all. His attempts to impress Daphne are reminiscent of the desperate plea of the narcissistic man to gain acceptance and approval in order to feel better about himself. Interestingly, it's in this context that Apollo's aggression first becomes overt — "You foolish girl, / You don't know who it is you run away from," he calls to the woman who's refusing to be impressed.

So here we encounter the logical if strange connection between self-involvement and aggression in men: in order to "love" themselves men must "hate" women. That is, in order to feel accepted they must prove their masculinity to women by denying their own vulnerability and by projecting it onto the women from whom they seek acceptance. While they are desperate for acceptance, they will not receive it if freely given, because from their defensive perspective it's only worthy when conquered.

When Apollo finally captures Daphne, he loses her. Yet Ovid speaks of no mourning. Rather, he tells us that even after Daphne turned into a tree,

> Apollo loved her still. He placed his hand
> Where he had hoped and felt the heart still beating
> Under the bark; and he embraced the branches
> As if they still were limbs, and kissed the wood
> And the wood shrank from his kisses, and the God
> Exclaimed: "Since you can never be my bride,
> My tree at least you shall be!"

So to the extent that unconscious motivation can be inferred from the consequence of the action it inspired, the purpose of the chase was not to love and be loved but rather to get the girl — dead or alive. It's not that the chase is better than the catch, it's just that it's not so bad if the catch is damaged goods — at least you don't need the wood's cooperation to kiss it. Or to do other things with it. Apollo, for one thing, declared the laurel to be the wreath that would adorn his own hair and that of victorious Romans. In other words, though he had lost in love he was still a winner, a physical conqueror, if you will — a fact which will be forever attested to by the celebratory display of the loser's body parts.

So though we are often moved by the romantic sufferings of love's emotional underdog, there's no denying that there's aggression in loving someone who doesn't want to be loved, in chasing another person — physically or psychologically — in order to make them love you. And while unrequited love or even the aggression embedded in it is hardly the exclusive province of men, in their case it more often takes the form of overt, hostile objectification.

The idea that this kind of masculine love is about conquest and possession gains a tragicomic expression at the conclusion of Ovid's tale when "Daphne" the tree accepts her destiny to become Apollo's: "He said no more. The laurel, / Stirring, seemed to consent, to be saying *Yes.*"

Now this male aggression, it's important to remember, is only one side of the coin, often the unconscious side. In our mind we must retain the beginning of the story as well and give male love and generosity its due. In reading Ovid, I suspect, only the radical feminist — and the feminine part of myself — would fail to identify with Apollo's quest and sufferings. In fact, the entire story of Apollo and Daphne was construed by Ovid as a punishment administered by Cupid to Apollo, not to Daphne.[13]

Nonetheless, as vulnerable as a man in love (or in lust) might feel, he's the one who's chasing, possibly frightening the woman away. True, unrequited love does not discriminate, and women who chase men evince their own brand of hostility. Nonetheless, most people will probably still say that when a woman is following a man she's masochistically hurting herself, whereas when a man does the following he's also hurting the woman. Once again, this might be an offshoot of the conflict of masculine insecurity, where the man, for internal defensive reasons, needs to feel he is ostensibly on top.

While my eight-year-old son sometimes expresses his love for his mother by hugging her so hard that he literally knocks the wind out of her, my five-year-old daughter often flirts with me by shrinking or running away from me, laughing and yelling, "Boy germs! Boy germs!" Though they also express their love in other, more versatile ways, with these particular modes of expression it's hard to imagine them trading places.

A Portrait of the Artist as a Don Juan

This patient was not really an artist. A young and promising underwriting manager in a large insurance company, "Keith" actually had few or no artistic inclinations. But in my mind, at least in his relationships with women, he was some sort of artist. Like a sculptor he was able to carve, mold, construct, and reconstruct images of women to fit his own psychic requirements. He was also sensitive, perceptive, and introspective, so you might say he was temperamentally artistic.

In his thoughts, Keith would turn the women he dated into compelling statuesque figures of various types — large and maternal, curvaceous and sexy, or slight and virginal — shaping them out of the white marble he unknowingly projected from his own unfeeling heart onto his perception of femininity. And he would fall in love with these images only to discover again and again that the heartbeat he had "hoped and felt" was not quite there.

Because the patient was very self-involved, he was searching for an ideal woman who would reflect well on his idealized self. But he carried plenty of aggression with him, too, because he had replaced the real person he was dating with a "thing." The first such "thing" he talked about in therapy was a big, abstract thing — a mother. In our first session together the patient explained that he needed therapy because his girlfriend of six years was ready to get married and he wasn't — he didn't know why. In that session he swore up and down that he loved his girlfriend and that she was incredibly sensitive and caring. And as if to prove the point, in the second session he brought her along. But while she seemed to be nice, I failed to see what was so special about her. That should have been my first clue that the patient was a "sculptor."

By the third session Keith had broken up with the girlfriend — she gave him a marriage ultimatum and he said no. But it was only a while later in therapy that he was able to articulate why he wasn't ready at the time. It had nothing to do with practical concerns like age, job security, or money, and nothing to do with romantic concerns like emotional ambivalence or lack of attraction. Rather, it was because the relationship with this woman made the patient feel like a child. The woman was, in fact, a caring, giving person, but the patient couldn't help but turn her into a "thing" — in this case, a mother — which made him feel like a little boy. Well, that was the end of that Rubenesque creation of his.

The irony was that after this breakup, for a period of several years the patient's idealization of this woman only intensified.

While he realized he couldn't have married a woman he conceived as so maternal, he became more and more convinced that he would never meet anybody as special as she was. So from being merely "a very special" mortal, she now became a goddess, or a wistful, marbleized construction of a goddess.

Of course, I shared these observations with my patient, and at least intellectually he agreed. But as he entered his next relationship, he continued sculpting, this time by casting the opposite mold. What's the opposite of a thing called mother? You might raise an eyebrow. Freud thought it was a thing called whore. Freud observed what he called the Madonna/Whore complex, which, the sexual revolution notwithstanding, is still a problem plaguing many men. In this situation the man treats his wife or girlfriend with so much respect that he is reluctant to sexually objectify her. He will engage in certain sexual fantasies or acts only with other, less respected women. This sexual split is an important way in which men manage their aggression, or more accurately, manage to hide their aggression — from others as well as themselves.

So my patient's next "thing" was a whore. Not literally, in this case, but certainly in terms of the dynamic of the relationship. This time his creation (or discovery, depending on the extent to which you think his image of the woman corresponded to the reality) was physically and psychologically quite different: young, curvaceous, and sexually daring. As Keith put it, she was a sexual animal who would do anything — begging, seducing, exposing — to get him into bed. But strangely, though she was anything if not hot, this woman left the patient emotionally cold. So after a year of long, uninhibited, fantastical nights the patient broke up with her.

"I've never been more aroused before," he explained, "but I would never marry someone like her." Interestingly, as he was an honest and straightforward man, the patient never hid this from the woman — which helped him to rationalize the guilt he felt. But the guilt didn't completely go away because his guilt wasn't about leading her on. It was about his hidden aggression — hidden brilliantly in his openness about his lack of commitment. That aggression, of course, consisted in his desire not for sexual exploration *with* a woman but rather for sexual objectification *of* a woman, once again transforming her into a "thing." Ultimately, it was that guilt that motivated the patient to break up the relationship — he eventually concluded that even if it was okay with a woman to be objectified, it was not okay for him to objectify.

After this relationship Keith decided that he had had enough sex for sex's sake. He thought he was now ready for marriage, and he began to look for the right person to fall in love with. Amazingly, he quickly found such a person in the form of a fellow churchgoer whom he excitedly described as "beautiful, creative and *so* open — really special." This woman he turned not into a sculpture, but a poem. Or perhaps I think that because after their second or third date she shared with him a poem she wrote — about him. So maybe it was a mirror he turned her into — like the mirror in the Snow White story — which he could ask, "Mirror, mirror, on the wall, who's the fairest of them all?"

If I'm a bit cynical now about this new creation of my patient, I wasn't at the time. Like the patient himself, I thought he was finally developing a real love relationship. But within a few weeks the patient began to feel doubt and ambivalence. His sexual interest was waning, and his sexual fantasies were suddenly reoccupied by images of his previous girlfriend, the one who was the "sex thing."

So once again Keith broke up a relationship. This time, though, he began to worry, and rightly so, about his ability to love. And this worry was greatly reinforced by a subsequent series of similar relationships, all with youthful, virginal, admiring women. In all these relationships he had fallen quickly in and out of love, though there was a great deal of good intentions and open communications. The reason he fell out of love was that, once again, what he had fallen in love with in the first place was not a person but a thing — in this case, an idea; the idea that these women were "marriage material" and that it was time to get married. Also, once again, his sexual fantasies were invaded by images of his old, "just sex" girlfriend.

After a couple of years of this Keith had to admit that even though he had no such conscious intention, he suddenly found himself with an impressive number of romantic experiences under his belt. "But all I really want is to be with someone I love," he said with great sincerity. So was he on a quest for love or in love with conquest? Was he longing for a woman or hunting laurels for his head? Don Juan's classical defense is that he loves women and therefore can exclude none of them! He too doesn't really keep count of his conquests — his servant does. In Mozart's version of the story, Don Giovanni's servant, Leporello, sings to one of his employer's victims: "Little lady, this is the list of the beauties my master has courted, a list I've made out myself: take a look, read it with me. In Italy six hundred and forty, in Germany two hundred and thirty-one, a hundred in France, ninety-one in Turkey; but in Spain already a thousand and three." And, says Leporello, Don Giovanni courts some of these women only for the pleasure of adding them to the list.

So like Don Juan, my patient was beginning to develop a list, and while this was not his conscious desire, he did let out a mischievous smile when I told him about Don Juan's list. Yet unlike Don Juan, he had never violated, forced, or deceived any women to get them into bed. In fact, his conscious intent was nothing if not noble. The problem was, he was too noble and couldn't integrate his aggression into his relationships. So his aggression came out in the unconscious ritual of conquest consisting of (1) gaining acceptance and (2) dumping. It also appeared as a sexual split in which only a "forbidden" woman or fantasies about that woman could truly arouse him. Paradoxically, it was only when the patient allowed himself to see and accept his hostility to women that he was able to commit to loving them — or one of them. The one he ended up marrying, by the way, was in fact special. Not "really special," but special enough to move out of the mold of the patient's casting and to rebel against her creator.

The Second Date as a Clinical Interview

Dealing with this kind of unintended, unconscious Don Juan is very challenging indeed. For one thing, the women my patient dated, like the patient himself, didn't have a clue that he was amassing a list. When he was dating, this man didn't talk about sex, but about love. He charmed women not with his body but with his mind. In fact, his body was not one of traditional male appeal. Though he was not unattractive, his short, slight build had caused him great grief as a teenager — he felt inferior to other boys and overlooked by girls. Even at the beginning of college no girl wanted to go out with him. But then — clearly out of necessity — he developed his skills in the field of gentle mind seduction.

This syndrome is quite common. Some of the most "successful" Don Juans I've seen are men with a physical inadequacy or with a self-perception of one. They might be, or feel, too thin, short, nerdy, effeminate or boyish, or a variation on such a theme. They are often driven to conquest by a history of being teased as a child by other boys and being rejected as a teenager by girls.[14]

In dating, turning his liability into an asset, this type of man is quick to open up. He is introspective and gentle and he seems comfortable with his vulnerabilities. He might even describe his own sensitivities and hang-ups. Consciously or not so consciously, he has learned that what did him in as a child or teenager can now work to his advantage. That being boyish, poetic, and defenseless goes a long way to disarm and charm women, especially those who are apprehensive about overt male aggression. Now as in the case of the patient I'm talking about, most times this dating style is not a show or a conscious manipulation. Nor is it always a forgone conclusion that this type of man will end up hurting the woman he is courting. What ultimately helped my patient to make a commitment was that I — as well as the woman he was dating at the time — held out not a good but an ugly mirror to him. A mirror which not only showed him the pattern of his aggression but one which also refused to be victimized by it. This is not an easy task for the therapist, let alone the woman involved. First, you need to have your evidence all lined up so that your guy will not think you're crazy — in his mind he's a really nice, sensitive guy. And he *is* those things, which leads to the second difficulty, that in presenting the evidence to him you can easily hurt his feelings. And third, in mirroring his aggression you must not be too angered or wounded by it. If your presentation is too affected by such feelings, you've been conquered and the man will lose interest and move on.

The woman whom Keith ended up with was one who quickly saw his aggression ("got his number"). In actions and even in words she pretty much told him, "I see where this is going, and I'm not the type to get hurt, so don't go there." And she was also someone who was comfortable with ambivalence. When he began to have doubts about her, she began to have doubts about him. When his sexual interest began to wane, she became aware (and told him!) that sometimes during sex she felt like she was with a child. And when he needed space, she felt relieved, not rejected. So by responding in kind, this woman was inviting the patient to bring his aggression into the relationship — she was not going to shrivel because of his expression of ambivalence. Now clearly, as was the case with the patient himself, this was not a conscious manipulation or a game — she simply had her own aggression and ambivalence to express. In short, she was the right person for this patient. But she also showed up at the right time — when the patient's own journey had brought him to the point of confronting his hostility toward women. And — to complete the cliché — together with the patient she worked very hard to create the right place, a place where straightforward aggression was preferable to unconscious sneakiness.

That place, of course, mirrors the therapeutic place in which the therapist works with the patient to be less fearful of his aggression and to integrate it into his relationships. Needless to say, this doesn't always look pretty. The "work" in this kind of relationship is not about trying to be kind and helpful and cooperative, but rather, about allowing oneself to be mean and angry and disagreeable. Put another way, the partners in this relationship need to learn how to fight without destroying their faith in each other and in love. As I often tell patients, everybody thinks that "open communication" is such a great thing, associating it with love, affection, and understanding. But the reason we don't communicate, in most cases, is not because it's such a wonderful thing, but because it can be a rather unpleasant thing. Who in their right mind would want to express negative emotions and thoughts — anger, aggression, or depression, to name a few, to the people they love? But like it or not, we do express them, and the only question is how we choose to do it.

For those who feel that this is too negative or too much work, the only avenue in dealing with the Sensitive Don Juan is that of an early exit. The problem with this strategy is that the whole point of this man's seduction is that you don't know it's happening — you're too busy talking about poetry or spirituality. So you won't know you need to exit. When a man loses his temper on your second date, you pretty much know you should stay away from him — unless, of course, you are so used to abuse that you don't even recognize it, which unfortunately too many women are. But if the man is nice, sweet, and supportive, you have no reason to expect aggression — except for the fact that most men are aggressive. So the first line of defense in dealing with nice guys is to look for and accept some form of male aggression. Of course, what will be acceptable will vary from woman to woman.

Some women who've been subjected to abusive men and who are aware of it are so fearful of any signs of aggressive or "negative" male behavior that they slam the door on any such expression from a man. But unwittingly they end up letting it in through the back door. This has something to do with the dynamics of opposites I discussed in the fourth chapter. If you are drawn to caring, passive, and sensitive men it might be because you are afraid of the opposite. The problem is, these men might be those who are afraid of their own aggression, and often for a good reason. So the unspoken deal of "no aggression" in this kind of relationship is based on fear of existing but denied or repressed aggression.

For a woman in this situation, it's possible that she's afraid not only of the aggression she experienced in a previous relationship, but also of her own retaliatory aggression or anger, which for some reason — perhaps she was a child, perhaps she was otherwise powerless in that relationship — she couldn't act on and therefore had to repress or repudiate. If this is true, the more she continues to choose "nonaggression," and the harder she works to escape the anger that's inside of her, the closer she gets to being hit over the head with it. The psychological principle here is that opposites contain each other, the reason being that the more we try to avoid something in ourselves by becoming its opposite, the more it needs expression. This is why on the 11 o'clock news, the murderer next door is often described by neighbors and friends as "a real nice, quiet guy." Or on a more poetic note, it's also a way of understanding Macbeth's "Fair is foul and foul is fair."

So we must expect and accept some aggression in men. At the same time, there's more that we can do to evaluate the nonaggressive man, especially the one who seems sweet, naive, and open beyond belief. If you know what to look for, you can apply the techniques of the clinical interview — asking questions about the person's past while looking to confirm or not confirm certain hypotheses about his character. Specifically in this case, you want to look for a pattern consisting of (a) a nice, gentle, or intellectual guy plus (b) many short-lived relationships plus (c) no explanation or insight involving himself as to why the relationships didn't work out. The third part of the equation is more difficult to ascertain, as our unintended Don Juan is quite good at employing psychological clichés, half-truths, and pseudo self-analyses such as "I wasn't ready for a relationship," "I was in a different phase of my life," and "I now know what it means to take responsibility." So if after establishing (a) and (b) you're still interested in the guy, consider that the key for genuine insight is an acknowledgment that the person has a problem which he does not completely understand but is committed to working on.

Now single women might raise an objection here: you can't start interviewing people about their past relationships on your first date! Okay, I say, I understand. How about on the second? Actually, I'm not really suggesting an interview. I think that if we trust ourselves and let ourselves see and feel what's there, the information will present itself. Scrutinizing the other person doesn't really work anyway — there are always faults to be found. But neither does second-guessing ourselves and rationalizing away the other person's behavior. On a second date, as elsewhere, we could be killed with kindness. So if we feel uncomfortable — for whatever reason — we have to listen to and explore our feelings rather than explain them away. As one of my supervisors in graduate school once said, "If you feel attacked, it's because you are *being* attacked."[15]

Listening to feelings in such a manner is not some kind of sixth sense, or mystical intuition. Nor is it a passive, evaluative mode. Rather, it's a state of mind that prompts us to act so as to test the validity of our emotional reactions — which ultimately is how we get to know the other person. For example, one female patient dated a man who was reliable, honest, and sensitive. He always called when he said he would, never stopped saying how great a person the patient was, and always said he was ready for a commitment. And yet, the patient felt irritated by him. Nonetheless, her friends told her she was just too picky, so she plugged away and tried to force herself to reciprocate his feelings — after all, he was such a nice guy. Yet the more she tried, the more resistant she grew and the more she felt attacked by his affection and admiration. The truth was, his roses were not without thorns — he was killing her with kindness. A truly sensitive man would have known that his advances were not fully reciprocated and would have backed away. This guy, on the other hand, stuck to his strategic kindness and continued to assault my patient with his guilt-inducing showers of love.

Needless to say, this relationship did not survive. But had the patient listened to her feelings early on, she would have saved herself and this man some time and pain. Which was something another female patient of mine, who was in a similar dating situation, did do. This woman told the man after a couple of dates that she was having a hard time with his being so effusive when he didn't really know anything about her. The man, responding with even greater accommodation and affection, said, "I completely understand why you feel this way — it will never happen again. I would never want to hurt your feelings because you are obviously such a special person." That confirmed her (emotional but not fully articulated) hypothesis that this man's overly positive disposition was not to be trusted — so she got rid of him.

This does not mean that a relationship with this initial dynamic has to go that way. Had the man responded with appropriate anger rather than with more accommodation, and had he turned off some of his unwelcome enthusiasm, my patient, in all likelihood, would have responded positively. This would have given the two of them a chance to build a relationship containing both love and aggression.

Man-to-Man Conflict

In my experience, sooner or later most women find the correct balance of war and love in their struggle to neutralize men's aggression. Men, on the other hand, find it particularly hard not to engage other men's aggression when it clashes with their own. As a starting point we might think of how men drive next to each other on the highway. The male driver seems to define good driving as the technical aptitude for achieving maximum speed and maneuverability. The female driver, by comparison, is more likely to include in her definition the notion of safety and courtesy.

But in addition to this offensive potential that men share, something else kicks in for them when the "opponent" is another man — they often become even more aggressive. On the one hand, you might say that they fight harder in such a case because they feel that a man is a more worthy competitor than a woman. On the other hand, it's often the case that what they fight for, literally or figuratively, is the attention of a woman.

Now if you're Freudian, you'd say that this is a residue of the Oedipal conflict, in which the boy competes with his father in order to win the mother's affection. And if you're a biological anthropologist, you'd say that this is just another way in which we are apes — male chimpanzees are reportedly particularly brutal and competitive in their fights with other males. What they fight for, interestingly enough, is leadership, which as we noted earlier translates into the acquisition of reproductive power. In some human societies this is rather concrete — for example, in the isolated Venezuelan/Brazilian tribe of the Yanomamo, the more male enemies you kill, the more wives you seem to be rewarded with. In others, such as ours, it's more symbolic. So it's quite possible that the tendency of many men in our society to compete harder when women are in the audience is metaphorically about the same thing.

But regardless of its origins, there is little doubt that man-to-man conflict has its own flavor, often one with greater competitiveness and combativeness. One of my patients, a successful and openly aggressive businessman, always demanded that I tell him what to do in different situations — never mind that I repeatedly explained to him that this was not how I saw my role. "Okay, so this is a process and I need to figure it out on my own," he would say impatiently, if not contemptuously, "but what am I paying you for? You have the experience and the expertise — at least I assume you do, but who knows? So you should be able to give me some advice." And he would get frustrated and angry and devalue me when I wouldn't.

But one time — when he got involved with his best friend's sister, who also happened to be a drug addict — I came very close to telling him what to do. His plan, at that time, was to build a life with this woman and to rescue her from her addiction. Accordingly, a few weeks after they started going out, acting on his sense that this was a caring and committed woman, the patient entrusted her with keys to his house. He also shared with her an important business secret. I initially explored with him rather gently and objectively his feelings about her addiction. He acknowledged it was a problem, but said he felt he "could deal with it." But then, remembering how he always demanded concrete information, and feeling that I could meet his aggression with my own, I told him a thing or two about drug abusers. While what I said was true — that is, that active drug users are manipulative and deceitful — there was nothing gentle about my approach. I thought he was in denial and I felt I needed to confront him, so I hit him hard with my "experience and expertise."

He did not react immediately, but later during the day he left a furious message on my voice mail, saying he was devastated by the session and asking that we meet again as soon as possible. When we did, he explained that I had destroyed his hopes and dreams about this woman, and that after the session he had become depressed and paranoid. He began to wonder if she was after him for his money, and when he interrogated her about his doubts and suspicions he almost ruined the relationship.

The patient then went on to lecture me about my therapeutic technique: "As a psychologist, and somebody who knows me by now, you should have known how depressed I can get. And you should have known to go slow with me. You can't just pummel someone like me, you know, I'm sensitive! I know you were trying to be helpful, but what you did was wrong. You have to be much more careful with me." Needless to say, he was right. But in my own male stubbornness, it took me some time to acknowledge it. First I had to show him that he had provoked my aggression, and that this was what he did elsewhere in his relationships. Then I had to explain how his denial invited a confrontation. Then and only then was I ready to apologize. Now while I still think I had a point or two there, what I also had, as the patient was only too happy to point out, was a problem in admitting that I was wrong. It was my own aggressive reaction to my own masculine insecurity. And it had collided with my patient's.

When I finally said, "You're right, I was insensitive and I didn't consider your feelings, I'm sorry," the patient graciously accepted my apology. But the patient was also right that as a psychologist I should have known better. In listening to my masculine insecurity I made the wrong call; sometimes when men are aggressive what they need is acceptance and reassurance, not an invitation to a duel. This factor, by the way, plays a critical role in helping aggressive men to talk rather than to act in psychotherapy. When they are able to talk about such "girl" things as relationships and self-esteem without experiencing themselves as wimps, men can internalize an accepting and curious attitude toward their own femininity. This, in turn, reduces their need to stake out their masculinity with aggression.

Even overtly aggressive men are not just bullies. Tough on the outside, they are often soft on the inside. Admiring strength, yet craving to be weak, they will want acceptance only from someone in a position of power. And so once again, there are no shortcuts for successfully coping with difficult men. Developing one's own sense of power and (loving) aggression is often a long-term proposition.

The Penetrator

Physical penetration is a biological fact (or possibility) in sexual relationships. It is also a fact in other human activities such as boxing or burglary. Of course these penetrations can be aggressive and welcome, aggressive and unwelcome, or aggressive and violent. In the war between the human sexes, rape and other forms of penetrating violence are the exception, not the rule. Nonetheless, men are penetrators — if not physically, psychologically.

When Len, the explosive patient described earlier in this chapter, yelled at the top of his lungs, I felt as though I had been physically violated. But even in the absence of such vehemence, men seem to thrust themselves upon you in a manner intended to leave you feeling almost spatially violated. Some soft-spoken men who are afraid of their own anger often sublimate this aspect of male aggression, transforming it into the more erudite transgression of intellectual penetration. Men who are professionally or otherwise concerned with the internal world of others — psychologists, for example — are especially at risk for this type of aggression.

A Ph.D. candidate in clinical psychology whom I've supervised comes to mind. He was a sweet, soft-spoken, and charming man with an androgynous disposition and didn't seem to have an aggressive bone in his body. He was treating in therapy a female patient whom he found difficult to reach — she frequently argued with his observations and didn't seem to "get it." After trying different angles, he decided he had to confront what he thought was her defense — her lack of openness to the process. Not realizing how frustrated and angry he was, he matter-of-factly — and I'm sure even sweetly — expressed to her what he felt was his objective understanding of her defense: "I think you don't really want to have insight into your own behavior because you don't want to see how nasty you are so that you can continue to be nasty."

The patient was understandably devastated and she left treatment. Whatever merit it had — and I think it had some — this therapist's comment came from his own unconscious anger toward the patient's lack of openness to *him,* which he felt compelled to break down by penetrating her mind. So in discussing this with him, while trying to walk the fine line between critiquing his work and doing to him what he had done to his patient, I said, "I think there was some truth to your observation, but the way you said it to the patient makes me wonder if you were angry with her, in which case what you said to her was also true about yourself — you didn't want to see your own nastiness toward her so that you could act on it." Now to the extent that I did cross that line and penetrate his mind, it must have been because I didn't want to see that I was angry with him for his stupid comment so that I could act on my own nastiness toward him.

If this begins to sound abstract, convoluted, and disorienting, it's because intellectualized anger is that — as its perpetrator you don't really know what you're doing, and as its target you don't really know what hit you or why it did. This sometimes happens when you're talking to someone really intelligent and all of a sudden you feel stupid, naked, and violated. Without knowing it, you've been subjected to intellectual warfare and were just penetrated by stupid-making germs.

So men who are afraid of their aggression may sublimate it —

more or less successfully — into symbolic forms of penetration. When I started dating my wife, I had a series of dreams about breaking into her apartment. One of my patients who felt angry that he wasn't getting enough help from me had a dream in which he had sneaked into my house at night. And another patient, angered by what he felt was his girlfriend's inability to empathize with his feelings, dreamt that he had found a cadaver of a woman's head in his drawer, penetrated it with a fork, and stirred its brain.

This last patient was a film critic, a man described by colleagues as possessing a "penetrating and dissecting intellect." His dream was a powerful if disturbing metaphor for his wish to break into his girlfriend's head and rearrange it so that she could be more receptive to his needs. As in all dreams, details are of utmost significance — in this case the instrument of penetration was a fork — revealing the hunger associated with the patient's anger. This emotional hunger, while by no means unique to men, is often the motive behind their angry outbursts. Unlike women — who are more socialized to express feelings of dependency or neediness — many men express the anger resulting from such feelings first. They don't usually know it, but they penetrate your space in order to get the food — it doesn't occur to them to just ask for it. Not only do they think you're not going to give it to them, but they also resent the fact that they depend on it.

Over the years I've seen this most clearly in men's unconscious reactions to their wives' pregnancy or the birth of their first child. While much of psychoanalysis, obviously Freudian in particular, focuses on the child's Oedipal competition with the same-sex parent, not nearly as much has been said about the parent's competition with the child. It's self-evident, however, that three is a conflict-ridden number, as any affinity between two leaves the third feeling excluded. When the woman gets emotionally involved with her baby — in or out of uterus — the man often feels abandoned. Try as he may, he can't win this one: the baby didn't even have to penetrate the woman — it was nurtured inside of her. And the baby doesn't even have to ask for attention — it is given in totality, without expectations of reciprocity. And of course, the husband also experiences the qualitative loss of attention paid to him — there's only so much to go around.

Granted, many men have a hard time becoming fathers because of the nature of the commitment. And for many this becomes even worse with the birth of a second child, which seems to deal a final blow to the fantasy of life with freedom from responsibility. But for many, the arrival of the first child is accompanied by the loss of emotional goods from their spouse, leaving them feeling emotionally hungry and angry.

But not realizing that they are angry — after all, having a child is a great source of happiness, narcissistic gratification, and pride for most men — they act out on it, often enough by trying to get from another woman, in fantasy or in reality, what they can't get from their wife. Some men do take it out on the baby, especially when he or she cries, as they see it, demandingly. One patient had a dream in which he was biting his one-and-a-half-year-old child, a dream which once again demonstrates the connection between hunger, anger, and penetration.

When my own first child was born I went through a period of irritability and anger. I first attributed much of it to lack of sleep, but I eventually came to see that it also had to do with my feelings of loss of an exclusive relationship with my wife. But it was not until years later, when I saw how long it took my son to come to terms with the arrival of his sister — and recognized myself in him — that I fully realized what I had felt at his arrival. One time, when he was feeling distraught and overcome with feelings of jealousy for his sister, I tried to comfort him by telling him that even I had such feelings when he was born. But to that he only responded with "Great, so you wanted to throw me away when I was a baby!" Another brilliant intervention from the parent as psychologist!

The Survivalist

George Soros, one of the world's most successful financial investors, calls himself an "insecurity" rather than a security analyst. And he attributes much of his success and philosophy of life to what he learned from his father's style of coping with the Nazi occupation of Hungary when Soros was a young teenager. His father — who as a prisoner of war in the First World War survived and escaped Siberian imprisonment as well as the dangers of the Russian revolution — knew, according to Soros, that at times of war the normal rules do not apply. As Soros put it, "Obeying the law became a dangerous addiction; [flouting] it was the way to survive." This knowledge enabled the father to save his family (and others) from extermination by obtaining false identity papers and following other such high-risk/high-reward tactics. "It had a formative effect on my life," writes Soros, "because I learned the art of survival from a grand master." Even more interesting, from a psychological standpoint, is Soros's open admission that "1944 was the happiest year of my life." "This is a strange, almost offensive thing to say," he explains, "because 1944 was the year of the Holocaust, but it is true. I was fourteen years old. I had a father whom I adored, who was in command of the situation, who knew what to do and who helped others. We were in mortal danger, but I was convinced that I was exempt."

The "survivalist" is someone who is not only hungry and angry, but also someone who thrives on insecurity, instability, and risk. I've mentioned Wall Street as an example before. On the surface, many of the barracudas who inhabit it give the impression of strength, confidence, and exuberance. Indeed, when you meet a sample of this species, you want to ask him, "How can you take the stress — the ups and downs of the market, the risk of losing tons of money, the pressure to make tons of money?" But don't bother to ask — the fish is the last to know anything about water. It does know how to swim, though. In other words, for these men (and the women who in recent years jointly ventured with them) living on the edge is second nature. And they love it.

Whether they've been ignored, abused, or uprooted, or simply brought up by warriors, these men learned the skills of survival the hard way, and at an early age. For them satiation is nonexistent and risk-taking is a given. To some extent this is true for all men, because as boys they've received less protection from emotional and physical hardships than girls. But just because they've adapted so well to uncertainty doesn't mean they are not paying a steep price for it. Apparently, if you place a frog in warm water and slowly raise the water's temperature, the frog adapts so well that instead of jumping out, it ends up being boiled to death. This, in a nutshell, is the long-term risk run by the survivalist. In the short term, he is always subjected to the boomerang effect of his interpersonal aggression. I often tell my patients, "If you live by the sword, you die by the sword."

An acquaintance of mine once complained about New York drivers. "You know," he said, "it's bad enough that people cut you off or tailgate you, but have you noticed that it's always the guys who drive better cars, like Mercedes or BMWs?" At the time, I laughed with him about his bemused envy, but when you think about it, he probably had a point. You don't become rich by being nice, and you don't become suddenly nice when you're rich.

Yet ultimately, the survivalist's aggression has little to do with Wall Street, cars, or money. One of my patients could undoubtedly have been a wealthy survivalist, but money was not his thing. Life and death were. I first met "Larry" when as an undergraduate student in New York he was trying to decide whether to come out to his family — he was gay and he had good reason to think they would not handle it well. I saw him for a few months during his senior year and after that he went off to medical school in California. He then completed his residency in Boston and returned to California, where in a few years he became a very successful AIDS specialist, both as a clinician and as a researcher. He came to see me some time later when he was on an extended professional visit to New York.

This patient's background was somewhat unusual. He grew up in Brooklyn, New York, the third child in a highly patriarchal, closely managed, conservative family. His mother, who was an Egyptian Jew, died at home when he was sixteen. The patient was very close to her, and watching her spitting up blood and literally dying in front of him was obviously very traumatic. But while the loss shook him, the manner in which she died only reinforced his decision — which was already cemented at that age — to become a doctor. He had made this decision a couple of years earlier after watching the family dog dying, strangely, in a similar manner.

But even before these experiences, the patient grew up with death on his mind. For one thing, he had a recurring dream as a child in which he was bitten by a rattlesnake and was waiting to die. Amazingly, a version of this dream reappeared in adulthood in the form of hypnogogic images — dream-like pictures which drift into your mind just as you're about to fall asleep. In those images, while he was lying in bed, "a hand or some other presence" would open the door or window to his room and then slowly and quietly advance toward his bed with the intention of killing him.

"There's no mystery as to what I was — and I guess still am — afraid of," Larry said when asked about his fear of death. "When I was in second or third grade, I had to write a sentence using the letter F, and I'll never forget what came out of me — I wrote, 'Feel the fearful form of the father'!" The patient's father — who grew up in a small mountain village in southern Spain where "men were men [if not bullfighters] and women were women," was, in fact, fearsome. While he was just as devoted to his family as to the Catholic Church, he didn't tolerate any deviations from his values on the part of his three sons — or wife. And even though he never physically abused his children, his anger was explosive and frightening.

When Larry was about six years old, he asked his parents if he could have piano lessons. "That's for girls!" the father exploded and forced the child to come out and play ball with him in the street. Another explosion followed a couple of months later when the patient announced he would no longer play any team sports. "Maybe we should put a dress on you!" the father mocked and stormed out. And it was only a couple of years later that the father expressed his concern more directly — and violently. "I'd rather you be dead than gay," he told his young son at a family barbecue when someone was discussing a distant gay relative and his boyfriend.

This exchange, which took place before the existence of AIDS in America, established in the patient's mind a connection between being gay and death — a terrible connection in which the latter was the punishment for the former. At the same time, it was this terrible connection that years later motivated him to direct his academic talents to target AIDS. As a teenager, the patient quite consciously escaped from his father's wrath into the scientific detachment of medical books. But while he consciously thought he was going to become a doctor to save other people from the kinds of deaths he was exposed to — his mother's and his dog's — on a less conscious level he sought to cope with his own mortality, to escape from his own fear of deadly punishment and to save himself.

Driven by this admixture of concerns, Larry ended up specializing in infectious diseases, a field in which treatment can often be the difference between life and death. And when AIDS, "the gay disease," burst onto the medical scene — just as the patient was finishing his medical training — it was natural for him to join the fight. It was also natural for him to bring plenty of survivalist aggression to this fight. For months at a time, he would work pretty much around the clock, experimenting aggressively with patients, leaving no medical stone unturned. But he also fought hospital administrators, government grant bureaucracies, medical reviewers, and pharmaceutical research directors. Sometimes he fought for good reasons, such as trying to expedite bureaucratic processes, but at other times he fought for no reason — he was just a fighter.

Interestingly, his conscious motivation at that time was not explicitly to save lives — after all, back then most AIDS patients didn't respond to any treatment and died relatively soon after diagnosis. Rather, he was motivated primarily by his scientific interest in virology. This, along with his total dedication to his work and his high energy level, made him very popular with patients as well as colleagues. He therefore always had a huge caseload of patients, which by the way did not translate into money because, not wanting to give up on research and teaching, he declined to go into private practice.

Given the fact that he had witnessed his mother dying so agonizingly when he was young, it always amazed me that Larry was never fazed by death. Not only would he see it almost daily on his unit, but he would also have to discuss it constantly with patients and with their surviving families. And it seemed he never failed to confront it head-on with a perfect balance of medical composure and a fighting spirit. Like a true survivalist, he appeared to thrive on crisis.

But even though no one associated with him professionally could ever tell, in his mind the patient paid a steep price for his survival aggression. For one thing, like any workaholic he had little time for the softer things in life — whether emotional relationships or poetry. There were also those hypnogogic images at bedtime — fleeting and perhaps insubstantial but nevertheless disturbing. And then there was the flip side of the fundamental lack of security that drove him in the first place. While he had no trouble dealing with other people's physical fragility, he would become overwhelmed with anxiety in relation to his own symptoms. To an extent this is an occupational hazard undertaken by every physician exposed to serious illnesses. But in Larry's case it was particularly intense, pointing once again to his early fear of death. And this insecurity played itself out in other, nonmedical ways as well. For example, at one point, after receiving and accepting an offer from a prestigious Ivy League university hospital, Larry talked to me about his gut feeling that the new job wouldn't work out, and that he "might end up on the street."

This seems absurd unless you recognize that (1) success is often motivated by this kind of fear, and (2) the more successful you are the more there is at stake. So paradoxically, the survivalist's success doesn't buy him a sense of security — the more he has, the more he has to lose. And while he is never afraid of risk, he is always afraid of fear, so he keeps fighting. Some such individuals, when they reach a level of success, must shoot themselves in the foot in order to remind themselves where they came from and as a way of keeping themselves motivated. Bill Clinton, "the comeback kid," might be a good example of this — as political pundits will tell you, every time he was doing well as a President or even a candidate, he would let loose and get into trouble, only to fight his way back to the top with ever more astonishing vigor and success.

My patient — to return to the price he had paid for success — went through something like this as well, though fortunately only once. Just after he started the new job, he did something so horrifically stupid that it could have cost him nothing less than his life. He had become accustomed to having a drink or two every night at home, as a way of relaxing after work. But one night he had more than two and then went out to meet an old acquaintance for a drink. Then one thing led to another and they ended up spending the night together.

This was unusual for my patient. He was sexually conservative and not very experienced. But even more unusual were his lapses under the influence: he pushed aside his knowledge that the other man was HIV-positive and forgot that he himself was an AIDS specialist who knew a thing or two about HIV contagion and its consequences. He had unprotected, high-risk sex with a known HIV carrier!

In a straightforward way, this incident could and should have been attributed to alcohol abuse. And it was. But Larry was an intellectual, so he didn't stop there. He thought there had to be some sort of death wish operating in his mind for him to do something like this. Painfully, we didn't have to search too hard — it was there in the internalized voice of his father, condemning his sexuality and wishing him dead rather than gay. Obviously, from that point of view, the patient needed to work on rejecting his father's death sentence and accepting his own sexuality rather than the other way around.

But exposing himself to the risk of AIDS was not only a self-destructive act. It was also a regressive retreat into the fear he had grown up with, the fear that had always motivated him to survive — and to thrive. When he first told me about his sexual encounter, this aspect was more evident than any kind of death wish — he was so scared that he didn't want to get tested. But he did, and he was negative. Nonetheless, the fear was enough of a reminder for him: he stopped drinking, got involved in a monogamous relationship, and redoubled his commitment to work. All of which, of course, had us both worried, because it could well have been the planting of seeds for another round of self-destruction in the future.

Fathers and Sons: Kafka's Dilemma

For better *and* for worse, most boys learn about aggression from their fathers — or from father substitutes such as an older brother, a mother, a friend, or men on TV. They learn not only by observing and modeling their fathers' aggressive interpersonal style, but also by identifying with the aggressive manner in which their fathers treat them. As we saw in the case of the Sambia in New Guinea and as further detailed by Terrence Real in *I Don't Want to Talk About It,* in many cultures boys are expected to become men by means of a *via dolorosa* of abuse, often enough heaped upon them — or at least encouraged or permitted — by their fathers.

Terrence Real points out that whereas girls' initiation rites, such as genital mutilation, are usually about the marking of the woman's status as property, boys' initiation rites are intended to demonstrate men's capacity to tolerate pain. The warrior has to be tough. Now while modern society generally spares its boys (and girls) such physical abuses, the basic notions underlying these initiation rites are still with us. And changes in traditional sex roles notwithstanding, Real says — and I agree — images of men as strong, daring, heroic warriors (and the corresponding images of vulnerable women waiting to be saved by them) are still ever-present in our culture.

Apparently, by the time he turns eighteen, the average American boy has watched about twenty-six thousand television murders, almost all of which are committed by men. And as Real puts it, "In contemporary children's lore — the stories we tell them, the books they read, the television and movies they digest — the boy is almost always the pivotal character. Males are bigger, stronger, more daring and more interesting.... Boys and men are the heroes who sacrifice self.... Boys are Peter Pan rescuing Wendy from Captain Hook; they are the nutcracker who transforms into a handsome prince and rescues Clara from the frightening Mouse King...."

Now some feminist critics say that if we could only rid ourselves of such cultural prejudices and stereotypes, we would be able to erase the differences in aggression between boys and girls. There is little doubt that these cultural influences have an enormous impact on children. But there is also little doubt, at least in my mind, that we can never fully eliminate these cultural influences from our environment — cultural censorship is a thing of the past. And furthermore, even if we could expunge them, we couldn't expunge the grain of truth on which they are based. It is not only on TV that most murders are committed by men. And as a group, men *are* bigger, stronger, and, yes, even more daring.

Granted, these largely biological facts do not translate directly into psychological attributes. For example, men are not psychologically stronger than women. But in the internal developmental dialogue through which we discover who we are, boys must listen to and respond to their biology as much as girls must converse with theirs. And this happens with or without cultural influences.

In addition, children learn about aggression not only by passive absorption or modeling, but also by processing and transforming environmental aggression to fit their own psychology — and boys do it differently than girls. As we saw in the fourth chapter, the typical father's masculine harshness toward his son leaves the boy torn between two unpalatable options: passively feeling the hurt delivered by the father or actively minimizing it by becoming like his father and inflicting it on others. Now because boys are biologically more active than girls (this, by the way, is one of the most consistent and significant findings in studies of sex differences), they are more likely to opt for the latter. They are also more likely to go that route because they are threatened by passivity, although — or as we saw in the conflict of masculine insecurity, *because* — they unconsciously desire it.

Here, notably, we are solidly in Freudian territory; try as we may, we can't quite leave him behind. One of Freud's central ideas was that sometimes in response to trauma we try to master the experience by repeating it in reverse, that is, by doing to others what has been done to us, so that we can come out feeling on top. Now while both men and women can get into trouble by this "compulsion to repeat," because of their biological predisposition for activity and their psychological fear of their wish for passivity, repeating a trauma in the active is particularly appealing to men.[16]

This is one of the reasons why men who have been physically or sexually abused in childhood are more likely to become abusive adults than women who've been abused. The latter, at least in terms of their external behavior, are more likely to repeat the abuse without a reversal, in the passive. Or perhaps more accurately, they seem to actively — if unconsciously — seek opportunities for passive victimization.

But the repetition compulsion, like aggression itself, is not all about abuse. For example, many kids want to be teachers when they've grown up — in part, so that they can be in control and do to others what's being done to them. And of course, many adults have the same fantasy in relation to a powerful boss they might identify with. To give another benign example, when I was in graduate school, there was fierce competition among third-year students to become members of the student-faculty admissions committee. Unconsciously, I think, everybody wanted to interview prospective candidates in order to put them through (possibly a better version of) what they had gone through a couple of years earlier, when anxiously interviewing in a rather competitive admissions environment.

Now even though as a group boys tend to be more active than girls, ultimately this is a statistic — of the kind which allows us to state that you can drown in a pool whose average depth is twenty inches. In other words, just as some girls are more active than some boys, not all boys choose to repeat traumas in the active. It should also be clear that repeating in the active is not preferable to repeating in the passive. As with anything else, there are advantages and disadvantages to both. And both philosophically and practically, the two styles are actually the flip side of the same coin. Abusing others is corrupting to the self and usually brings about a retaliation, as much as allowing others to abuse you is corrupting to them and usually gets them into trouble. Or to take it to its logical extreme, the man who kills others ends up killing or otherwise destroying himself, and the man who kills himself ends up "killing" or otherwise destroying the lives of others — his family, friends, or those who've "done him wrong."

So when a boy "feels the fearful form of the father," he's in trouble, one way or another. For me, one of the most compelling renderings of this kind of trouble is to be found in the writings of Franz Kafka. In his autobiographical accounts, Kafka was not only conscious of his reluctance to repeat his father's legacy in the active, but was also able to explain why. In "Letter to His Father," an actual fifty-page letter he wrote to his father, Kafka undertook the task of confronting him with an analysis of their relationship.

> Dearest Father,
>
> You asked me recently why I maintain that I am afraid of you. As usual, I was unable to think of any answer to your question, partly for the very reason that I am afraid of you, and partly because an explanation of the grounds for this fear would mean going into far more details than I could even approximately keep in mind while talking.

With these simple words, Kafka invites his father to a dialogue and shares with him at once both the poignancy of his feelings and his analytic — one might say psychoanalytic — skills. In the next fifty pages, Kafka goes on to recall the experience of growing up with his father, who was — to use some of Kafka's own descriptors — a large, loud, self-satisfied, grand, hot-tempered, red-faced man. In addition to this personality, Kafka says, his father subscribed to "child-rearing methods" consisting of threats, irony, spiteful laughter, shouting, and humiliation. This, Kafka writes, could have produced different results with a child who was equally strong and oblivious. But in his case, his sensitivity and timidity inevitably led him to try to avoid anything connected to his father, including things he may have liked or desired, such as working in his father's business or even getting married.

It's in Kafka's explanation as to why he wasn't able to get married — he had canceled two or three engagements — that one sees most clearly his reluctance to repeat in the active or to identify with his father.

> Marriage certainly is the pledge of the most acute form of self-liberation and independence. I would have a family, in my opinion, the highest one can achieve, and so too the highest you have achieved; I would be your equal; all old and every new shame and tyranny would be mere history. It would be like a fairy tale, but precisely there lies the questionable element. It is too much; so much cannot be achieved. It is as if a person were a prisoner, and he had not only the intention to escape, which would perhaps be attainable, but also, and indeed simultaneously, the intention to rebuild the prison as a pleasure dome for himself. But if he escapes, he cannot rebuild, and if he rebuilds he cannot escape. If I, in the particular unhappy relationship in which I stand to you, want to become independent, I must do something that will have, if possible, no connection with you at all; though marrying is the greatest thing of all and provides the most honorable independence, it also stands at the same time in the closest relation to you.

There's much more to Kafka's letter. But in our context it suffices to say that even though his letter was more balanced than you might conclude from the above — Kafka did take some responsibility for his own undoing — in the end, he was too timid and too afraid of his father to actually send him the letter. He showed it to his mother but never to his father, and it was only published after his death.

Amazingly, Kafka's dilemma haunted not only his life, but also his entire literary creation. In his letter, Kafka himself says that in his writing he finally seemed to have gained some distance from his father, a feeling that was only reinforced by the father's aversion to his writing. But having said that, Kafka sadly adds, "Of course, this was a delusion; I was not, or to put it most optimistically, was not yet, free. My writing was all about you; all I did there, after all, was to bemoan what I could not bemoan upon your breast."

It's not for us to judge whether in his later writings Kafka the person has been able to separate from his father and escape his tyranny. As a writer, in his philosophical novels he certainly transcended the personal. On the other hand, when you consider the subject matter of these novels — for example, the tyranny of metaphysical powers in *The Trial* or *The Castle* — you can't help but trace it back to the Kafkaesque child-rearing methods of Kafka the father. Many literary critics, especially those of the deconstructionist school, as well as some artists and writers, do not like this kind of analysis. Understandably, they want to think that art can stand on its own, free of the artists' demons. But it's like our relationship to the apes — it's precisely when we insist on escaping our past that we end up being imprisoned by it.

In one of Kafka's stories, *The Judgment*, which some say gave birth to Kafka the writer — Kafka himself wrote that the story came out of him like a birth — an aging father objects to his son's intentions to get married and eventually "sentences" him to death by drowning. The faithful son bolts out of their apartment, runs over to the river, and executes his own sentence. A strange, unlikely, almost biblical story — like much of Kafka's work — and yet one with the raw logical precision of the unconscious.

If you can't meet your father's aggression with your own — and most abused or frightened children cannot — and if your sensitivity is inconsistent with the defense of becoming like him and aggressing upon others, what other psychic path can you take? Sadly, and almost tragically, *The Judgment* had a strong parallel in Kafka's life. Before his death he ordered a friend to destroy all his unpublished work. Luckily for us, if not for Kafka's father, his friend did not carry out his wish, giving the world some of its greatest literary masterpieces.

Unlike *The Judgment,* Kafka's letter to his father has little by way of the bizarre in it. As Kafka acknowledges to his father, there was never any physical abuse in their relationship, and much of the damage was merely collateral to the father's "strong" personality. Ultimately, for Kafka, the letter was very much in the genre of everything-you-ever-wanted-to-tell-your-father-but-were-afraid-to-say. And it still reads this way today, so much so that it's hard not to relate to it even if you didn't have an emotionally abusive father. For all these reasons Kafka's dilemma resonates with the inner conflict of many contemporary men who, in their loyalty to a destructive father, end up destroying themselves.

Self-Destructiveness

...I'm such a loser

The Idiot

A winter or two ago, on a family skiing trip, my wife and I took a couple of hours to ski without our children. Though we're both solidly intermediate skiers, on that occasion we were persuaded by a friend — an advanced skier and a fearless man — to join him in skiing down one of the more difficult trails on the mountain. It was tough. This was one of the highest elevations in the Rockies, and the trail had multiple areas of moguls and other "challenging" terrain. We had never tried anything like this before. It was physically difficult, emotionally exhausting, and generally not enjoyable. And it took us an hour and a half to ski down to the lodge, which was pretty bad because as soon as we saw what we were in for, getting down was all we cared about. When we finally made it and were taking off our skies, my wife — who is actually a better skier than I am — moaned, "That was such a waste of time." "Really?" I said in disagreement, "I'm glad we did it." And tongue in cheek I added, "It makes me feel like a real man." To which my wife responded, "Really, it makes me feel like an idiot." "That's the same thing!" I said, and we both laughed.

Now of course, had such a punch line come out of my wife's mouth, my reaction would have been unpredictable — possibly I would have erupted in anger and accused her of being a minimizing, castrating, phallic woman who harbors hostility toward men.

Which is not to say that I would have been wrong — I do believe that women who think that men are idiots, dicks, or morons do harbor such hostility. Nonetheless, as a man, it was apparently okay for me to say it. Well, not exactly. It was okay for me to say it because I didn't really believe it. Men's legendary self-destructiveness, as evidenced most notably by their devotion to drinking, drugging, reckless driving, and other forms of self-obliteration, is not simply a question of idiocy.

First of all, depending on its often unpredictable consequences, a questionable "masculine" action can be idiotic or heroic. If you resist a mugger and get shot you're an idiot, but if you resist and get him arrested, you're not only a hero but also an intuitive genius who knew that this mugger was not for real. Second, there are better, simple explanations for men's self-destructiveness other than idiocy. For example, perhaps men are more self-destructive than women because their stronger and more active physicality can cause more damage — to others as well as to themselves. This hypothesis, for example, could possibly explain why even though more women attempt suicide, more men actually kill themselves. But while simple is good, simple is not always good enough. And what looks like a split-second, spur-of-the-moment, hyperactive act of bad judgment is often the culmination of a slow-moving, underlying developmental current.

One patient, a young scientist who was as far from idiocy as you can get, entered my office one day smiling. "Another week like this and you may never see me again," he said. "What do you mean?" I smiled back. "Last week after the session I was mugged, and today, just now an older woman tried to pick me up!" I laughed, of course, and said, "I'm not sure which is worse." But I wasn't completely joking. This patient was an only child, and his father — to whom he was very attached — had left and moved to another state when he was quite young. From that time on the patient would see his father several times a year and would always have fun with him. But for the most part he was "stuck" with his mother, who happened to be a depressed psychologist, and who — with a volume of good intentions — had always made penetrating, intrusive comments about her child's innermost thoughts and feelings. So for this patient, being picked up by an older woman was in a sense more of an assault on his manhood than being mugged. Except that the mugging was, in fact, quite serious.

After the previous week's session the patient had left my office thinking about his anger toward his mother and how he had always avoided expressing it to her. The more he thought about it the angrier and more distracted he got. He was so deep in angry thoughts, he didn't notice the suspicious man crossing the street in his direction until this man, a gun in his hand, confronted him and demanded his money. Responding with ready-made rage, the patient whacked him on the head with his briefcase, which was heavily stuffed with scientific instruments. The mugger responded by hitting the patient on his head with the gun, and the two of them continued to struggle for a long couple of minutes, until neighbors began to gather, at which point the mugger took off and disappeared around the corner. The patient held on to his briefcase and his money — as well as to his aggressive defense of his masculine insecurity — all the way to the emergency room. He spent the night there, getting treatment for a superficial head injury. His deeper head injury was perhaps mental (I can say this only because in a way I admire the strength it revealed and also because it's so culturally prevalent): not wanting to upset his girlfriend and his mother, or perhaps because he didn't want to be vulnerable in the company of a woman, the patient didn't call them and ended up spending the night in the emergency room alone.

When he told me how he had whacked the attacker in the midst of angry thoughts about his mother, I was incredulous and joked that it reminded me of a Woody Allen movie. The patient smiled, but then he started telling me what it had reminded him of. When he was a young teenager, his father — who was a high-ranking State Department official — took him on a trip to Greece, to spend time at the beach and to visit the birthplace of democracy. One afternoon, while they were walking in a small island village together, the father was pickpocketed by a group of young men encircling them in the street. As soon as he realized what had happened, the father grabbed his son's arm and began to chase this gang through the narrow streets of the village — a pretty idiotic thing to do, especially with your twelve-year-old son! But the patient loved it and admired his father's courage and strength.

Needless to say, they didn't catch the pickpocketers. But many years later the patient made up for it by whacking his own mugger. More to the point, the patient's violent reaction to the mugger sprang not only out of his mounting anger at his mother, but also out of a triumphant identification with his longed-for and idealized father. In short, it was a moment in which he emerged as, or snapped into being, a man. At the same time, with a bit of bad luck it obviously could have been a moment of self-destructiveness, illustrating how the latter is sometimes a logical extension of aggression, which is a defense against masculine insecurity, about which men know very little because of their emotional absence and shame.

Another moment of self-destructiveness — of an all-too-common type in these days of stock market mania — was revealed to me with great shame and humiliation by a patient who came to see me for depression. This hard-working young man was in a significant depression because he had just lost $50,000 — practically his entire savings — in the stock market. Together with his wife, the patient had been saving this money for a down payment on a house. He initially invested his savings in conservative bonds, but then, as the stock market time and again climbed into record territory, he bought some mutual funds. These did well, but not as well as some individual stocks. So as the market continued to rise, he traded his funds for individual stocks of several large companies. These did really well, but not as well as some small Internet stocks. The patient ended up buying several hot Internet stocks "on margin," borrowing against his stocks to double the value of his investment. It was at that point, of course, that the market tumbled and the patient was left with a few thousand dollars in his account.

It so happened that the market fully recovered and even went into new record territory a short month or two later. But for my patient, it wasn't short enough — when he told his wife about the status of their investments, she was very upset, and pressured him to get out of the stock market altogether. He yielded and sold his stocks a week before the market began to bounce back. It was while he was watching the market moving up that the patient had sunk into depression, indicating that it wasn't so much the loss of money that bothered him but rather the fact that he had listened to his wife. He was angry with her for "making" him sell, but at the same time knew that it was his responsibility, and that he shouldn't have invested that money in the stock market in the first place. So not being able to blame her, he turned his anger inward, punishing himself with depression.

Putting aside his depression, what this patient really needed, you might think, was a financial adviser, not a therapist. Perhaps so. Except that when you scratch the surface you find that even such a financial loss — a version of which happens regularly to thousands of small and big investors — reflects not merely financial ignorance or naive enthusiasm but also a deeper, self-destructive process. One way to look at that process is that by listening to his wife and selling his stocks, the patient made the mistake of succumbing to feminine influence — if he had only stayed the course he would have been fine. But this was just the end of the story, whereas its beginning suggested the opposite explanation, that by constantly upping the ante on his investments, the patient made the mistake of allowing his idiotic male ego to drive his investment strategy. So which was it, offensive masculinity or defensive femininity? I think both.

The patient was born in Hong Kong and spent most of his childhood there. His father, an American, was a retired navy officer and a struggling, unsuccessful entrepreneur. He treated his son in harsh, unfeeling, authoritarian style. His mother, a Korean-Chinese woman, was independent, driven, and hard-working. She treated her son — her firstborn — by spoiling, overprotecting, and controlling him. When the patient was twelve, the parents divorced. The father remained in Hong Kong, where he continued to struggle and lose money in various businesses, but the mother immigrated with her children to the United States. There, in the New World, having to help his mother support the family, the patient was thrown into a premature manhood. Except that he was still under his mother's thumb — his afternoon and weekend job, practically to the day he left for college, was to help his mother run her fruit and vegetable store. Now while he resented having to do this, he was a good boy. So he respected his mother and never rebelled against her.

But he did rebel against his wife, or at least that's how I interpreted his impulsive, risky investment style: it sought to assert an independent, liberated masculinity. Of course, it didn't help that as a child he had no model of a more conservative, disciplined masculinity in the form of an emotionally inviting father. And naturally, his irresponsible masculinity was nothing if not an invitation for a controlling femininity to step in and nag him out of the stock market.

To generalize, many self-destructive men are hypermasculine. Paradoxically but logically, these men must reject their own femininity because there's always been too much of it around them, and now there's too much of it inside them. In many cases, then, this type of self-destructiveness is an attempt to say good-bye to an omnipresent, controlling mother and hello to an absent, irresponsible father. In this case, as in the previous one I discussed, there was a marital separation between the parents along with a geographical move which left the boy living with a physically close mother and physically distant father. However, the self-destructive process I'm exploring here is not about divorce and relocation. Nor does it require a physical stress or trauma. More than anything else, it's a question of the parents' personalities. And more specifically, it's a question of how the parents integrate their own masculine and feminine identifications. Let me illustrate.

John was an uncharacteristically sensitive and pleasant corporate lawyer. He grew up in an intact family and his parents, so he said, were everybody's favorites. They were hip, informal, friendly, and young. And they were always there for John and his older sister, with genuine concern as well as financial assistance. Nonetheless, from the beginning of college to the day he came to see me — a week after he turned thirty-eight — John suffered from a severe drinking and cocaine problem. I will not discuss the issue of substance abuse here, other than to say the obvious, which is that it's one of men's most common forms of self-destructiveness. And I won't discuss its treatment either, other than to say that with the help of AA, which he joined a couple of months after he started seeing me, John has been able to remain sober for the long haul.

What was clinically unique in his case was the fact that along with his substance abuse, John suffered from a "disorder" usually diagnosed in children — separation anxiety. As a young child, he had difficulties separating from his mother when going to nursery school, and in grade school he developed a full-blown "school phobia," complete with repeated running away from school in order to be at home with his mother. As a teenager, he was afraid to go to school because of a group of bullies who picked on him, and in college he was reluctant to do anything without his girlfriend. He went to college in San Francisco, away from his family in New York, and it was there that he started drinking, in his own words in order to alleviate his anxiety about being alone.

But while he was afraid of being alone, he also resented his own dependency. So in his sophomore year of college, he bought himself an old used car and started taking weekend trips on his own. He would get in his car with a case of beer and drive north to the mountains, drinking all the way, successfully turning dread into excitement. There, in the Sierra Nevada, he got into rock climbing, which at the time was less safe than it is today. He never drank while climbing, but when he would safely reach the peak or the end of a route and set up a tent for the night, all hell would break loose for him. Sitting alone on top of a giant Yosemite rock, he would freak out with fear and anxiety. Desperately craving to be back home with his girlfriend, he would then drink himself into oblivion.

On some of these trips, John stopped over in a roadside bar where he would continue to drink, sometimes hooking up with a girl and feeling tempted to have sex with her in the back room. But as soon as the thought would cross his mind, he would be struck by torturous feelings of guilt, which of course could only be alleviated with more alcohol. At some point, John came to the realization that he should break up with his girlfriend, but he couldn't let go, because of his separation anxiety. During that time, however, his roommate's sister from New York was visiting. The patient fell in love with her and they began to have a relationship. While she was there, he finally broke up with his girlfriend, and after the roommate's sister left, he continued to have a long-distance, telephone relationship with her.

By this time a senior in college, John was also in love with the outdoor life of northern California. He would never go back to the concrete, dirt, cabs, and elevators of New York, he decided. But his New York girlfriend envisioned for herself a career on Wall Street and told him that she would never move away. So fearing losing her, he moved back to New York and soon thereafter they got married. Over the years of their marriage, the patient made various attempts to control his drinking. And a couple of times he was able to stop drinking for months at a stretch. But his separation anxiety was always there. For years, he would wake up at 4:00 A.M. every Monday, with intense dread about beginning the work week. And while he always longed to be back in northern California, whenever he would go — his wife, by now a busy Wall Street analyst, never objected to his semi-annual long-weekend getaways — he would be overtaken with intense night-time anxiety. In more recent years, with the advent of the cell phone, he would struggle to not call his wife from the roadside, from his tent, or from the top of some rock. And while his more extreme self-destructive behaviors, such as drinking while driving, abated, he seemed to substitute other risky business. For example, although he was an expert skier, practically every time he went skiing he would end up getting hurt. And at work, too, every time he was about to close a deal he would end up saying something impulsive or stupid to his client, almost jeopardizing the deal at the last minute.

By the time he came to see me, John already knew that he was using alcohol to medicate his anxiety. And he called it separation anxiety even before I did. "Look," he said, "it's very clear to me. It all started at nursery school when I was afraid to let go of my mother. Ever since then it's been a struggle for me to be out there in the world." What wasn't clear to him was *why* he'd been so anxious about separation. But in therapy he gradually realized that when alone he wasn't so much fearful for himself as for the girlfriend, wife, or mother he left behind. He began to remember that when he would run away from school, he'd go home not to be taken care of by his mother, but rather to check on her. The same was true for the subsequent women in his life — when away he was afraid that something terrible would happen to *them*, not to him.

He then realized that it had all started in nursery school not because *he* had to separate from his mom, but because *she* had to separate from him. And his mother, it turned out, had just moved with her husband and two young children to New York, reluctantly separating for the first time from her own family and from the small upstate village she grew up in. It's generally true that many separation-anxious children are afraid to leave their mother's side because they receive an unconscious message from her that the world is a dangerous place. Yet an overprotective mother or one who's struggling with her own loss can hardly explain the severity of this patient's anxiety many years later. Indeed, when I first met the patient I was so impressed with his anxiety that I felt it was biologically driven and that treating it would probably require medication in addition to therapy. But amazingly, after three years of therapy (and abstinence) John was almost completely free of anxiety.

In my mind, one of the major reasons for this recovery was that John finally got to know — and to some extent to liberate himself from — the personalities of his parents. It wasn't so much that his mother suffered from separation anxiety herself and projected it onto her child that was the problem. It was that she projected her entire self onto him. In therapy, it slowly emerged that John's mother was blessed with an overabundance of feelings, impulses, and images. But she had little in the way of thoughts, concepts, or ideas. She experienced everything in life, good or bad, with great intensity, and never with cool detachment. In short, she was all color and texture and no form or structure. She therefore went through life in a state of perpetual merger with the universe, not excluding, of course, the people who inhabited her interpersonal space.

So as he was developing, John, the child, was always aware of his mother's feelings more than his own. Or more accurately, day in and day out, his feelings were edged out by hers. If she was cold, he had to dress warmly. If she was afraid of the dark, he had to sleep with the light on. If she feared that a mole was cancerous, he was afraid that she was dying. If she missed her mother, he missed his mother. If she wanted to cuddle in bed, he wanted to cuddle in bed. And if she complained that his father was a careless klutz, he felt that his father was a careless klutz.

So based on his mother's personality — which could be stereotyped as a caricature of traditional femininity — it should now be easier to see why John had such a severe case of separation anxiety. It was triggered not by a traumatic separation but rather by a traumatizing personality. It should also be easy to see that had John, the child, been able to develop his own feelings, they would consist not of fear of the world but rather of anger toward his mother. Perhaps predictably, John, the man, did develop such feelings in therapy. As he was beginning to feel less anxious, he was experiencing a lot of anger — toward his mother, his wife, or anyone else who he felt was trying to control his life. Unfortunately, though also predictably, his anger was just as intense as his anxiety, and he was now prone to attacks of rage, which were perhaps less self-destructive but were certainly destructive toward others in his life.

Now lest I be accused of mother-bashing, let me say that there's no problem mother without a problem father. John's father, while not physically absent or aggressive, did embody, with superficial clarity, many of the negative male attributes discussed in this book. He never spoke about his own or his son's feelings, and in fact, the only emotional thing he'd ever told his son was to control his emotions. When he did talk, he would tell war stories about his business, crack silly sexual jokes, make fun of John's mother, and reminisce about his youthful alcoholic adventures. In short, while socially smooth he was so emotionally underdeveloped that he offered John no shelter from his mother.

So with a bit more therapy, John also discovered his father's personality as well as how disappointed in him he felt — for not being a real, three-dimensional person. To take a snapshot of John's separation anxiety, then, it consisted of trying to become less of a woman than his mother and more of a man than his father. If in climbing rocks he was trying to get away from mother, anxiety had to follow because there was no father to protect him at the top.

In terms of John's therapy, it was no accident that his anxiety was "cured" by his anger, although both he and I felt that his therapy would not be complete — to the extent that there is such a thing — until it also cured his anger. What I'm alluding to here is another important connection between aggression and self-destructiveness. If so far in this chapter we visited men who were "idiotically" extending their aggressive hypermasculinity into self-destructiveness, we'll now turn to men who come to self-destructiveness from the opposite direction, that of not having enough aggression — I've touched on this type previously when discussing Kafka. But first, an important note about being angry with one's parents.

One of the most unflattering stereotypes of psychotherapy is that it's a process which teaches you to blame everything that's wrong in your life on your parents. Unfortunately, many people — patients and some therapists included — have a hard time distinguishing between anger and blame. In theory, the distinction is easy enough — anger is an emotion, whereas blame is a cognitive attribution of responsibility, really two different things.

But in actuality we often confuse the two. For example, if John is finally angry with his parents for how they related to him as a child, and especially if he expresses his anger to them, doesn't that mean that he's blaming them for his separation anxiety?

Well, the short answer is no, the reason being that no matter what cards we are dealt — and they are never all bad — how we play them is always our choice. So even as a child, let alone as an adult, John made choices about how to deal with his parents' limitations. Good enough therapy, in my mind, focuses on these choices and on how they can be changed, rather than on how we were victimized by other people's choices, about which there's nothing we can do. Of course, this is not about blaming the patient either. It's about taking responsibility instead of blaming your parent or yourself.

The problem with anger is that it's a very painful emotion, especially when directed toward someone you love and depend on. So many patients use the confusion between anger and blame to avoid feeling angry with their parents — "I'm not going to blame them for my problems now, thirty years later," they rightly say, while wrongly using the right to deny their anger. Perhaps they confuse anger with denial because they are so angry that they actually would like to blame. Of course there are those who do blame their parents, and in cases of severe abuse it's hard to argue with that attribution of responsibility — as long as they do not use that truth to lie to themselves about their own choices.

Winning by Losing: Sick, Angry, and Unattractive

A few years ago I had a dream about my own self-destructiveness. Ironically, but as we shall see not coincidentally, this was a period in my life when I was beginning to be professionally successful. Also significantly, the dream was triggered — I think — by a conversation I had that day with an older, rather successful friend who was struggling with a career setback. In the dream, I was driving with my family when I suddenly lost control of the steering wheel. I crashed and totaled the car. My wife, children, and I were okay, but there was blood, twisted metal, and ripped clothes everywhere. At this point there was a fadeout, and in the next scene I was having wild sex with my wife.

In thinking about the dream it immediately came to me that in my family, I was the only man who didn't total my father's car. Both of my older brothers did when borrowing it in their late teens or early twenties, and so did my father. Now no one in my family took these accidents lightly, and my brothers didn't receive prizes for wrecking the cars. At the same time, these events didn't prevent my father from proclaiming some years later that one of these car-crashing brothers was the best driver in the family. The truth is that for many years I felt less comfortable with my aggression — a fact which was reflected not merely in my driving style — than did my brothers. It's not that I felt less competitive or hostile than they did, but rather, that I was more conflicted about these feelings. As a result, my self-destructiveness consisted not in the idiocy of wrecking the car, but rather in the lunacy of wrecking the self.

For example, in my junior year of high school I worked hard to be elected president of the student body. But as soon as I got the job, I chose an agenda that would get the student council into a collision course with the school principal. Under my "leadership," the student council demanded that the school cancel its mandatory uniform policy and establish a smoking room for students. When the school refused both demands, we resigned in protest, merely two months after we were elected, demolishing the whole notion of a student council in the school for a couple of years. Clearly, I had some interest in power and authority, but when I got some, rather than use it to my own and others' benefit, I threw it away, thinking, "That will show them." Well, it only showed myself, as I missed an opportunity to learn about leadership.

A perhaps more subtle, if more consequential, example was my choice of major in college. While my brothers galloped away to aggressive law careers, I went to study filmmaking. Obviously, there's nothing wrong with that, unless, of course, you have no cinematic talent, which was pretty much my case. Somewhere, somehow, I knew that filmmaking was not for me, but I didn't listen to myself or to my parents. It was only later, when confronted on my own with the full implications of my choice — including the realization that I was a highly practical person who could never live with the lack of structure and stability inherent in the entertainment business — that I changed course.

Fortunately, it worked out well for me, so I can't say I regret the early detour. When I recently told a friend that I could see myself being in other fields, he responded in disbelief, saying that I seemed to be so much into my work that he couldn't see me doing anything else. He may have had a point there, which brings me back to the dream. Apparently feeling I'd found my own success, I wanted to switch from my own lunacy to the idiocy of the other men in my family. You might say, then, that the dream was about a rite of passage. To become a man — remember, I got the woman in the second part of the dream — you must first wreck the car. Or more colloquially, you gotta have balls if you want to have sex. Interestingly, there is also a cultural context to this dream which goes beyond my own family, as Israelis, by and large, are truly mad drivers — more people get killed in Israel by car accidents than by terrorism and war put together. But then again, hypermasculine self-destructiveness is very much part of the Israeli psyche as a whole.

Over the years, I've had my own personal difficulties and pain. But my family and I were spared the more serious abuse and self-destruction which plague so many families from all walks of life. Nonetheless, the dynamics of my own male self-destructiveness described above are fundamentally no different than those of the cases described below. As I said, in my youth I really wasn't comfortable with my aggression, and I still have some work to do in that area, although when I recently expressed this to a (female) friend, she laughed and said, "I shudder to think what you'd be like when you're more comfortable with your aggression!"

Why are some people self-destructively uncomfortable with their aggression? The ultimate answer comes from a patient who for years struggled heroically to recover from multiple childhood traumas, not the worst of which was his father's suicide. Throughout his childhood, the patient's father had been physically abusive to both the patient and his mother, and so on several occasions the mother took the patient and his younger brother and left the house. But each time, when the father sent emissaries begging her on his behalf to return, she did. One night, when the patient was about twelve, after a day of particularly explosive abuse, the mother took her children and left, "this time for good." On their way out, the patient — who had witnessed his father savagely beating his mother earlier in the day — called out to his father, "I hate you." A couple of days later, even though there were no emissaries this time, the mother and children returned home. When no one answered the doorbell, the mother sent the patient to climb through the window — they lived on the ground floor — and let them in. When the boy squeezed his narrow body through the half-open window, he saw what he's never been able to forget since, not even for one day or night — the body of his big, powerful father hanging from the ceiling with a trickle of red blood still coming down from the side of his mouth.

Though the patient was old enough to know otherwise, in his mind he had killed his father. He had finally gotten up the nerve to express his anger to his father, and look what happened. The painful truth was, he did not hate his father — he loved him. And he continued to love him as an adult, as was evident by the nostalgic dreams in which his father would visit him on many a night. (Yes, there were also the other, frighteningly violent father dreams.) The fact is, in the language of children, "I hate you," "You're not my friend anymore," and "I wish you were dead," are rather common expressions of anger. But when the child's anger is of a certain intensity and depth, and when its expression is followed by suicide, is it any wonder that the child feels that the father killed himself because he, the child, made him feel so bad?

And is it any wonder that the child is forever afraid of his anger? And that he'd therefore prefer to blame himself into a depression rather than have an angry disposition? This patient certainly blamed himself. Just as the classical theory of depression would predict, he had turned his anger inward and punished himself with depression for his mental murder of his father. But while there's more to male self-destructiveness than depression — which generally tends to afflict more women than men — there is a conceptual kinship between the two: self-destructiveness is a close cousin of depression. In both, the person is struggling with unacceptable negative feelings toward an important person in his life and ends up taking it out on himself. The big difference, though, is that in self-destructiveness, these negative feelings consist more of rage than anger, and so the person — who may have been beaten down by some form of ongoing abuse as a child — is too "weak" to contain them within his internal mood. Rather, he feels compelled to act on them in the external, physical world.

For example, when this patient felt angry with me, he would not only get depressed, but he'd also not show up for the session — he would genuinely forget about the appointment so that he wouldn't have to tell me he hated me. Or when his wife criticized him for spending too much money on CDs he'd tell her she was right, but the next day he'd buy more, this time without telling her. More significantly, when he was frustrated for not being promoted fast enough at work, he developed a habit of taking "sick days" without calling in. And when his boss called him on it, he acknowledged his wrongdoing but continued to do it. And then, with every disciplinary action that followed, he escalated his absences, raising the ante as his job status continued to deteriorate. Until he was fired.

Another patient with similar dynamics came from a less abusive home. Hence, his self-destructiveness was more along the depressive end of the continuum. This patient was from a politically unstable South American country, and just before he came to the U.S. to go to business school, his father was arrested for an "antigovernment" activity. At his family's insistence — and apparently for his own protection — the patient did not postpone his studies and came to New York.

Shortly after starting graduate school, the patient learned that the government back home had offered to release his father if he'd agree to cease all political activities. The father refused and was subsequently sentenced to two years in jail. The patient was furious — with his country, to be sure, but also with his father. While on the one hand he admired his father for his principles and moral integrity, he also felt that he was out of touch with the real world and that he took no responsibility for the financial well-being of the family.

For months the patient debated what to do about his anger but always came down on the side of wanting to protect his father from any emotional harm while he was in prison. But, finally, he decided to write his father a letter, telling him that if he didn't stop his political activity and start working for his family (the patient had two young siblings) when he was out of jail, he should no longer consider himself his father. The patient ended up writing and not sending the letter, but in contemplating it, he felt so disappointed and angry that he even had the thought that everyone in his family would be better off if his father just died in prison.

A week later the patient got a call that his father had died, of a heart attack, in jail, seven months before his term was up. So here, too, a death wish was materialized. And while the adult rational mind knows better, the unconscious conclusion that anger kills mandates that we turn it around into a punishing depression. In this case it was particularly difficult for the patient to remain angry with his father — after all, he was a man of principle who was persecuted and essentially killed by an oppressive authority whom the patient himself feared and hated. And it was relatively easy for the patient to hate — and therefore sabotage himself — if for no other reason than his feelings that his father's ultimate sacrifice for the benefit of others rendered his own pursuit of self-interest meaningless.

Now this patient initially resisted the notion that his depression was actually a lingering anger with his father — by the time he came to see me he had managed to idealize his father and to feel sorrow rather than anger. But as we reconstructed this history, he rather quickly came to see it my way. And in what he felt was a therapeutic milestone, he dreamt of a reunion with his father, in which the father told him, "Don't blame me," and the patient responded with, "I don't," at which point they hugged and reconciled. As I told the patient, I wasn't sure whether this Hollywood-style dream was a real resolution of his anger or a denial of its depth. But either way, it confirmed the hypothesis that the patient was, and didn't want to be, angry with his father.

One of the more subtle similarities between these two "father" cases was the fact that, while presumably not consciously intended, the father's action had sent a powerful message to the child that there was something fundamentally wrong with him. In the case of parental suicide — certainly under the circumstances of this particular case and perhaps in most cases — the message is "You are not enough of a reason for me to be alive." And in the case of choosing prison over taking care of the family — or even choosing principle over self-interest at the same time that your son is choosing business school — the message to the child is also not exactly affirming. In both instances the message is analogous to that of the Kafka father who "sentences" his son to death by drowning. And in both instances, very much like the Kafka son who ends up throwing himself in the river, the patients' self-destructiveness is in compliance with the unconscious message of the father.

Now what parents, you might protest, would want to see their child self-destruct? Surely none, in any conscious way. On the contrary, even the "worst" parents truly do their best, and there's nothing more rewarding to a parent than to see his or her child blossom. But therein lies the paradoxical and most problematic aspect of self-destructiveness: while aggression is turned toward the self, its hostile intention toward the parent remains intact and is in fact even more effective than straightforward aggression. By becoming "a loser," a man is not only punishing himself, but also, first and foremost, his parents, or those parent substitutes who "want nothing more than seeing you happy." As any parent knows, there is no better way for a child to make his parents miserable than to become truly miserable himself. When a parent administers a punishment, say, no Nintendo for a week, the child clearly loses something. But if he is willing to tolerate some extra loss, he can win something else, something even more gratifying than Nintendo — the chance to punish his parents back, big time. "Here's your Nintendo and all the toys you ever gave me — I don't need any of it!" he can say. He can give it all up and hang tough, knowing that it won't be too long before his parents practically beg him to play Nintendo.

This may be more difficult to identify in adults, but if you're personally involved with a self-destructive man who keeps pushing the envelope even when the odds are clearly against him, perhaps you can see that he is trying to win — by losing, because his loss is also yours. In my mind, no psychologist, psychiatrist, or AA enthusiast could ever describe the peculiar, pathetic mixture of heroism and vindictiveness which characterizes the self-destructive mind-set as well as the Russian author Fyodor Dostoyevsky did. I once recommended Dostoyevsky's book *Notes from the Underground* to a patient who was not fully self-destructive but who tended to sabotage himself along these lines. The patient, a nice, charming man, responded with a thinly disguised snicker. "Dostoyevsky, ha!" as if to imply that he was too stupid to read such a thing and that it was intellectual superiority on my part to suggest it — the reverse of which was his true intention, as he was putting *me* down by putting himself down! It was precisely this unconscious attitude on his part that made me think of the book, which, frankly, is more down to earth than intellectual. Here's how it starts:

> I am a sick man.... I am an angry man. I am an unattractive man. I think there is something wrong with my liver. But I don't understand the least thing about my illness, and I don't know for certain what part of me is affected. I'm not having any treatment for it, and never have had, although I have a great respect for medicine and doctors.... No, I refuse treatment out of spite. That is something you will probably not understand. Well, I understand it. I can't of course explain who

> my spite is directed against in this matter.... I know better than anybody that I am harming nobody but myself. All the same, if I don't have treatment, it is out of spite. Is my liver out of order? — let it get worse!

This goes on and on, and I'll resist my own self-destructive temptation to inflict more of it on you. But this only is critical: when the sick man explains how we can actually find pleasure in pain, he hits the nail on the head. When a person with a toothache groans on and on even when he knows that everyone in the house is already sick of listening to him, this Dostoyevsky character explains, it's because he enjoys the message to his "audience":

> "I'm disturbing you," he seems to say, "I'm lacerating your feelings and preventing everybody in the house from sleeping. Well, don't sleep, then; you ought to be feeling my toothache all the time. I'm not a hero to you any longer, as I used to try to seem, but only a worthless good-for-nothing."

Like the angry child, this type of man knows that the best way to defeat the people who care about him is to make himself miserable. Feeling unable to experience and to express aggression directly, he actually strives to fail so as to make others feel guilty about, and unhappy with, their success.

Invisible Man

One patient, a doctoral candidate in international relations, reported a dream during the NATO air war against Yugoslavia. In his dream he was flying an air force jet over Yugoslavia, circling military targets and hitting them without being hit. In searching for "day residues" — events from the previous day or two which could have triggered the dream — the patient remembered watching TV footage of a plane facing antiaircraft fire, and thinking, "These pilots really have guts to continue to do their job even when there's real risk." The patient related this thought directly to his conflict regarding what to do with his life after he got his Ph.D. His fantasy was to move to Washington, D.C., and get involved in international affairs at the highest levels of government. But he felt that he was too risk averse to delve into Washington's power politics. So he concluded that he would end up in academia, probably teaching in a college.

Clearly, in the dream the patient somehow found the guts to take the risk and do what he wanted to do. "Why were you able to do that in the dream?" I asked him, suggesting it wasn't merely for the same reason that we are able to fly in our dreams even without an airplane. We then wandered around the subject together until I asked him what kind of a jet he was flying in the dream. "It was an F-117," he said with a barely disguised smile as if pretending to hide something we both knew. "The Stealth!" I almost jumped out of my seat, impressing even myself with both my military and psychological acumen. You see, as fellow news junkies, both the patient and I knew of the secretive, self-protective Stealth. The so-called invisible bomber was the only plane in the world built to evade the enemy's radar!

So while this patient wanted to go to Washington, where the real action was, he felt he couldn't do it without a measure of evasive protection. It's not that he didn't like Washington or what it represented, it's just that he didn't want to get hurt there. This was unfortunate because these days academia is hardly an ivory tower free of power politics. But the real question of the dream was why the patient experienced his career conflict in terms of warfare. Yes, Washington is probably a very aggressive place. But the truth is, you need aggression to be successful at work, no matter where you are or what you do for a living. You need to be able to do what survival demands, sometimes even at the expense of others. But of course, as aggression invites aggression, you also need to have a pretty thick skin. So this patient's self-destructiveness consisted not in turning his aggression on himself, but rather in his reluctance to unleash it on others, for fear of retaliation. Of course, pursuing a Ph.D. in international relations is hardly a meek enterprise. But in the patient's mind, it felt like a risk-free hiding place.

Speaking of hiding, whereas conventional wisdom has it that all men would like to have as large a sexual organ as possible, it is also the case that many men desire to "shorten," or altogether hide, their penis. Some men are so fearful of the demands of aggressive performance — as defined by the conflict of masculine insecurity — that they attempt to express it in disguise or while being a moving target. Certain kinds of workplace acting-out, for example, embezzling funds, stealing, or vandalizing, while by no means exclusively male, fall into this hit-and-run category.

If the abusive boss is someone who displays too much masculine aggression in his management style, the "abusive employee," as we might call the type of man I'm referring to here, doesn't show enough of it. Feeling unable to "step up to the plate" and "act like a man," he expresses his aggression in secretive, invisible ways. To use an analogy from the world of male adolescence, he's like the boy who is so anxious about becoming a man that he tries to hide or do away with his secondary sexual characteristics, for instance, by shaving off new and threatening pubic hair. This, or variations on this theme, are a fairly common reaction to the pressures of entering manhood in our society. One patient recalled that when he began to get erections in puberty he was so worried that there was something wrong with his penis that he wrapped it with masking tape to "reduce the swelling." Obviously, these kinds of reactions are more likely to occur in the absence of family discussions about sexual development. But interestingly, that very absence can be an indication that the family is ambivalent or anxious about the son becoming a man.

True, in traditional cultures there was less talk about sex in the family, suggesting the problem may be more generational than psychological. Unlike my eight-year-old son, I don't recall ever asking my parents, "Do we have to talk about sex again?!" On the other hand, it's precisely because sex (unlike other aspects of sexuality) is fundamentally an adult act that orthodox societies are so threatened by it. Clearly, orthodoxy — be it religious, intellectual, or political — has a vested interest in keeping its followers childlike. As long as they're emotionally and intellectually dependent on the rigid truths espoused by a higher authority, followers are less likely to question the legitimacy of the entire system.

Now if we expand the definition of orthodoxy to include any kind of extreme, rigid, or inflexible environment, we can see that psychologically speaking, orthodoxy is a breeding ground for invisible men. To start with a religious example, a Jewish patient in his forties, a professional man with his own family, describes what it's like to go out to dinner with his strictly Orthodox parents. As the patient tells it, even though his parents know he is not observant, he has an unspoken agreement with them not to discuss it. So when they go out to eat together, the patient will order only kosher food, even if he's really not in the mood for it. The patient explains, and it's hard to disagree, that he does this out of respect for his parents — there's obviously no need to offend them. The problem is that he doesn't feel that they respect *him* — they seem to expect that he pretends that he is someone different than who he really is. So how can he respect them if they don't respect him? The truth is, he doesn't really respect them — he's just pretending to. He doesn't respect them because, by definition, unless you are orthodox yourself, you don't respect orthodoxy. It's not anything that you do, it's just who you are in the orthodox mind if you don't happen to be orthodox yourself. And therein lies the problem of growing up with orthodoxy — if you don't follow *its* agenda, you can't have *any* agenda. Unless of course, you develop an underground, secret, or invisible agenda.

For men, the oppression of orthodoxy brings the issue of aggression into sharp focus. For what's a boy to do if he cannot openly play rough-and-tumble with authority? One man, after receiving a less than perfect performance evaluation on his job, left a copy of an article about a disgruntled employee who "went postal" on his manager's desk. Of course the manager suspected him, but he couldn't prove anything. Another man, a young banking executive who tested positive for cocaine on a random urine test, proceeded to beat the system by using a friend's urine in several subsequent drug tests. Before every test he would warm up the friend's urine in a microwave oven in order to fool the thermometer which was used to verify that the urine was fresh!

These men — like many others who transgress with deception rather than with aggression — have received rather early in life, from one orthodox authority or another, extensive if unintended training in the art of subversive warfare. In our culture, the orthodoxy which trained them is likely to be less religious and more psychological, taking such forms as the militaristic father, the hyperemotional mother, the sexually abusive grandfather, or the physically abusive brother. A less obvious but just as deadly form is that of the "normotic" parents, who, as described by psychoanalyst Christopher Bollas, are people who value strict adherence to normalcy, reasonableness, and objectivity above all else. This type of orthodoxy is particularly hard to "diagnose" because by nature it's completely dedicated to nonextreme behavior.

While these environments are in fact quite different from each other, from the viewpoint of the developing child they all share one central and psychologically ever-present component: the child is subjected to so much external pressure that he cannot emerge but only submerge. Since he is bombarded by so many overwhelming stimuli, he can only be reactive, never proactive.[17]

Another way to conceptualize the development of the invisibly self-destructive man is as a product of a narcissistic environment. The more self-important, glamorous, or imposing the environment, the less room there is for the child to shine. He then paradoxically seeks to be "seen" or noticed by disappearing altogether. One patient who had a rather chaotic early home life recalled always wandering away and getting lost as a child — apparently in order to be found. Another patient was always lost as an adult — professionally speaking. A man with many talents, he kept changing jobs and even careers, not because he would find something more interesting or better but because he desperately wanted to be seen and recognized but could never "make a splash" in any of these jobs. Of course, he never stayed with any of them long enough to actually achieve success. This act of disappearance always reminds me of a character in Thomas Bernhard's novel *The Loser.* A writer, this character had made so many corrections and erasures in his manuscript that in the end the only thing left of the manuscript was the title, which was — you guessed it — *The Loser.*

The Accommodating Cockroach

It's impossible to discuss disappearance from tyranny without an honorary mention of this most famous of male insects. In Kafka's perhaps most well known story, *Metamorphosis,* Gregor Samsa wakes up one morning to find himself transformed, overnight, into a gigantic cockroach. Before this transformation, we are told, Gregor was the perfect son. Living at home and working in a job he hated to pay off his parents' debt, he basically sacrificed himself to support his dependent parents and sister. But even now, as a cockroach — notwithstanding his family's selfish disgust and lack of concern for his new predicament — Gregor continues to work hard on trying to please them, for example by hiding under the bed in order to spare them the repulsive sight of him when they come in to clean his room! Yet nothing he does to disappear is sufficient to please his family, except for his ultimate act of disappearance, his dying, after which he is literally thrown out of the house by the cleaning woman.

Among other things, this story also shows the positive side of self-destructiveness. In his own way, the self-destructive man is often a caring, passionate, and idealistic individual. Free of conventional concerns, he can be courageous, creative, and accepting of individual differences. And when he doesn't choose disappearance as his defense, he is likely to be at the forefront of fighting tyranny.

But Kafka's *Metamorphosis* is also a fantastical illustration of one of Freud's most controversial ideas, the so-called death instinct. Amazed by the general intensity and perseverance of self-destructive behavior, Freud speculated that we all have an innate drive to reverse our growth and to return to the inanimate state from which we were conceived. At first, this seems like a rather strange concept, born out of frustration with the inability of psychoanalysis to explain, let alone cure, some self-destructive conditions. But if you think of it as a drive toward regression — a desire to return home to the familiarity, safety, and dependency of childhood and babyhood — it can go a long way to explain why people resist growth and why they shrink in self-destruction.

In struggling to understand why his self-destructive behaviors had been so resistant to therapy, one of my patients, a scientist with a strong philosophical bent, asked for my explanation of it. Exasperated myself, I mentioned the death instinct. I told the patient that much of contemporary psychoanalysis doesn't like the idea and that at least one important psychoanalytic textbook warns clinicians that mentioning this unuseful concept to patients only leads to nonproductive intellectualizations. "Well, I rather like it," he began to intellectualize, but ended up acknowledging, rather emotionally, that he liked it because it was consistent with his experience that his self-destructive patterns were not under his control. Now as any of the millions of AA and other twelve-step programs members will tell you, acknowledging this kind of powerlessness is the first and probably most critical step to recovery from addiction. In my mind, this is an important step not only in fighting addiction but also in coping with any self-destructive desires. This is so because the self-destructive man insists on trying to control what he *cannot* — for example, his feelings of anger or his aggressive impulses — and on not trying to control what he *can* — that is, his behavior.

While I cannot elaborate here on the treatment of self-destructiveness, I'd like to briefly discuss a few principles which help me deal with it not only clinically but also in everyday life. By way of doing that, let's first examine and decode some of the more common interpersonal messages issued by the actions of male self-destructiveness.

Actions Speak Louder than Words

- Your boyfriend stands you up again. *Translation: (1) I'm such a loser, (2) You have nothing important to do with your time anyway.*
- Your husband bought you earrings on Valentine's Day but

you find a pawn note on his night table. *Translation: (1) I'm such a loser, (2) I never meant to give them to you in the first place.*

- Your husband drives past a stop sign. *Translation: (1) I'm such a loser, (2) What's the big deal, it's only your life.*
- You get a phone bill with repeated calls to a certain number 1-900-6969-SEX. *Translation: (1) I'm such a loser, (2) What's the big deal, it's only your body.*
- Your husband calls you from the street — he lost his wallet and needs you to come get him. *Translation: (1) I'm so disorganized, (2) Your time is mine.*
- Your boyfriend whispers on the phone in the other room. *Translation: (1) I'm such a scum bag, (2) You are such a sucker.*
- Your husband mentions he's once again late to his job. *Translation: (1) I'm such a loser, (2) I'm sick and tired of supporting you.*
- After promising a million times he'll never do it again, your husband goes out with the boys after work. He comes home at 2:00 A.M. reeking of alcohol. *Translation: (1) I'm such a jackass, (2) And so are you.*
- Your husband forgets to put out the garbage again. *Translation: (1) I'm such a baby, (2) You do it!*

This list, I'm afraid, is interminable, which is not even its worst characteristic. What's really bad about it is what it says about the prospects for coping with, not to mention helping, the self-destructive man. First, since he uses actions rather than words to express his feelings, this man doesn't really respond to verbal communications. Second, since his actions are inherently not only self-destructive but also destructive toward others, why would you want to be with him in the first place? Indeed, in our culture it's generally considered okay to walk away from a self-destructive man, and many of us do. But it's not always that simple, is it? The therapist, for one, cannot abandon his patient because he refuses to get better. And can a parent simply throw out of the house the drug-addicted or alcoholic son? And is it right or feasible for a loving spouse to leave her husband of twenty years because he has developed a gambling problem? And should a single woman in her thirties throw out an otherwise good and promising relationship when she realizes her boyfriend drinks too much? And should Hillary leave Bill? And what about that garbage — should you do it yourself or let it stink up the house?

Putting Actions into Words

The first job of the therapist or of anyone choosing to deal with self-destructive men — or really any man — is to be a translator. Since male self-destructiveness is a substitute language, you need to develop skills in interpretation and translation. Luckily, it's not a complicated language. As seen in the list above, the communication, while nonverbal, is actually quite straightforward. The more difficult task is to communicate your translation back to the foreigner, who, as you know, doesn't really want to hear it. Nonetheless, if you can show him with some degree of distance and objectivity that he is voting with his feet, he might eventually get it. In case you wonder, "distance and objectivity" does not mean that when he leaves you the car with the gas tank warning light on you snap at him for not caring about anybody in the house but himself. A more bemused observation, such as "I guess you'd like to think it's my job to fill up the car," would be better. Granted, it's extremely difficult not to get angry with such behavior. But try to remember the child who punishes his parents by making them miserable. If you're angry, he got to you, which means he got what he wanted — misery loves company. So when it comes to dealing with self-destructiveness, it's critical to develop the skill of obliviousness.

In moderate cases of self-destructive behavior, putting your man's actions into words can make a huge difference. For example, one young man told his girlfriend that he was having some strange problems on his job. His manager told him that while he was doing a good job, he seemed to have a problem getting along with coworkers. "My boss said I don't speak up in meetings, I'm always a few minutes late, I always spend lunch by myself, and that I never smile," the boyfriend explained. "I don't get it," he continued, "this is just the way I am, I'm there to do a job, not to hang out." "This is not the way you are," said the girlfriend. "You're pretty outgoing and friendly with me or with your buddies. Maybe you just don't want to be in that job." "Maybe I don't," he said. "I guess I never really liked the corporate world." And that evening he started looking in the paper for a different kind of job.

One man was in marital therapy with his wife. A corporate lawyer, he had finally found his dream job in the mergers-and-acquisitions department of a prestigious New York firm. He was initially excited and happy, but a couple of months into the job he made a mistake evaluating a client's stock transaction and ended up endorsing a legally questionable procedure. Fortunately, the procedure was not executed, no law was broken, and the patient's mistake was not noticed. Nonetheless, he entered a state of extreme anxiety and was convinced that the government Securities and Exchange Commission — known among investment professionals as a hard-core, relentless investigatory body — was going to come after him. For several weeks the patient was tortured about this, obsessing that he was going to be fired, debarred, and prosecuted. And for months, his wife and I tried to understand his fear and to reassure him that he was blowing things out of proportion. But it didn't help. Finally, the wife came up with the winning formula. "Maybe the real question is why you made that mistake in the first place, and maybe the answer is that you don't really want to do this kind of work but you can't admit it to yourself because it's something you wanted for such a long time." "That's an interesting theory," the man said, almost dismissively. But that night he slept like a baby, and the next day his anxiety was gone. By the next session he was talking about making a career change.

Failing just on the verge of success, as this patient did, is a relatively common display of the simple logic of self-destructiveness — unconsciously, the person does not want to succeed. And with many men, as in the case of this patient, there is something fundamentally wrong, for *them*, in their life choices — wrong career, wrong marriage, or wrong sexual orientation (false straight or gay lifestyle) — which they want to destroy. The problem is that on his way down, the self-destructive man wants to take whoever stands in his way with him, including, most particularly, the helpful translators.

The Road to Hell

Psychoanalyst Phillip Bromberg tells of a patient who came for a consultation and related a dream in which his house was on fire, and he, the patient, was standing on the roof and throwing rocks on the firemen who were trying to put out the fire. In a sense, like the child who punishes himself to get to his parents, the ultimate goal of the self-destructive man is to destroy anyone who is trying to help him. So the second task in coping with men's self-destructive streak is to be indestructible, which oddly enough, for the therapist as much as for the spouse, friend, or parent, means stopping being so goddamn helpful.

In their zeal to help self-destructive men, many therapists, like well-intentioned parents and spouses, learn the hard way that the road to hell is paved with good intentions. I did, recently, with a patient who's a heavy marijuana user and who had previously refused my recommendation for a rehab admission. One day, when I felt the patient had made enough progress in his sessions with me, I took the initiative — against my better judgment — to actively help him stop smoking dope. The patient was greatly appreciative and moved by my concern. He agreed enthusiastically to my plan. But in the next session, he reported that a big part of his motivation to quit was to gain my approval, and that just before he "crumbled," he told himself, "Fuck Dr. Gratch, I can smoke if I want to."

But withholding help from self-destructive people is easier said than done. Even with this patient, every once in a while, I can't help but let my helpful or concerned attitude sneak into the session. For example, when the patient once expressed what seemed to be genuine pain about his lack of direction in life, I interjected — instead of biting my tongue — that he wouldn't have any direction until he did something about his smoking. The patient agreed and, needless to say, continued to do nothing about his smoking. Interestingly, every once in a while, he comes to a session with the thought that this will be the day I "fire" him from the therapy, a thought which, of course, is part of his self-destructive wish. And since he might need to hit bottom before getting better, I might very well grant him his wish one day.

Another patient didn't appear to be self-destructive when I started working with him shortly after he graduated from college. Good-looking and articulate, he didn't seem to have many problems. But he came to therapy at the recommendation of a college counselor whom he'd seen regarding career choices and lack of sexual experience. Now while no counselor could tell him what career to choose or even how to choose one, the same did not apply to dating. As the patient reported it, his college counselor suggested that the next time he took a girl out to a movie, he should just put his hand on her leg. The patient thought it was a reasonable idea but never carried it out.

My approach with him was different. Together we began to explore *why* he hadn't had any sexual experiences so far and *why* he didn't know how "to make a move" on a girl. As we covered the usual territory of the patient's history, including the unusual and traumatic loss of his mother at a young age, our basic assumption was that the patient's avoidance of intimacy was motivated by some fear, for example, the fear of being too aggressive with women. But this led nowhere fast, so we began to explore the opposite hypothesis, that is, that his avoidance was motivated by a wish.

Here we seemed to be getting somewhere, as it quickly became evident that the patient simply didn't want to become intimate with a woman. His sexual fantasies were always about a woman seducing *him* and often about older, unavailable women. In a word, he was waiting for his mother to come back, and therefore didn't want anyone else. But even this hypothesis, which rang true to the patient, led pretty much nowhere. The reason: the patient was also waiting for me, the therapist-turned-mother, to do it for him. Unfortunately, though perhaps unavoidably, I initially didn't see this. So with time, and in my frustration, I found myself more and more allied with the college counselor, whom I had discounted before. And while the patient made progress with his career issues, as he accumulated therapy years, his complete passivity led me to a make a series of escalating suggestions — from calling potential dates to answering personal ads, from trying group therapy to consulting with another therapist.

The patient, you may have guessed, declined to act on any of these ideas, which eventually forced us to see his self-destructiveness: he needed to bring back to his life not only a mother who would take care of him, but also one whom he could punish — for abandoning him — by rejecting her care and by torturing her with his failures. In turning me into such a mother, the patient's "symptom" — the waiting for mother — had defeated the therapy which was supposed to cure it. When I realized this I shared it with the patient and he agreed. But this time I didn't ask him to do anything about it — I asked myself. I stopped generating suggestions once and for all and began to withdraw from the case in every possible way, until I was reduced to the caricature of the bored, silent analyst. And while the patient complained bitterly about my lack of interest — once again his mother abandoned him — it was this withdrawal that eventually allowed him to take charge of his romantic life and to start dating. Interestingly, another patient of mine who went through a similar therapeutic process concluded that he wasn't really interested in dating anyone, and that other than feeling external social pressures to be married, he was perfectly happy to be on his own. So this patient stopped wanting what he didn't want, which from my point of view was also a positive therapeutic outcome.

But do we always have to spend years "enabling" the self-destructive man before wising up? Unfortunately, sometimes we do — because hard lessons can only be fully learned from our own mistakes. Nevertheless, there are at least two things we can do to avoid playing into the self-destructive hand of the important people in our lives. The first thing is extremely difficult to do, because it requires that we do nothing. This is particularly difficult in times of crisis, which the self-destructive man produces rather regularly. For that reason, in thinking about my advice to the reader for coping with men's self-destructiveness, I toyed with the idea of filling a whole page with one line: THERE'S NOTHING YOU CAN DO TO HELP A SELF-DESTRUCTIVE MAN; THERE'S NOTHING YOU CAN DO TO HELP A SELF-DESTRUCTIVE MAN; THERE'S NOTHING YOU CAN DO TO HELP A SELF-DESTRUCTIVE MAN; THERE'S NOTHING YOU CAN DO.... I thought of doing this as a reminder, to myself as much as to anyone else. But instead, let me drive the point home in the words of a slightly better writer. Once again, Dostoyevsky:

"Where did all the sages get the idea that a man's desires must be normal and virtuous? Why did they imagine that he must inevitably will what is reasonable and profitable? What a man needs is simply and solely *independent* volition, whatever that independence may cost and wherever it may lead."

In other words, in acting self-destructively, men try to preserve their intellectual independence, or at least their ability to choose. So the more *you* believe life is the only choice, the more *they* must choose death. And to the extent that your help is trying to influence their choices — which it does — they must reject it. But if you withhold your helping hand — believing, as it were, in the reality of both life and death — you leave them with the choice to help themselves or not, which is what they really need.

The second thing we can do to reduce our natural inclination to help the help-rejecting man (or woman) is fortunately a bit more active. Instead of trying to help *him*, we should try to help *ourselves*. To the therapist I say, heal thyself. And to anyone else whose life project it is to care for a self-destructive man, I say, get a life. This does not necessarily mean separation or divorce. Nor does it mean a selfish lack of interest in others. All it means is finding an emotional or spiritual or intellectual or whatever purpose for being alive other than this project. This is a difficult objective for many people and especially for women, most of whom are still raised to take care of others, not themselves. But if you want to launch such a journey, the first step is to ask yourself not why you want to change the status quo, but why you don't. In other words, what's in it for *you* to let a self-destructive man destroy you.

One couple came to see me for marital therapy following a series of crises in which the husband failed to meet financial obligations and deceived the wife about it. In one session, the woman — an extremely bright and successful professional — turned to me and said, "Tell me if this is inappropriate for me to say this, because I'm certainly no shrink, but my theory is that David [her husband] actually wants to fail." "Well," I said, "it's not inappropriate of you to say this — anybody can be a shrink, and I actually agree with your theory. But what *is* inappropriate is that you don't have a theory about yourself, a theory about why *you* want to be with someone who wants to fail." When we explored this, we fairly quickly developed a theory, and a good one, about her. Her father was rather abusive in his perfectionism, and throughout her life had always put her down. So by being with someone who was failing, she could do to him what her father had done to her, thereby avoiding her own feelings of inadequacy as well as the painful anger in relation to her father. It's as if she were saying, "My father was right about how important success is — look at that bum I'm married to!"

For this woman, the development of such a theory boded well, both in terms of the prognosis for her present relationship, or if it ended, for a future one. In many cases of separation or divorce, the wife walks out, understandably fed up with the husband's series of self-destructive acts. But to the extent that she views herself as the passive victim of his abuse, chances are that in the future she will find herself in the same situation again, or in no relationship at all.

The Cactus

After being fired from an executive position — which he didn't really like and therefore unconsciously sabotaged — a patient of mine had a dream about a cactus in the desert. "The cactus is me," the patient analyzed his dream, "transplanted from fertile soil to a barren landscape, where I now have to survive with so little nourishment." I couldn't have agreed more with this interpretation, but unlike the patient himself, I didn't quite feel so sorry for him. While he had reasons to be worried — he had a family to support and it was unlikely that he would find such a high-level job in another company — I saw the cactus as a more complex symbol. The patient's self-pity was also other-punitive — "You, an oak tree, wouldn't even understand what it's like to be a cactus," it seemed to be saying. The truth is, the cactus is a rather prickly survivor.

In case you wonder, I told this to the patient, even though his depression and anxiety after losing the job were genuine. My experience is that the best time to beat up on self-destructive men is when they're down — otherwise, they just don't listen to you. Also, telling it to them like it is speaks to their notion of heroic masculinity. Strangely, criticizing them at their weakest moment is a form of support — "I know you're tough enough to take it" is the implied message. And when they're down and out and have no illusions left, it paradoxically strengthens them to hear that they are not victims but rather screw-ups: if their destruction was of their own making, so could their resurrection be.

When the self-destructive man hits bottom, it's also the best time to finally exercise your irresistible desire to help others. But you should not take it beyond a basic level of intervention. Offering someone the name of a therapist might be helpful, calling the therapist for him is not. Giving him a place to live might be okay, giving him money is not. Telling him he's just about to miss the exit on the highway is helpful, but only the first or maybe second time around. And reminding him to change a light bulb once in a while might be wise, but doing it for him and then complaining about it is not.[18]

Sexual Acting-Out

...I want sex now

Concluding with Sex

Showing me into his office and motioning me to sit down, my boss looked firmly into my eyes and asked me how many times I had sex in the past week...." My patient, a salesman who normally might be asked how many buyers he visits in a week, was relating a dream. Did the dream tell us that sex was on his mind more than work? I don't think we need dreams to confirm to us that men think about sex during work. And of course, they think about sex during love: referring to Erich Fromm's book *The Art of Loving,* which I had previously recommended to him, another male patient proudly reported to me, "I finally read *The Art of Lovemaking!*"

So before resting my case — which is that men are after all nothing if not men — let me sum up with sex. Leaving sex to the end, I should say, was not an accidental act of omission. Nor was it a postponement of having to deal with the inevitable cliché that men have sex on the brain pretty much all the time. Rather, it was based on the idea that by its very nature, male sexual acting-out offers a condensed summary of the six male attributes I've explored so far. The same concept applies to women just as well, because sexuality is the ultimate playground of gender differences, the meeting place of biology and psychology, reality and fantasy. But due to a combination of biological, cultural, and psychological factors which render them emotionally mute, men tend to sexualize their psychology to a much greater degree.

So in summing up, I will visit some of my patients' sexual disorders (and orders), along with plain old fantasies, thoughts, and dreams, and I will analyze or desexualize them back to their emotional origin. In that respect, if you've skipped all the previous chapters to read about sex, you might be disappointed — everything is about sex, except for sex, which is about.... Let's see.

Before proceeding it might be useful to reflect on some of the possible reasons that men experience sexuality differently than women. Without the pretense of a scientific discussion — and I do believe that science can help us here a great deal — let me just mention a few variables. From an evolutionary standpoint, it's a fact that males, much more so than females, can further their reproductive agenda simply by having more sex. No matter what they do, females cannot have more than one pregnancy at a time. From a cultural perspective, as discussed by psychiatrist Robert Stoller, boys in our society are expected to be sexually naughty. This is evident, for instance, from the fact that girls are taught to protect themselves from boys rather early on. Biologically, there are generally well known hormonal differences, as well as important genital differences. For example, men usually need a shorter period of time and less direct stimulation to become sexually aroused. This, by the way, is particularly true at a younger age and with less experience, which is when and how men, or really boys, develop the "skill" of sexualizing mental contents. In other words, the simplicity of boys' sexual responses — on top of weighty evolutionary, cultural, and hormonal pressures — makes it more likely that they will seek the powerful reward of arousal and orgasm to escape, or cope with, emotional conflicts.

A simple example is one of a patient who grew up in a home with physically abusive, emotionally erratic, and, periodically, altogether absent parents. This patient recalls having "constant erections with lonely feelings of anticipation" from as early an age as six. And he remembers his young teenage years as a time "when [he] was always naked, having an erection, at home or in the pool, desperately wanting someone to touch [him], and once even allowing this older gay man to masturbate [him] in the locker room." This sexualization of his starvation for love had set the patient on a course shared by many men with depressive tendencies. Confusing sex with Prozac, as a grown man, he would lose himself in the warm, sensual bodies of pretty women, using them much as an antidepressant.

Shame: Times Square Revisited

"When my firm decided to explore relocating to the Times Square area a few months ago, I volunteered to be on the exploratory committee — I thought it would be good for me to work more closely with the partners. And a couple of weeks ago when we decided in favor of the move, I volunteered to write the report. I'm bringing this up because I was supposed to write the report this weekend, and I had a complete writer's block — which I never have. I just couldn't do the damn thing, and I had a miserable weekend because of it."

George was a young professional, a driven, hard-working associate in a large New York firm. Smart and perceptive, he was always the cotherapist, speculating with me about his unconscious motives and analyzing them. But on that particular issue he was vague and inarticulate. He had no idea why he was unable to write the report and in fact showed no interest in finding out why. He moved on to talk about something else, and my assumption at the time was that because the report was not a business matter but "extracurricular," he didn't think it was all that important.

A couple of sessions later, George reported a dream. In it, he was watching Channel J — the local porno channel — when his girlfriend walked into the room. Grabbing the remote, he tried to change the channel, but the remote wasn't working. He woke up frantically pressing his finger on the bed. The dream led to a couple of relatively trivial memories, one from Catholic school and one of watching a movie with a sexual scene several years before with his parents. Then, as the session wound down, seemingly reaching for more, even farfetched associations, George assumed a distant, speculative tone: "I don't think this is related to the dream, but who knows. The day before yesterday, after work, I went to a Times Square establishment — you know, a peep show." He paused and in the absence of a reaction from me, added, "But I don't see that as a big deal."

"How did you feel about it?" I asked. "I felt good," he said. "How do you feel talking about it with me?" I asked. "I feel fine about it," he said. After a brief silence I said, "What's going on? This kind of staccato talk is a bit out of character for you." "Well," he said, "I guess I feel a little embarrassed, I guess because I think you might judge me — perhaps you think it's morally wrong." He then went on to say that on that night he ended up in a private booth with the girl from the show, "fondling her breasts, wrapping myself around her and coming in my pants." Uncomfortably, with those words, the session too came to an end. "I hate to do this at such a climactic moment," I said, laughing, "but we have to stop." "That's okay." The patient laughed back and got up to leave.

In the next session, George revealed that he had actually visited this, and "other establishments of its kind," a few times before. The fact that he felt ashamed of these visits was evident in his communications, which were not inconsistent with how many men talk about sex: vagueness, sudden lack of articulation, halting speech, indirect allusions, denial of feelings, and verbal obfuscation. A more subtle indicator of George's shame was the indirect, almost accidental nature of his Times Square "confession" — the purpose of which was not only to reduce his feelings of shame but also to cover them up. Yes, men feel ashamed of their shame about sex. Finally, there was also the projection of his feelings of shame onto someone else — denying he felt bad about the "visits" but fearing that I would judge him for them.

It should now be easy to see why George was unable to write a report concluding that Times Square was an okay location for his firm — he didn't feel it was an okay location for himself. And it was shame about the whole issue that had prevented him from discussing it with me before his inadvertent confession. How to "confess" about sexual issues without feeling shame is a major preoccupation of men, in and out of therapy. Indeed, George was hardly my first or last patient to resort to indirect or coded language in a doomed attempt to bypass sexual shame. Here are some examples.

- I have some sexual anxieties. *Translation: I can't get it up.*
- I have some sexual anxieties. *Translation: I come too quickly.*
- It's hard for me to get close to a woman. *Translation: I can't get it up.*
- I'm beginning to think I drink too much. *Translation: I can't get it up.*
- I had a horrible dream which I can't even talk about. *Translation: I have sexual fantasies about men.*
- I love women. *Translation: I'm a sex addict.*
- I may have a thing about getting old. *Translation: I'm only attracted to sixteen-year-olds.*
- I don't know how to put sex and love together. *Translation: I love rough sex.*
- My wife doesn't like to experiment. *Translation: I can only come if I tie her up.*

As evident in these examples and as we saw in the second chapter, men generally feel shame about being vulnerable, not performing, and deviating from what they perceive as conventional normalcy. In the bedroom, this translates into shame about not being in control of their equipment, not doing a good job as a lover, and fantasizing about anything other than the missionary position plus or minus. My patient George, it turned out after some discussion, felt ashamed of the fact that he had to pay for his sexual exploits — in his mind, more than anything else this was evidence of his lack of control over his sexuality. He also felt shame about the pathetic aspect of the experience — his vulnerability — and about the pornographic aspect of the experience — the supposed deviation from what mature, healthy sexuality was all about.

But, of course, the case can be made that all men pay *something* for their sexual gratification, that their sexual desperation is inherently pathetic, and that their sexual interest is fundamentally pornographic. Indeed, most men display some evidence of sexual shame in most sexual encounters. Using hands rather than words; silently moving to position themselves in a particular way; saying "nothing" when you ask what's wrong; frantically trying to enjoy something; cracking nervous or self-deprecating jokes; and criticizing the other person's sexual technique or body are all common examples of evasive maneuvers aimed at bypassing shame.

In the second chapter, I discussed several therapeutic "techniques" which could be used to break through men's wall of shame. All apply equally well to sexual shame. The single most important thing you can do if you want your man to talk to you openly about sex is to become comfortable with your own sexuality, or at least comfortable enough to talk about it. One of my patients once mentioned that I seemed quite comfortable talking about sex. Of course I was comfortable talking about it with him — it wasn't my sex life we were discussing! Actually, these very therapeutic boundaries, while protecting the therapist from exposing his own sexual embarrassments, often disadvantage him in helping patients to open up. There's nothing like talking about your own sexuality to help someone else talk about his. Being open-minded about alternative lifestyles, asking detailed questions, listening without judgment, and using humor to acknowledge and dissolve silence are also natural techniques anyone can use.

Some men have no shame. Expecting gratification as if it were their constitutional right, demanding that their partner indulge their every whim without regard to her tastes and criticizing her for any reluctance, these men project their shame on the partner, making her feel she's sexually repressed or deviant for not wanting to do it all. These men could use some shame, which is another way of saying that sexual shame is not all bad. If nothing else, it's part of what makes us civilized.

Emotional Absence: 2001 Space Odyssey

If shame is about hiding something from another person, emotional absence is about hiding something from oneself. Sexually speaking, the latter is often evident in men's infamous goal orientation and in their mechanical approach to lovemaking. As many a woman in couple therapy tells her husband or boyfriend, "I don't feel you're really there when we make love." In the third chapter, we saw that men's reluctance to feel — their emotional absence — is based, first and foremost, on their fear of losing themselves in a woman. We also saw that this fear is also a wish, and that this duality is at the core of what I call the conflict of masculine insecurity. Sexually, the desire to lose oneself in a woman is all but evident in the length to which men go to gain admittance into a woman's inner body. The other side of the conflict, the fear, is less evident because it's often more unconscious.

Nonetheless, from the common "wham-bam-thank-you-ma'am" approach to lovemaking to the more rare condition of "vagina dentata" — the belief that teeth inside the vagina will clamp down on the visiting penis during intercourse — there exist a large variety of more or less socially sanctioned behaviors and attitudes which reflect that fear. One patient was extremely aroused by his girlfriend for the first couple of months of their relationship. But then, as the girlfriend started talking about wanting to see him more, his attraction began to wane. And it didn't help matters that she soon thereafter started hinting about getting engaged. But the fate of this couple was sealed when — in an attempt to revive their faltering sex life — they had unprotected intercourse. The idea that she might be pregnant — a mother no less — was enough to turn the patient off completely. Sadly, this kind of loss of desire — to an attractive, even loved, woman — is a common problem of men in psychotherapy.

Other forms of sexual absence can be seen in the ways in which men limit, if not lose, their desire. Some men are attracted only to petite or young women — unconsciously protecting themselves from feeling bodily overwhelmed. Others are attracted only to "bimbos," or intellectually inferior women, who allow them to use their own intellect as a shield or partition behind which they can preserve sufficient emotional space. And yet others are attracted to only a certain part of the female body, also protecting themselves from too much intimacy. Finally, there are those who are aroused only by sexual activities which limit the potential for losing oneself in the other. In oral sex, for example, one is only engaged with a small part of the other person's body. Similarly, while in the "doggie" position, one cannot be engulfed by an embrace.

There are also more uniquely individual variations on the theme. For example, one patient, a college student, had some sexual experiences but was committed for religious reasons to not having sex before marriage. Yet even in his dreams — and he had plenty of sexual dreams — he could never "complete the act" as there was always some interference or distraction before penetration. At one point, there was even an intruding, and certainly not arousing, image of his therapist — me — in an armchair. It turned out this was not only a religious issue but also fear of intimacy. A pat Freudian interpretation of these dreams — supported by the intrusion of an older father-figure type into the action — would be that the patient's fear of intercourse was Oedipal: the unconscious wish to sleep with the mother leads to a fear of punishment, by castration, from the father. According to such an interpretation, the patient avoided intercourse because he was afraid to lose his penis. A deeper interpretation, however, was that he avoided it because he was afraid to lose himself. Interestingly, the patient's history supported both. His father died at the height of the Oedipal period, which means that, as a child, the patient didn't have a chance to see that his father wasn't going to punish him but was in fact his buddy. And his mother, overprotective to start with, reacted to the death of her husband by clinging to her only child as to a lifesaver — leaving the patient in a permanent struggle to get space from her and from all subsequent women.

One of men's most favorite means of extricating or distancing themselves from feelings of intimacy is to objectify women. For instance, men often treat real women as objects of pornography, asking them to put on this or that item so that they'll be more arousing. Perhaps this is just an extension of wanting someone to look sexy, but in my mind it's also about men's tendency to protect themselves from the reality of female sexuality by using mental pictures which they can control. This is one of the reasons why visual enhancements of one's actual sex life often work only temporarily — once reality conforms to the mental picture, the man often needs a new and improved one.

Sadly, for some men, even the mental picture is not good enough. One patient tragically lost both his parents at a young age in an accident. He was so devastated by this that even as an adult he had a hard time feeling anything. Sexually, while he avoided getting involved with a woman, he would savor the opportunity of seeing an attractive woman in the street so that he could take a mental picture of her, to be used later at home for masturbation. This man genuinely didn't seem to need more by way of a sex life, except that at times, the picture he would bring home would "fade out" on him and he couldn't be aroused. This upset him greatly because he knew it meant he wasn't even connecting to people in his fantasy life. This, incidentally, is an example of emotional absence stemming primarily not from a defense against losing oneself in a woman, but rather from a general emotional shutdown following a catastrophic loss.

Interestingly, some men do the opposite of objectifying women. Treating objects of pornography as if they were real people, these men subjectify or personalize pornography. Having elaborate sexual fantasies, or responding to pornographic material in which the arousing elements or even the orgasmic punch line is not hard-core sex but rather an emotional moment, is a common example. These emotional moments, or symbols, can involve wistful scenarios with illusive or reluctant women, images of body parts accompanied by painful yearnings, and dialogue lines such as "Let me show you my dick," or "Tell me you want me, baby." Often, the woman in the fantasy talks, expressing sentiments of sexual devotion and submission.

And, of course, when men visit prostitutes, they sometimes try to use the power of money to turn the sexual exchange into a non-pornographic relationship. One such patient related trying to discuss with the prostitute he'd just had sex with "the politics of sex, including the nature of the financial transaction between us." When I smiled at that, the patient said, "Why are you smiling, Doc? The lady thought it was rather sweet of me!" Another patient developed a long-term relationship with a prostitute. While constrained by his limited finances and her other professional obligations, the patient's attachment to this woman was as romantic as it gets, with gifts of flowers and jewelry. He once even wrote her a poem. And a third patient used prostitutes to "feel sensual and alive," valuing the touching and hugging more than the sexual release.

In truth, personalizing pornographic objects and objectifying real women are not opposites, but rather one and the same. Psychologically speaking, both buy men the critical commodity of space — from women — without having to completely give up on women. Nowhere is this more evident than in the tendency of many men to enhance their sexual arousal by fantasizing about imaginary women while having sex with their real partner. One patient, a musician in his early thirties, was very much in love with his girlfriend, who was not only incredibly beautiful — he showed me pictures — but also a rising star in her field of academic study. But when making love to her, he somehow needed the extra stimulation of fantasizing about other women. Perhaps not surprisingly, those other women were usually "less challenging," ranging from some of his music students to some of his parents' cleaning women. It seemed, then, that the purpose of these fantasies was to bring into the relationship a greater sense of equality: unconsciously feeling outshone by his girlfriend, the patient was trying to reverse the balance of power. Of course, sexualizing these feelings meant they would remain unconscious and that he wouldn't actually feel any of them. Indeed, on a conscious level he experienced his fantasies merely as sexual aphrodisiacs enabling him to perform better with his girlfriend.

Now if you think about this patient's relationship with the imaginary, pornographic women, you can see that by using them during actual sex with his girlfriend he was trying to make them real. And if you think about his relationship with his girlfriend, you can see that by fantasizing about imaginary women while with her, he was trying to make her pornographic. So in both "relationships" he maintained a protective degree of emotional absence from the sexual experience: the pornographic women could never become real, and the real woman could never become pornographic.

As we saw in the third chapter, men's emotional absence originates in its opposite, boys' emotional vulnerability at a young age and their conflicted desire to separate from the first woman in their lives. One patient, a man with OCD (obsessive-compulsive) tendencies, depicted his sex life with his wife as particularly intense. He would describe sex with her as an experience of complete fusion, with fantasies of immersing himself in her insides and of being emptied out of his semen. And all this in hours of unremitting, wholly enviable bliss. But he would always add some sort of detail which would cast a shadow over the whole thing. For example, once, after discussing going down on his wife for "at least" two to three hours, he said: "Do you wanna know what went on in my mind during that time — it will definitely tell you something about how my mind works. What I did while eating her out was *count!*" Then, as if not believing it himself, he explained, "I was counting how many times I was licking her — it actually came to two thousand and one. I swear, two thousand and one!" Well, there's nothing like a bit of arithmetic to keep the mind occupied, and nothing like an occupied mind to draw a boundary around one's own psychic space.

There is another sexual aspect to the defense of emotional absence, one which might well be based on evolutionary value. By not feeling much, men may avoid empathizing with their partner, which is an advantage if thrusting your agenda on her unilaterally gets you closer to what you want. If you ask your partner if she's up to it, the answer may be no. But if you get into bed with the assumption you're going to have sex — thus thinks the male mind — you'll overcome her objections and get what you want. In reality, since we are more than just chimpanzees, this often backfires. But hope springs eternal. For women, the implications of this aspect of emotional absence is that they must be clear and unambiguously expressive with their desires or lack thereof. Because when it comes to their sexual needs, men are anything but subtle.

This brings to mind the case of a university student who was accused of sexual assault after spending a night with a female friend in the women's dorms. It all began innocently enough when, after staying up all night talking, the two went to bed with only their undergarments on, and with the intention of going to sleep. But once in bed they started fooling around. At some point, the man put his hand inside her underwear and started touching her, to which she responded with heavy breathing and increased arousal. He continued to do so until all of a sudden the woman jumped, sat up in bed, and started yelling at him. It turned out that unbeknownst to him she had fallen asleep when they just started to fool around! So when she woke up with his hand in her underwear, she felt assaulted. At that point, the man didn't know what to think. He tried to explain himself, but she demanded that he leave immediately, which he did. The next day she filed a complaint with the dean of student affairs. Though no criminal actions were taken, the man was subsequently "convicted" by the university authorities and received certain disciplinary actions. (Later, on appeal, he was exonerated, and those actions were reversed.)

This man — who grew up in a liberal Jewish home in New Jersey and who had a sweet, gentle disposition and many female friends — was so shaken up by the whole thing that he decided to seek help. After several months of therapy with me, he and I established that underneath his softspoken, female-friendly exterior, there was actually a great deal of unconscious aggression toward women. We then came to see what happened to him on that fateful night in the women's dorms: his emotional absence while in bed with his female friend enabled him to *act on this aggression without feeling it.* Of course, whether or not this was a sexual assault is a different matter — the fact was that he had not been sensitively attuned to where his friend was — asleep. The woman, on the other hand, was perhaps too subtle in communicating her objections, although falling asleep in the middle of fooling around is a pretty strong message. But then again, from his point of view, she never indicated she didn't want to be touched, and she never said she was going to sleep. And while she was asleep, her body continued to respond favorably.[19]

So one implication of sexual emotional absence for women is that they must communicate their own sexual agenda loud and clear. But there are other implications as well. As we saw in the third chapter, emotional absence is a more powerful defense than shame, operating instantly and unconsciously, which means it's much more resistant to external intervention. So the first thing you've got to do is to strike while the iron is hot, which means that if your man wants to talk about sex — go for it. Go for it even if he wants to express anger and frustration about your sex life — as long as he's not blaming (only) you. Go for it and *listen,* and then seize the moment by discussing the issue in his, not your, language. Remember, what he needs is emotional space. So rather than discuss your feelings about it — you can do that later — talk about what you and he are going to do to fix it. More time alone, more foreplay, get a book, go to counseling — whatever it is, use the logic of the situation to make the case. And be objective if not detached: "I just don't work that way; maybe if we spent more intimate time together I'd be more up to it."

This approach, to the extent that you have it in you, will speak to your man's goal-oriented, bottom-line philosophy. It will do more to loosen his intellectualized defenses than would asking him what he feels when you're in bed together. If you ask him how he feels about you when making love, he'll think you want to swallow him — and he'll start counting some numbers! So paradoxically, being less emotional on your end is an invitation for him to be more emotional.

Finally, and perhaps most important, while a sex therapist or a book may help you with some sexual techniques, to cope with whatever emotional absence plagues your bedroom you need to think of nonsexual equivalents. One of the problems with sex is that it's extremely susceptible to psychological pressure: general stress, specific emotional conflicts, and poor communication all play a major role in the bedroom. The good news, though, is that if you address these, sex will improve on its own. In addition to pursuing therapy for such issues, this has a practical implication, best described as putting sexual actions back into words. In terms of emotional absence, suppose your man begins to show a lack of sexual interest in you. Before you start thinking there's something wrong with *you,* consider that there might be something wrong with *him*. For example, a man may lose sexual interest in his partner when he suffers a career setback or when, for whatever reason, he is struggling with a sense of failure at work. Rather than feeling he's no good, he "chooses" — not quite consciously — to feel *you* are no good. The transition from "I'm not a good provider" to "My wife is not attractive" is narcissistically natural for many men.

So in this case when trying to help your husband or boyfriend — and more important, yourself — your job is to stop or reverse the direction of this transition. This is not as difficult as it sounds. All you need to do — assuming it's not a deeper problem — is to listen to him talking about his work. Somewhere he will express in words, and therefore no longer in sexual inaction, his disappointment with himself. Of course, if you can be genuinely supportive, even admiring, of his struggle, chances are he will open up even more, with sexual actions following nonsexual words.

This notion, that solutions to sexual problems lie outside the bedroom and involve a nonsexual intervention, will become even more evident as we proceed with our sexual review away from the defenses of shame and emotional absence and toward the underlying conflicts. As we do this, keep in mind that sexual acting-out, while based on a biological drive, is also a defense of sorts. A defense, because it protects men from feeling certain conflicts. Of sorts, because it doesn't really do the job too well — they end up acting on these conflicts anyway. Another way of saying this is that sex has meaning — interpersonal meaning. So as I explore and decode the messages underlying various sexual activities or fantasies — from oral to anal sex, from "painting with your penis" (an enrichment technique recommended by some sexual awareness books) to pinning down your partner — it's important to remember that this analysis of meaning, even when it uncovers aggressive or selfish elements, doesn't render these sexual expressions illegitimate or pathological. Of course, you can make the case that when someone's sex life consists entirely of, say, oral sex, or for that matter of missionary-style intercourse, they are limiting themselves and may also make their partner unhappy. But that's hardly a pathology.[20]

Masculine Insecurity: Lesbian Man

One of my patients reported a dream in which he had sex with a coworker who in reality was a lesbian. Perhaps anticipating a challenge from me to his heterosexuality, the patient commented that while he believed that everybody had bisexual potential, he didn't think that this dream was about that. "I agree with you on both counts," I said. "So what do you think the dream is about?" he asked. "Well, if this woman is a lesbian," I answered, "she sleeps with other women who are lesbians, which makes you...a lesbian." But I wasn't joking, and the patient knew it. "Great," he said, "wait until I tell my wife that my doctor said I'm a lesbian!"

I wasn't joking, in this case, because, as I went on to explain to the patient, this was a nonsexual, or more accurately a presexual dream, stemming from his early identification with his mother. As we saw in the fourth chapter, before they are catapulted by their own desire and societal pressures to "become men"— somewhere at the beginning of grade school — boys are quite girl-like, especially in relation to their mothers. And as we saw throughout this book, this early identification with their mother and men's need to both preserve and repudiate it is at the heart of the conflict of masculine insecurity. So while most men have homosexual potential, all men have lesbian potential, which is to say, they have the capacity to experience themselves as a woman loving a woman or, historically speaking, a girl loving her mother.

Now while essentially nonsexual, this potential is not always free of sexual conflict. In order to become sexual, the boy has to separate himself from his mother, which involves, among other things, accepting that he has different sex organs than she does. Intellectually, of course, boys know that from a very early age, but emotionally they are not always prepared to accept it, because it shatters their early feelings of bliss and security in being one with mother.

One patient mentioned that once while walking in the park and passing by two police officers, he suddenly had a frightening image of being sodomized by them. This fear repeated itself in the therapy as well, when at one point we decided to use a more analytic approach, with the patient lying down on the couch without directly seeing me. When he first tried it, the patient developed severe anxiety, twitching and turning on the couch, eventually verbalizing the fear that I would attack him and rape him. Now as we saw before, a fear is often a wish, which was true for this patient as well. Except that in his case it wasn't a sexual wish. Rather, it reflected the patient's emotional interpretation of his early childhood experience. An only child to a single mother, he grew up feeling "trapped" by her soft attentiveness, always longing for a powerful male presence. For this patient, neither the problem nor the solution — which was to develop stronger male friendships — was sexual.

But even when the problem seems to be sexual, it often isn't. These days it's hardly news that anal stimulation or intercourse is not in the exclusive domain of gay men. What's perhaps less widely known is the desire of many straight men to be penetrated — by a woman. Some men actually pursue this with their partner, the latter employing some kind of penis substitute, while others leave it to fantasy or dreams. And yet others experience it more indirectly, for example, by finding it more arousing to be on the bottom during intercourse. Whether a reality or a fantasy, these scenarios can be sexually charged with great intensity, as the anus is an erotic zone. Nonetheless, they also represent a nonsexual memory and desire. A memory of being no different than a girl, and a desire to repeat the experience of being known — sexualized to the biblical meaning of the word — by the mother.

While sexually this may not be a problem, as discussed by Stoller and others, for many men this kind of identification is conflictual. With it comes anger and fear. *Anger* for having to give up on the illusion that "Mommy and I are one" and for her putting them in this predicament. And *fear* of not being able to escape her influence. It's easy to see how this unconscious conflict in relation to one's mother gets played out in men's sexual experience. For example, many men are angry when their girlfriend or wife doesn't want to do the same thing in bed they want to do, or if she doesn't know how to stimulate them — she should be one with them. They are also angry about "having to give up" on other women when committing to a relationship, unconsciously blaming their partner for it, as if it's her fault. And of course, they are afraid of what it means to lose out on the possibility of sex with other women when making a commitment to one.

This dynamic is a major reason why many men have extramarital affairs. By having an affair, they angrily assert their right to a sexually more understanding woman as well as to sexual freedom. And they also alleviate their fear of being doomed to have sex with the same woman for the rest of their lives. It doesn't seem to occur to them that you cannot get emancipated in secrecy, or by substituting one master — I guess mistress — for another. While we are quick to condemn men (or women) who cheat on their partners and to think of them as emotional freeloaders, clinical experience shows that these men are in a great deal of pain, mostly because they are prisoners of their own making. Sooner or later, most men find out that the hypermasculine defense is only a proof of its opposite, or in sexualized terms, that the multiple showings of their penis multiply not its size but rather the perception — including their own — that it's small enough to require multiplication. On the other hand, it's easy to see that it's precisely through the use of the sexual organ that a boy can prove to his mother, and to himself, that he is different and separate from her.

The idea of seeking space from one woman by making love to another is as paradoxical as the very conflict of masculine insecurity: men want it both ways — to be a man and to be (with) a woman. The stereotypical relationship in which the man is reluctant to commit and the woman is pushing for a commitment is only true when viewed from a conscious perspective. Unconsciously — and this is easy to show in couple therapy — these men set up the woman to push them, because they want to repeat their relationship with their First Woman, Mom — a relationship in which the woman committed, protected, and engulfed, while the boy reluctantly tried to get away. Let me illustrate — with sex.

One patient, a professional man in his thirties, grew up with a mother who out of her own need to be needed was extremely helpful and supportive — so much so that she facilitated a certain emotional dependency in him. Now while as a young man this patient was able to overcome the desire to be taken care of by his parents and was able to attain self-sufficiency, remnants of this dependency still colored his sexuality. This came to the foreground in therapy when he related a dream in which a childhood friend by the name of Samuel cut off the patient's feet as a punishment for some wrongdoing. While the patient was perplexed about the dream, his associations to it easily dissolved its mystery. The day before the dream, the patient, who was not Jewish, had had a conversation with a coworker who happened to be an orthodox Jew by the name of Shmuel — the Hebrew equivalent of Samuel — in which the latter mentioned a new book about "kosher sex."

Taking a shot at a premature interpretation of the dream, I said, "Is it possible that you had some nonkosher sex and that your 'organ' — in what Freud would have called a downward displacement — is being cut off as a punishment?" The patient laughed, but to my amazement went on to say that he actually had. A couple of weeks earlier he had had sex with his ex-girlfriend, which he felt was wrong because he had previously broken up with her when he realized that he couldn't commit to the relationship. But there was more to it than that. The night before the dream, the patient went on to say, the ex-girlfriend called to tell him, not without angry sarcasm, "In case you were worried, I'm not pregnant." I thus found out that they didn't use birth control — which in the patient's own words was "extremely irresponsible" and in mine, another nonkosher aspect of their lovemaking. Their failure to use a contraceptive was particularly striking because it had never happened in the two years they had been together — only now that they were apart.

So this is what I told the patient: "Let me get it straight. You break up with your girlfriend because she is smothering and you need space, but then you not only see her, not only have sex with her, but also try to get her pregnant so that you also have a child with her?" The patient protested a bit, but then came to see that unconsciously he had done what he had always done with women, starting with his mother — setting them up to depend on him and to need him so that he wouldn't have to let go, or more accurately, so that he could angrily demand to be liberated without knowing that it was his own dependency on them that was holding him back.

This angry dimension in the patient's struggle with separation came further into focus when he told me about the circumstances of his nonkosher act with the ex-girlfriend. Apparently, the ex-girlfriend still had keys to his apartment and on that night, pretty much after the patient's bedtime, she let herself in, unannounced — ostensibly to pick up something she had left behind. The patient was still awake but hanging out in his underwear.... So one thing led to another.

"I guess there was something angry in fucking her," the patient now recalled. "Like I was telling her, 'If you think you can enter my space like this and be so intimate with me, then take this — take what intimacy is really all about.'" As I told the patient, this brought to my mind a picture of a child in his underwear, angrily fantasizing about how he's going to show the mother who had just barged into his room that he is no longer a little boy. It also gave another meaning to the girlfriend's telephone call — or at least to the patient's interpretation of it in the dream. If in fucking her without a condom he was saying, "I can show you I'm a man by making a baby," in reassuring him that she wasn't pregnant, she was saying, "No you can't, no you can't — your dick was cut off!"

A different kind of example is that of an actor in his late thirties who came to see me for a sexual problem. This man was genuinely in love with his girlfriend. He described her as smart, spirited, and attractive and was in fact all ready to propose to her. The problem was that during sex he felt compelled to pretty much forbid his girlfriend to talk, make noises, or move too abruptly. His explanation was that if she became too intense or overpowering he would lose his concentration and erection. As we explored this in therapy, it became clear that in order to perform sexually the patient needed his girlfriend to be "smaller" than he was, or submissive, so that he could feel "big" and on top. But of course, the more he demanded that she restrain herself, the more frustrated, needy, and angry she felt, eventually exploding during sex into a loud burst of emotional demands — at which point he lost his erection completely and irreversibly. So in instructing her to shrink, he set her up to expand; in expecting her to be a good, quiet girl, he turned her into a difficult, hysterical woman.

For this couple, too, the "cure" was not in a sexual technique but rather in finding and defining the nonsexual equivalents of the sexual problem, which in this case, wasn't hard. As they were getting ready to become engaged, the couple began to discuss such issues as when they might have a baby and where they might live. But in these conversations, just as in bed, the patient would set up his girlfriend to become an emotional, demanding woman, a mother of sorts. In discussing having a baby he would say, "Why don't we wait a couple of years, so that we can be more settled and so on," which the girlfriend — who had just turned thirty-two — would interpret as "Maybe he's not so sure about me and wants to buy time." So she would naturally react by saying, "No! I'm not going to wait and risk having fertility problems; if you're not ready to commit, then maybe we should just forget about the whole thing." Similarly, in discussing where to live, he would say, "Why don't we stay in the city as long as we can — it's so convenient; besides, the suburbs are like death to me!" which she would interpret as "Maybe he's not ready to settle down with one woman," and react by saying, "Well, if you don't really want a family life, you'd better say this now, because I really want to have children and a house and a dog — that's how I grew up and that's what I want!"

It was in working with him on his nonsexual ambivalence — his desire to be *with* and *without* a woman in his mother's image — that I was able to get this patient to see that in his communications with his girlfriend he was unwittingly training her to become his mother, and that it was the successful result of that training program that caused his impotence. When he realized this, the patient was able to stop seeing his mother everywhere, and to start seeing his girlfriend for who she was — including the exciting and arousing young woman she was in bed when he first met her.

In the fourth chapter, I described impotence as the quintessential metaphor of the conflict of masculine insecurity. "I must do my work — but I'm tired of being on top" is what the afflicted man unconsciously communicates through his symptom. But to be sure, for many men impotence is not only a metaphor but also a painfully concrete problem. What to do about it short of getting into therapy? Once again, find the nonsexual equivalent. One technique, which was popularized in several variations by sex therapists and which I've used with my own patients, actually starts with the sexual, or the physical, though it usually doesn't stay there. Without getting into the actual technique — it's available in many books about sexual awareness — the basic idea is to start with exercises of physical touching which are specifically nonsexual while at the same time completely forbidding intercourse, and very gradually moving into exercises involving more sexual touching. Eventually this culminates in intercourse, first with the woman on top, guiding the penis into her.

Many times when couples go through these exercises, some unexpected things happen. First, already at the beginning phase of the exercises, the man almost immediately regains his erection. There are two reasons for this, both of which are nonsexual: (1) there is no pressure to perform, and (2) because the negative side of the man's ambivalence, that is, his fear of losing himself in a woman, is taken care of by the prohibition of intercourse, he can allow himself to experience the positive side of the conflict — his wish of losing himself in a woman. Now if in discussing these exercises the therapist departs from their narrow physical path, he can almost always find the nonsexual equivalents. In terms of performance, impotence is often triggered by mounting performance pressures at work. The actor who gets a bad review, the lawyer who loses an important case, the doctor who loses patients, and the sales rep who loses an account are prime possible examples. And with regard to ambivalence, as we saw in the cases above, the man often feels dependent on or engulfed by the woman, and he struggles to separate from her — all of which can be real or in his head, as a displacement from a previous important relationship.

The second interesting thing happens not infrequently at the end of a successful series of exercises, when the man is erectly prepared for intercourse: the woman gets the proverbial headache. Inexplicably, the woman loses interest in sex. Or she might be otherwise preoccupied or she might unconsciously undermine the prospects for intercourse. When this happens, it confirms that even in this very individual male domain the invisible hand of a woman is at play — as an Arabic proverb goes, you can't clap with one hand.

While some of this can be resolved only in therapy, these two essentially nonsexual issues — performance anxiety and ambivalence — have important practical implications for a couple dealing with erection problems. For example, discussing and genuinely reassuring a man about his performance at work, or about his value as a man regardless of his performance at work, can do more in the bedroom than would discussing his sexual problem. Second — and this is especially true when the problem is more than transitory — the woman will be wise to explore whether she herself is ambivalent about sex. Possibly, she herself has a "feminine insecurity" conflict which plays itself out by avoiding sex when the man is actually ready for it. For instance, she may want to be married to a powerful, successful provider so that she can feel secure, but at the same time may wish that he defer to her about all family and household matters. This may work in their daily living if the husband is interested in the same arrangement. But in the naked reality of the bedroom, they may not be able to define or divide such areas of influence — physically speaking, the male body is likely to be bigger, stronger, and harder. So to the extent that the wife wants the man to be both strong and weak, impotence might be the outcome, as it allows her to feel both sides of the conflict — her desire for male strength *and* her wish to be on top of male weakness.

In other words, when your man has erection problems, the best thing you can do for him is to explore whether in some sense his impotence is just fine with you. Paradoxically, getting to that place may lift the pressure from him and may even facilitate a spontaneous recovery of erection. Ultimately, however, especially with a long-lasting erection problem, both of you will need to work on integrating the nonsexual aspects of the masculine-feminine split.

The other common sexual male problem which could be looked at through the prism of masculine insecurity is rapid or premature ejaculation. Many men learn to become rapid ejaculators rather early in their sexual development. "Among adolescent boys, for example," writes sex therapist Barry McCarthy, "masturbation is a secretive, hidden activity, haunted by guilt and the fear of discovery. For this reason, most young boys try to reach orgasm as quickly as possible. In the so-called circle jerk, when a group of adolescent boys masturbate in unison, the winner in terms of being most masculine is the one who ejaculates the fastest and farthest." As further pointed out by McCarthy, this "push towards rapid performance" often carries over to the first intercourse experience, which is likely to be hurried, unplanned, or under pressures of time and privacy. Yet rather than being merely circumstantial, this push is propelled by the young man's desire to prove himself sexually, a desire which often enough overshadows the need to have a pleasurable, let alone an emotionally meaningful, sexual experience.

Now since having sex doesn't really prove anything, most men feel they must continue to prove themselves, over and over again. And ironically, the greater the push to perform, the more rapid the ejaculation, and the more bitter the sense of failure. Psychologically, it's as if the rapid ejaculator views orgasm as a shortcut to masculinity — "Why waste time being a boy," his unconscious says as he becomes aroused. Which is what the nonsexual equivalents of rapid ejaculation are all about. In fact, as we seem to live in a culture of premature ejaculation — at worst one of instant gratification and at best one where, in search of some ultimate future outcome, we sacrifice the pleasures of the present time — it's easy to see what these equivalents are. Perhaps the best analogy to rapid ejaculation is the unsuccessful entrepreneur who dreams up pie-in-the-sky business ideas which never fail to fail — always just as they are about to materialize. Or maybe it's the young, just-out-of-school MBA or lawyer with the starting salary of $150,000 — after all, like the premature ejaculator, they actually get somewhere. Or maybe it's the teenage computer nerd catapulted into wealth and fame by the combined speed of the information revolution and the stock market. Although in reality these examples are the statistical exceptions in our society, they still illuminate all of men's desire to circumvent and shortcut the process of developing from boy to man. Indeed, the everyday language of men is full of expressions which equate the quick attainment of an outcome with masculinity: "scoring," "hitting a home run," "making it," "the bottom line," "the finish line," "the big one," "the pinnacle"... and on and on.

Given this, it's hardly surprising that many men struggle to prolong intercourse, and that they do so in a typical male, "bottom-line" way. Whether out of consideration for their partner or because they view intercourse itself as the pinnacle of sexual pleasure, they try to slow down their arousal by focusing their thoughts on such unpleasant ideas as taxes, the in-laws, or the boss. One patient, a physician, said he had tried to reduce the intensity of stimulation before orgasm by fantasizing about one of his patients — an obese man who during examination would pick his nose and then put his finger in his mouth. These techniques, like biting one's tongue or pinching oneself, can get the job done, but at an obvious cost. Fortunately, as sex therapists will tell you, there's a better technique which in a sense is the opposite, because it involves focusing on pleasure rather than on pain. This technique is based on the fact that we can keep our mind fully occupied on only one thing at a time. Rather than occupying his mind with something unpleasant or even unrelated, in order to prolong intercourse all the man needs to do is focus his mind on the sensations of intercourse. The more he does that, the less immediate the need for orgasm. As McCarthy puts it, "The difference in approach is roughly that between a sprinter straining to reach the finish line and a person strolling at a leisurely pace through a lovely, enthralling countryside and using all his senses to take in as much of the experience as he can."

As evidenced by this analogy, the sexual technique for the treatment of premature ejaculation — the details of which I will once again skip — can easily be applied to nonsexual techniques in living. Slowing life down, enjoying the process, the moment, the journey, the view, the children, the shower, the sun, all this as opposed to subjugating all present-time experiences to the purpose of getting somewhere, is a nonsexual way of prolonging intercourse, and also of enjoying it more. And since women are often less inclined to view life as a race, they can play an important role in demonstrating to their man that the only finish line in life is death. Or, as put by the famous "woman" Peter Lynch — the celebrated Magellan money manager — when explaining his early retirement in an interview, "I never heard of anybody on their deathbed saying they wished they'd spent more time at the office." But in trying to influence their man to appreciate the moment, women must never be demanding. So instead of asking for more time with your husband, you're better off demonstrating to him — in action, not in words — the "value" of free or intimate time, by enjoying it yourself, with or without him.

Now if we consider that there aren't really any shortcuts to masculinity, we can see that much like the impotent man, the premature ejaculator is someone who's reluctant to perform as a man. So on behalf of all their brethren, whether they want to remain boys or even to be girls, men with sexual dysfunctions unconsciously say, "We're tired of being on top." As we saw in the fourth chapter, the idea that men struggle to accept their feminine desires raises the question as to the relationship between masculine insecurity and homosexuality. For example, many men have erotic dreams in which they are shocked to discover, as clothes are taken off, that the woman they're with has a penis. Does this kind of dream signal an unconscious homosexual desire or rather a feminine identification, a wish for being taken care of, passively or receptively? Well, depending on the individual, it might mean either or both. Certainly, some men in therapy — men in my own practice included — uncover their own suppressed or repressed homosexuality and assume an active gay lifestyle. But others employ homosexual fantasies as a way of escaping what they perceive to be the pressures of masculinity. Though there appears to be some connection between gender identification and homosexuality, ultimately no one knows much about the nature of such a relationship. For one thing, both gay and straight men can be more or less female-identified. Nevertheless, gay psychoanalyst Richard Isay draws an important distinction between "defensive" and genuine homosexuality.[21]

My own understanding of this distinction can be best illustrated by the case of a patient who was straight but who had a dream in which he was having anal sex with a younger man. The patient came to treatment because of doubts about his relationship with his fiancée as well as his heavy drinking. As the wedding date drew nearer, he said, he was beginning to lose his sexual attraction to his fiancée. Given this, the dream — which he had early on in the therapy — could have been interpreted as a signal that the problem was that he was with the wrong sexual partner. In my experience, such an interpretation could have easily been supported by the fact that the patient was drinking — before coming out, some gay men try to suppress their sexual orientation with a haze of alcohol and/or marijuana.

However, the specifics of this case pointed to a different interpretation. First, the dream was an obvious reaction to a particular situation. That day the patient had told his fiancée that he planned to go out that Saturday night with a male friend he hadn't seen for a while. The fiancée took offense, saying he didn't spend enough time with her as it was. The patient felt smothered and angry, and they had a fight. Viewed in that light, one can interpret the dream as an angry message of liberation from the patient to his fiancée, something along the lines of: "Not only will I go out with my friend, but if I want to, I'll even have sex with him." Alternatively, the dream could be interpreted to mean that under the demand for more intimacy with a woman, the patient felt the need to get closer to a man — basically, in order to reaffirm his masculinity. Interestingly, when you consider the patient's family constellation, both interpretations seem relevant. First, the patient was always angry with his mother for being overprotective and smothering. But second, he was chronically hungry for a masculine association with his father, who was an absentminded, self-absorbed scientist, as well as with his younger brother (the younger man in the dream?), who was an ambitious law student completely consumed by his own career.

In addition to all this, other, perhaps more obvious circumstances mitigated against a genuine gay interpretation of the dream. Not only did the patient deny ever being attracted to men, but he also recalled no sexual pleasure in the dream. And significantly, he was not particularly resistant to exploring his potential homosexuality — in discussing the dream he was neither frightened nor defensive. In fact, one of his closest friends was gay, and they had openly discussed the fact that the patient was neither tempted nor threatened by their relationship. So for this patient, being on top of a man was not a *homo*sexual thing. In a strange way, rather, it was the ultimate *hetero*sexual expression: proof that he could be on top of a woman — his fiancée. If you can wrestle with men and come out on top, many a man would concur, surely you need not be afraid of a woman.[22]

Self-Involvement: From Peanuts to Penis

It's been said that 90 percent of men masturbate and that the 10 percent who don't, lie. I don't know what the statistics are for male versus female masturbation, but anecdotally, even if they don't really do it more, men certainly talk about it more — at least in therapy. And it's hard to think of a better sexual illustration of men's self-involvement than their obsession with this autoerotic practice. While most men will not discuss this with others beyond adolescence, in therapy, where they are less fearful of being judged, it is often the topic of the day.

Now even though it doesn't stop them from doing it, many men feel guilt and shame about masturbating. They may feel so because of their perception that unless you "get to home base" you're immature and because of the "forbidden" content of their sexual fantasies. But they also feel guilt or shame about it, because it is what it is — an unrelated, self-involved, sexual activity. Now lest you think I'm saying men *should* feel bad about masturbating, let's remember what I said in the fifth chapter, that is, that up to a certain point, self-involvement is not only a good, but also a necessary thing. Certainly, whether on your own or in lovemaking, it's good to try to have your sexual needs met. And women, it seems, can still learn more about this from men.

Over the years, several women in my practice have discussed their wish to "explore," "try," or "practice" masturbation. This, after the sexual revolution educated all of us that women are just as sexual as men — which they are even if they experience it differently. The thing is, I've never met a man who needed to learn how to masturbate, which I suppose could be attributed to the simple — some say primitive — nature of male anatomy, as well as to the historical cultures promoting and reinforcing male self-involvement. Women's history, by contrast, at least until very recently, has not been about self-exploration, but rather about playing a behind-the-scenes, supportive, facilitative, or manipulative role, always *in relation* to the more frontal, center-stage role of men.

While self-gratification, sexual or otherwise, is at the core of narcissism, the interpersonal impact of narcissism stems from its defensive nature — the overcompensating desire to gratify oneself by impressing others. When I first asked my wife out — I was twenty-eight at the time — I naturally felt nervous, and like many men thought I needed to impress her. So as soon as I asked her what she wanted to do on the date, and before she had a chance to answer, this is what came out of my mouth: "You know, they say breakfast is for friendship, lunch is for business, and dinner is for sex — which would you like?" Not skipping a beat, my then prospective date answered, "How about an afternoon snack?"

Well, in addition to my more or less conscious need to cover up my insecurity by impressing her with my bold, if questionable witticism, in retrospect it seemed that another, less conscious dynamic was at play. By hinting at the possibility of romance as one of the options, I was signaling my intention regarding a sexual conquest and checking out the response. The response, by the way, was perfect because it indicated a potential without a guarantee — a winning combination when it comes to dating the self-involved man. In general, the more narcissistic her dating or relationship partner is, the more a woman should be like that T-shirt which proclaims, "I'm not *playing* hard to get."

So even when they step away from the autoerotic and extend their sexuality to include others, men still hold on to their self-involvement. In dating, they do so by appreciating the challenge of an independent woman — one who will not scare them with open emotionality and who will present them with a winnable challenge. Winnable so that they don't feel like a failure, and a challenge so that they don't devalue the laurels of their conquest.

Unfortunately, even after a successful conquest, many men do not shed their sexual self-involvement. This was all too evident in the old days — which in many quarters are only as old as yesterday — when women were not supposed to actually enjoy sex, and men needed to concern themselves only with their own gratification. But it's also omnipresent in the new days in the form of the anti-narcissist who works hard on refining his sexual technique so that he can bring his partner to multiple orgasms or other uncharted sexual peaks. While this man's partner is likely to enjoy the sex, she may ultimately find it emotionally empty, because his sexual giving is motivated by the self-involved purpose of perfecting his own performance in order to feel good about himself as a man. Of course, there's nothing wrong with feeling good about oneself as a man, and as long as it's not the only or primary goal of the sexual exchange, the woman might be happy to facilitate such feelings.

The trouble is that unconsciously men do not necessarily expect women to facilitate such feelings. If anything, as I explained before, their early relationship with the all-important first woman in their lives reinforces not feelings of manhood but rather the opposite kinds of feelings, those of being more like a girl. Because of that, men sometimes feel that they must preemptively impose and expose their masculinity upon women. In my practice, I've found that many self-involved men have a history of physically exposing themselves as children. In reconstructing their history, it seems that in early childhood — say from age four to eight — these patients tried to regulate their self-esteem by showing off their penises to other children. Often, these patients were insecure about their gender identity because their narcissistic mothers had treated them as a girl, or more accurately, as a pretty, gentle, and idealized extension of themselves.

In most cases, this type of early exhibitionism simply fades away with childhood. But it often leaves behind a variety of nonsexual traces: the need to be admired, a focus on body building, an enjoyment of skinny-dipping, a desire to exhibit wealth, or a wish to expose oneself creatively as in the writing of one's memoir or in the painting of self-portraits. One of my patients was an extremely talented, African-American film student. Well dressed, stylish, and gentle, he made a short, autobiographical film about growing up with an abusive older brother in Harlem. As I sometimes do with artist patients, I suggested that he bring me the script. I told him I would treat it as a dream — I would analyze it as his mental creation. But instead of bringing the script, the patient brought me a video copy of the movie, which I then watched at home. It was an amazingly powerful movie — visually and emotionally — which immediately made me feel excited, not just for the patient, but also for myself. I felt impressed and proud that he was my patient and I wanted to celebrate his talent, so much so that in discussing the content of the film with him, it was hard to distinguish between objective analysis and subjective praise.

I first rationalized this by thinking that it was good to recognize and celebrate a patient's talent — which I still think is true. But then, when the patient continued to want to show me various aspects of his work, I began to feel uncomfortable about it. It seemed I was no longer with a patient whose job it was to help me get to know him, but rather with a celebrity whose job was to be seen and admired. And it somehow paralleled his sexual fantasies, most of which consisted of a nurse-type figure finding him naked in her bed and "discovering" and admiring his body.

But I didn't fully grasp what was happening until the patient, who also drew and photographed, offered to bring in some of his drawings, "a series of erotic self-portraits." Clearly, the patient was "seducing" me, essentially so that I would serve as a celebratory mirror of his masculinity. Though I was tempted to see these drawings — he was very talented — I resisted because I felt there would be something pornographic about the exchange. And it was in the next session that the patient — who, by the way, was neither gay nor bisexual — told me that as a teenager he used to masturbate on the windowsill in full view of the next-door neighbor, an older, "mother-type" woman, who unlike me did not decline to watch.

It may be of limited use to generalize from this symbolic narcissistic seduction of the therapist — where no sexual arousal took place — to real physical relationships. Nonetheless, the dynamics are similar. In pursuing a woman, the narcissistic man is not interested in who the other person is, but rather in whether she can credibly celebrate him. Ironically, then, the gender or sexual preference of the therapist in this case is irrelevant. Similarly, both the personality of the woman who is seduced by the self-involved man and even her physical attributes are irrelevant. Yet a woman may not realize this until late in the game because she may be very excited about celebrating the man's unusual mind, talent, body, creativity, or whatever. She may also confuse his openness with generosity, interpreting his vibrant sexual presence as a giving of himself rather than seeing it for what it is — a showing of himself so that he can be admired.

This physical narcissistic generosity is probably more feminine than masculine — as women in our society are more encouraged to focus on and show their bodies. But these days, more and more men share with women this form of self-involvement. Now regardless of gender, the awful truth is that narcissistic people — unless they are extremely unattractive, and perhaps even if they are — are often unusually compelling. Sexually, this can be so because (1) they spend more time on building or beautifying their bodies, (2) they exude self-confidence, which makes them seem more desirable, and/or (3) they were attractive children who therefore received special attention, which taught them how to use their looks to get more. For these reasons, when I find myself sexually aroused in a session — once again I must admit to being human — it's not unusual for me to conclude that I'm in the company of a narcissist. So perhaps we should all question our attractions, especially if we find ourselves in the midst of an intensely physical seduction. When sexuality and sensuality are idealized, we may very well be in the presence of someone needing to be admired — for their gender — rather than loved for their person.

Statistically speaking, I suspect most men never literally expose themselves. But as we saw in the fifth chapter, they do it in a multitude of nonsexual ways. I once had a dream that my children called me up in the office, while I was in a session, to ask if they could have peanuts for lunch. My initial association to the dream was an obvious one: the day before, my wife had told me that our babysitter had paged her in the middle of a session to ask if the kids could have a peanut butter and jelly sandwich for lunch. In mentioning it to me, my wife described how she was talking about it with the babysitter on the phone while remaining appropriately elusive so as not to force upon the patient knowledge about the therapist which the patient may have preferred not to know. In light of that association, the interesting thing about my dream was that in it, unlike my wife, I didn't protect my patient from my life. "Peanuts? For lunch? Yes," I told my kids on the phone, right in front of my patient, who was amused but also irritated that I had answered the phone. There was nothing else to the dream, but I later had a second association which clinched my understanding of it. A couple of days earlier I had gone over to a neighbor's to borrow some peanut butter to make my kids a sandwich, and while I was waiting in the living room, my eyes were drawn to a book about sex which was lying on the coffee table. When I remembered that, I could no longer resist the cliché that "peanuts" sounded awfully much like "penis." In short, in this dream I was exposing to my patient evidence of my masculinity — my children, and of course, my "peanuts."

This brings to mind one of my patients, a man who was obsessed with what he felt was his peanut-size penis. The patient — a young, aggressive businessman — received complimentary tickets from a client to a World Series game and invited his relatively new girlfriend to join him. But the girlfriend declined, saying she wasn't into baseball. The patient didn't say anything to her, but he told me that he was disappointed and angry with her. And that night he had a dream in which his penis was hanging out of his pants and a woman was touching it. "She wasn't impressed." He frowned as he was relating the dream to me. This little dream shows (1) that what looks like generosity may actually be an attempt to regulate one's self-esteem and (2) that this attempt can easily be sexualized. Or as I put it to the patient: "So in offering her a ticket you didn't really want to give her something — you wanted her to be impressed with your big dick!" The patient agreed and went on to say how his entire business success was an attempt to compensate for his small penis. "Yeah yeah," I said, "I heard enough about your small penis — I wish mine made so much money for me!" The truth was that even I couldn't agree with this simplistic, stereotypical, and masculine view of success. My own simplistic view of success, at least for this patient, was that he forever and in vain strove to impress his demanding, critical mother. In fact, in the week before the dream, his mother had come for her first visit to his new Manhattan apartment — a penthouse condominium with a wraparound view — and all she said about it was, "The kitchen is so small!"

Another patient, a gay man in his late twenties, avoided sex almost completely because he couldn't find a man who would meet his physical standards for sexual attractiveness. Amusingly, in one of our sessions together he reported the following dream: "I had sex with Danny DeVito, which as I'm sure you can imagine, was not the most pleasant experience. He had hair on his back and also a zit on his chest. I didn't want him to fuck me. He kept trying to grab my hair as if trying to remove it. I then told him I knew Marlon Brando — I guess I was kind of name dropping." As you may have guessed, this patient had some reservations about his own imperfect body. Specifically, he didn't like the fact that he had body hair, although as he himself acknowledged, he wasn't very hairy. And as you also may have guessed, he couldn't feel sexually attracted to men with body hair or other skin imperfections. When he did attempt to go out with such men — because he liked their personality — he became painfully and acutely aware of their and therefore his own, self-perceived, unattractiveness. In truth, he was rather handsome and in fact many gay men found him attractive. But like most people's, his body wasn't perfect. Now rather than accepting this fact, he was intent on coping with it by looking for a lover who would offer him an improved and idealized version of himself.

In the words of the dream, this patient was trying to turn

Danny DeVito, the devalued image of himself, into Marlon Brando, the idealized lover. But as I told him, much like name dropping, having sex with beautiful men — or not having sex at all until he met a Marlon Brando — wasn't going to do the trick. If anything, it was only going to make him feel worse about his body, because the more you compare yourself to a Brando, the more you end up looking like a DeVito. Now if you think that the dynamics of this patient are exclusively gay — because you can only look for an improved version of your own body in a same-sex partner — think again. As we saw above, for the self-involved man the reality of the other person is basically irrelevant. Magically, a woman's beautiful breasts can instantly enlarge a man's penis — and we're not talking erection here.

Aggression: The War Against Seminal Extraction

As exemplified by the exhibitionist's hope for a shocked reaction in the females to whom he exposes himself, waving one's "peanuts" is not only a narcissistic but also an aggressive act. I already discussed in the sixth chapter why men sexualize their aggression. But here's a quick reminder in the form of a patient's dream, as related by the patient to his wife in a marital therapy session: "I was abducted by a space ship, and it was a classic alien-abduction scenario, except that as part of the brainwashing, the alien extracted my semen. The only other unusual thing was that at the end of the dream it turned out that the alien was you!"

Paradoxically, many "educated," refined men find it hard to see that their sexual interest in women has an aggressive, even hostile component. By way of denying it, they prefer to talk about "lovemaking" rather than "fucking" or "doing her." One patient, a lawyer, went through a series of girlfriends whom he considered to be "your basic, uninspiring but attractive bimbos." When I tried to point out to him his hostility toward women, the patient countered with, "Well, Dr. Gratch, we can hardly consider this a premeditated act of hostility. Perhaps you mean a negligent disregard or some such transgression, but surely not intentional hostility." Well, no, I did mean intentional — if unconscious — hostility. Intentional, because at least in the male mind, this hostility is part of a defense strategy to ward off those dangerous, semen-extracting aliens.

An example of this sexual dynamic comes from a female patient whose husband was laid off shortly after their wedding. A few weeks after he lost his job, the two of them went out to dinner with another couple. During dinner, the wife casually mentioned that her husband was laid off, and when they got the check she made some reference to their need to watch their budget. When they came home at the end of the evening, the husband — whom the patient described to me as a loving, gentle man — expressed to her feelings of shame over his job situation. "I feel bad that we need to watch every penny like this, and that I can't be a better provider," he said. The patient reassured him that he would be back on his feet soon and that everything would be all right.

But what the husband didn't say — because he didn't really know it — was that he was furious with her because as he experienced it, she emasculated and humiliated him in front of their friends. This only occurred to him in a subsequent conversation — actually a bad fight — which the two of them had when trying to deal with what happened between them in bed the next morning. That morning they started making love as they often did on Sunday mornings. But then, in the middle of foreplay, the husband jumped up with excitement, and sat on top of the patient. "Our sex life is a bit boring these days, how about experimenting?" he proposed. The patient smiled at that, which the husband took as an agreement. He then pinned her down, thrust his penis into her mouth, and ordered her to "Swallow it!" As this was not at all her thing, the patient was quite upset.

As we saw in the sixth chapter, when we're not in touch with our aggression, it gets in touch with us. And it can reach us in rather unexpected places. One couple, both hospital workers in their early twenties, came to see me sometime after their engagement but before their wedding. As is often the case, it was the woman's initiative to seek counseling. But her reason for doing so was less typical. Glancing apologetically at her fiancée, this is what she said: "I hope you don't mind me being blunt, Doctor. Mike and I have a very good relationship, and we really love each other. And I know he's going to be a wonderful husband. Even my girlfriends say it. You couldn't ask for someone more supportive, sensitive, or caring. And he's even great with children, like, he really knows how to play with my nieces and nephews. He'll be a great father. And we can also talk about everything. There's only one problem — Mike is not really interested in sex — and he can't tell me why. We had sex a few times, and there's nothing wrong with him, if you know what I mean. But then it kind of petered out. He always has some reason — he's stressed, he's tired, he's worried, but I think he kind of lost interest in it. And it's not like I think there's someone else or anything, and I know he loves me. And it's not as if sex is the most important thing. But I'm worried about it — we're not even married. And I don't think Mike would tell you a different story, would you, honey?"

Not only did Mike not tell a different story, but also his lovely, soft-spoken manner and his quiet intelligence confirmed that he was an unusually kind, committed, and giving man. He vowed he loved his fiancée and he insisted he was very much attracted to her. And he acknowledged that he was resisting sex. "But I don't really know why," he said, looking at me with big, sad, perplexed eyes. While he couldn't articulate his feelings on the matter, he showed none of the guarded aggressiveness many men bring to their first therapy session.

Now even though all three of us agreed to explore the problem in marital therapy, after a couple of such sessions we were at a dead end — I had no more clue than his fiancée as to what was going on with Mike. So I suggested terminating the couple therapy and offered to see Mike individually. This was the right move, because as it turned out, Mike did have a different story to tell after all. Basically, he explained when we met alone, he had a sexual problem, which was that he could only get aroused when fantasizing about raping or wrestling with women. He hated himself for these fantasies, he said movingly, and while he felt it was somewhat acceptable to masturbate to them, he wouldn't "use" them to get aroused while having sex with a woman he loved. So that's why he was avoiding sex with his fiancée.

This symptom was the only problem Mike had ever had with his fiancée or with any other woman. He was always the model boyfriend, showing none of the anger, hypercriticalness, defiance, or insensitivity imposed to some degree or another by most men on their partners. It followed, then, that the therapeutic goal for Mike was to integrate his repressed or "split off" rage with women into his emotional dialogue with them, so that eventually, it could be desexualized.

This case of sexual hostility may seem rather extreme, and in fact it arose out of a childhood history of severe emotional and physical abuse. But let's not forget that this patient knew the difference between fantasy and reality and that for various reasons he was not at risk for acting on his fantasies. And furthermore, let's remember that the interpersonal meaning of his fantasies — the idea of sexual domination — is rather universal. When I started my own analysis, I had a dream in which my analyst, a woman, was conducting the session while lying on the couch with me. Wisely, my analyst's interpretation of the dream was that I wanted not to make love to her, but rather to fuck her, meaning, to equalize us or bring her down to my level — I was a beginner at the time. Along these lines, I once made an embarrassing slip with a patient who previously referred to his penis as a truck — I recalled and referred to it in the next session as a tank! In my defense, as illustrated by the dream and the slip, in my case this stuff is mostly unconscious. After all, you may remember, I was the sensitive youngest child in my family, with the two aggressive older brothers!

Many of my patients express the feeling that while they can be directly aggressive or angry with other men, they are afraid to do so with women, either because they view women as fragile or because they view them as all too powerful. In the former case, they are reluctant to hurt a woman's feelings, and in the latter case, they fear that unlike the directly aggressive response of a man, the wounded woman will retaliate insidiously through some sort of invisible manipulation. But in either case, men who find it difficult to be directly aggressive with their partner are likely to displace it onto the disguised arena of sex.[23] A simple example: a patient was angry with his girlfriend because she was preoccupied for months preparing for a professional examination. But having grown up constantly fighting with an emotionally overreactive, domineering mother, the patient was reluctant to express his anger to his girlfriend. So he was supportive and understanding throughout that whole period. But after the exam, when they went out to a celebratory dinner, he found himself busily checking out other women in the restaurant and feeling more attracted to them than to his girlfriend.

As we can see from this example, like it or not, men do end up communicating their aggression to women. But when they do it through sex, it's generally hidden from view — their partner's as well as their own. Or at least that's what they'd like to believe. Nowhere is this strange form of communication more evident than in men's sexual fantasies. The sexual fantasy is private in that it's inside your head but public because it involves other people. It's also public because as we already saw, it always has nonsexual, external equivalents in the real world.

A not uncommon male fantasy: "I'm in some kind of a palatial estate with beautiful grounds and gorgeous women. There's a pool, a wet bar, Jacuzzi, food — anything you want. And I'm with two knock-dead women. One is sucking me, the other one I do in the ass. Nasty stuff." Among other things, such a fantasy demonstrates the evolution of self-involvement into aggression, moving from a defensive self-aggrandizement to the domination of women. In relating this kind of a fantasy, one of my patients, a conservative MBA type, described it as "your basic heterosexual stuff." The patient was less sure as to whether his other favorite fantasy — that of ejaculating on his partner's face — was also basic stuff. He felt guilty about that fantasy, he said, especially because when he was with a woman, he would often "sneak up on her" and try to come on her face. "As I'm about to come, I literally hold my dick like a gun and aim at her face," he explained. "So am I some kind of a sick fuck or what?" he then asked me.

Whatever he was, the fantasy of penis-to-face domination is hardly rare. In the case of this patient, though, it had an interesting origin. When he was growing up, his mother would walk naked in the house. She also had an extramarital affair, or at least the patient thought so. Finally, as a child, the patient discovered in his mother's closet a stash of porno tapes and dildos. In short, her sexuality was in his face — which he apparently was trying to reverse in his sexual relationships with other women. This kind of reversal illustrates what psychiatrist Robert Stoller describes as the perverse element of male sexuality — the turning of trauma into triumph. In actual perversions, as well as in nonperverse sexual hostility, Stoller says, the trauma has to do with the difficulty for the young boy of forming a gender identity different from his mother's. The triumph, he says, is in finding orgasmic pleasure and revenge in that very difference.

This particular patient, a good-looking man in his late thirties, was constantly dating with the presumed goal of meeting the right woman for the purpose of marriage. He was tall, blond, and outgoing, and most women responded to him favorably. But strangely, after a couple of dates he would lose all interest. In trying to understand why, I first speculated with him that as he was getting to know these women, the prospect of being dominated by a motherlike creature turned him off. This seemed reasonable enough but was of no help. Then, after about a year and a half of such speculations, the patient revealed to me that he actually did have a girlfriend, or at least "a kind of girlfriend." "You do?" I responded in disbelief. "Yes," he answered, and went on to explain: "I've been seeing this girl for more than a year now. She's really nice, and we have a real good time together. But I basically know I'm not gonna marry her, so I keep thinking I should break up with her. Except that I don't, which I know is not fair because as far as she's concerned, I mean, she would love to marry me."

"Why didn't you tell me about her?" I was perplexed. "I told no one about her," he smiled. "I guess I feel ashamed about the relationship. I'm not sure why, but the fact is no one knows about her. She hasn't met any of my friends, and I don't even answer the phone when she's in my apartment."

"I guess like your mother," I offered, "you're having a secret affair." "I guess so," he said. "But this woman is not at all like my mother," he observed. "That makes sense," I said," because in this relationship *you* are like your mother — *you're* the one who's on top." Then, as if to confirm this in the sexual realm, the patient revealed that the reason he was ashamed of the relationship had something to do with the fact that his girlfriend was indeed the physical opposite of his mother. While the mother was a large, matronly woman with "huge, protruding breasts," the girlfriend was short-haired, petite, and flat-chested. "Sometimes I think she looks like a boy," he said, "which makes me wonder if I have a problem or something."

So in addition to illustrating the reversal of trauma into triumph, this case shows that even if a woman is not bothered by a man's sexual aggression — this patient's secret lover didn't object to being squirted by him — she cannot avoid being targeted by its nonsexual equivalents. In this case, the girlfriend had repeatedly tried to break up the relationship, but would always recontact the patient and resubmit to his terms. So if this woman was my patient, while I would not necessarily be impressed if she told me that her boyfriend liked to squirt her with his gun, I'd be on the lookout for other, nonsexual ways in which she'd let him shoot her. And of course, I would analyze her interpersonal masochism or whatever it was that drew her to this kind of relationship.

As we've seen, much of men's sexual aggression is an attempt to reverse their early balance of power with their mother. But it's not all about mother — men are perfectly capable of becoming sexually aggressive when threatened by a sense of powerlessness not associated with their mother. An example comes from a patient who is a physician. "Yesterday when I came home from moonlighting in the ER I had this sexual fantasy that I sometimes use when I masturbate — it's about a beautiful young woman who's begging me to have sex with her. But something weird and disturbing happened. As I was about to ejaculate, the head of this elderly woman — a patient of mine who died in the ER that night — popped into my mind and replaced the head of the woman in the fantasy. Granted, I was a little tired after working all night, but still, it kind of freaked me out."

When I asked the patient about the elderly woman, it turned out that she was an Alzheimer's patient in her eighties whom he had approached for an examination minutes before she died. "Go away," she rudely dismissed him. "I need to examine you, please," he almost begged. "Go away!" she repeated in her delirium. He went away and later that night found out she had died. As a doctor, the patient knew that her death was unavoidable and, in fact, unrelated to his failure to examine her. But as a man, he felt powerless in the face of death. Also as a man, he felt emasculated by a woman who wouldn't let him perform his job even when he begged. So in his fantasy, he reversed all that by assuming the extraordinary powers of (1) bringing her back to life, and (2) having *her* beg *him* to perform. He thus turned the anguish of defeat into the pleasure of orgasm.

At the extreme end of the continuum of male sexual aggression lies sexual sadism. While technically outside the scope of this book, sadism does overlap with aggression and is likewise present in everyday life. The high frequency of fantasies and/or actual role playing of bondage is an obvious example, as is the most benign of sexual teasing during foreplay. Underlying these are clearly the pleasures of control, power, and domination, all of which, we have seen, play a role in the battle between the sexes, in and out of the bedroom. Perhaps a scary word, sadism is nevertheless a useful one here, especially when it couples with its opposite — masochism. For women, this is important because it's this coupling which results in such syndromes as "women who love too much," and "men who hate women and the women who love them." But as I've tried to show all along, neither gender has a monopoly on the psychological attributes associated with it, sadism and masochism included. In terms of men, as I've discussed before, Freud theorized that sadism is one of those male-related concepts which can turn into its "female" opposite, masochism. But whether we accept this theory or not, it's hard to argue that when men turn their aggression on themselves the result is at all enviable. Let's conclude by revisiting this issue in the language of sex.

Self-Destructiveness: Coming Outside

There's an old joke about an Israeli foreign minister. After seeing him having sex with his wife on their balcony, the joke goes, the foreign minister's neighbor asks him why he did it. Well, the foreign minister answers, I heard it was good for birth control to come outside. This joke, which probably has racist undertones — the foreign minister is a Moroccan Jew — alludes to the man's lack of formal education and his former career as a construction worker. But the truth is that when it comes to sex, men's stupidity knows no racial or educational bounds. Indeed, sexually speaking, all men are at risk for coming in the wrong place, or at the wrong time, or in the wrong person, or not at all — when they're supposed to. Nor is men's sexual stupidity limited by nationality or language. It's as evident in the Spanish of Don Juan of Andalusia, Spain — where a joke has it that when a man's lower head (a linguistic allusion to penis) is erect, he loses the one above — as it is in the Yiddish of Eastern European Jews, with its saying that "when the putz goes up, the brain gets buried in the ground."

But as we saw in the previous chapter, men's self-destructiveness is not simply a matter of idiocy. Like self-involvement and aggression, it's a direct outcome of the conflict of masculine insecurity. Sexually, this can be seen in a patient whose favorite sexual fantasy was that of entering a woman with his head — the one above — and swimming inside of her. In the case of that patient, whereas the wish of losing oneself in a woman was evident in his sexual fantasy, the fear of it was evident in his sexual reality: to prove his masculinity he was particularly fond of having sex in dangerous places — on his boss's desk, in an Empire State Building elevator, and once, barely three feet away from the actual drop of the Grand Canyon.

The same conflict can be seen from the opposite direction when a man retreats from what he perceives as a dangerous reality to the safety of sexual fantasy. For example, one patient, a lawyer in his late thirties, always aspired to work in the corporate area of mergers and acquisitions, although in some ways he was too sensitive a man to actively pursue such an aggressive path. Nonetheless, when he finally took the leap, he landed on a pretty powerful job — as a partner in a major firm. But already on the first day of the job he began to have fantasies of screwing up and of being fired. That night he dreamt that he was back at his childhood home, going to the bathroom but peeing on the floor, with "a hard, strong spray coming out like from a hose, making a mess and not cleaning up, while [his] mother was watching." Clearly, it felt safer to be bold and make a mess at home, where his mother would clean up after him, than to do it among the penis wavers of Manhattan's M & A lawyers.

To elaborate on this dynamic, consider the case of a thirty-four-year-old patient who for several years equivocated about how ambitious he wanted to be and how much risk he was willing to take in his career. Finally, as he was about to get married, the patient decided to "take the plunge." He made the difficult transition from being a financial adviser to becoming a portfolio manager at an investment house. The latter job was a high-risk, high-reward proposition where you live or die by your performance — in short, a dangerous place. But by combining his great analytical and people skills, and with the help of a soaring stock market, the patient's performance in the first year exceeded his wildest expectations. "Welcome to Wall Street," his boss told him as he handed him his first bonus, which was close to $500,000. The year before, the patient's entire salary had been $75,000. But paradoxically, this success didn't make the patient feel more secure. On the contrary, realizing what the stakes were only made him more nervous. So he continued to work hard, taking no vacations and no advantage of the corporate perks offered to him. And he did even better in the second year.

It was at that time that he went to Montreal to attend a professional conference on stock selection. Since he loved skiing and as he'd had no vacation in two years, he decided to leave New York a day early and go skiing before the conference started. But because of his insecurity he didn't tell his boss he was taking a day off, figuring the boss wouldn't know the difference. Then, once on the slopes, he called the office on his cell phone to check in with the boss, thinking the boss would assume he was calling from the conference. But the boss said, "Good thing you called, David. There's nothing happening here. Call back tomorrow when you're off the slopes."

That night, alone in his hotel room, the patient was quite anxious, even depressed. Fearful that he was going to be fired, he couldn't stop obsessing about the incident. So to escape the pain he went out for a walk in town, ending up in a local nude bar, where he had a backroom lap dance with one of the girls. The patient — who by now was married and whose wife was pregnant — didn't think that going to a nude bar or even dancing with a naked girl was such a big deal. After all he was fully clothed. But during the lap dance he orgasmed, and that freaked him out — he felt he had crossed the line. So now his escape backfired, as he was more tortured than before — imagining not only that he would lose the job, but also that he was infected with AIDS, and that his wife was going to leave him.

As it turned out, the patient's boss, body, and wife were more forgiving than he thought, and in the end he lost none of them. But I think it's fairly easy to see that this patient was unconsciously trying to sabotage himself, probably because he experienced his masculine achievements — at work and at home — as dangerous endeavors. In that light, then, sexual self-destructiveness can be seen as an escape from responsibility into an imaginary or momentary place of safety. Of course, when you cross the line — wherever that line is — the fantasy may become a reality, at which point it's not so safe anymore. One patient — a particularly kind, honest, and responsible man who was also married for just over a year — mentioned in a session that he was "checking out women in the street." This disturbed him because he had been married for such a short time and because he had a great relationship with his wife. "Why would I be looking at other women, when I finally found the woman of my dreams?" he asked me. "Well," I responded with what I thought was a rhetorical question, "why are you so worried about it? Do you think you might end up cheating on your wife?" "I wouldn't initiate anything like that," he surprised me with his answer, "but if one of these women came up to me and said 'You wanna take me for a drink or something,' I'd probably have sex with her — or at least I'm not sure I wouldn't." "I guess only time will tell," I summarized, "whether you're a Jimmy Carter or a Bill Clinton."

In Stanley Kubrick's film *Eyes Wide Shut,* the character played by Tom Cruise walks the fine sexual line between fantasy and reality. Prompted by a marital fight in which his wife reveals a sexual fantasy she had about another man, the Tom Cruise character undertakes a night of exploration in New York's sexual underworld. But every time he comes close to action, something dangerous happens. A naked woman he helps revive at a party ends up dead. A prostitute he almost sleeps with turns out to be HIV-positive. And when he manages to attend — as an uninvited observer — a secretive masked-ball orgy on a Long Island estate, his life is threatened. Yet in watching this movie, one doesn't get the sense that it's some kind of morality tale about the dangers of infidelity. Rather, it strikes you more as a statement about the relationship between sexuality and danger, which is hardly a surprise when you consider that the movie is based on an Arthur Schnitzler novel, written and set in Freud's Vienna.

Freud's ultimate view of human nature was that of a battle between forces of good and evil, the former being associated with Eros, the sexual life force which seeks to perpetuate and renew life, and the latter involving Thanatos, the "death instinct," which as we've seen could be interpreted as the desire to shrink from responsibility and to return to earlier, safer states of being. So it's not that sex itself is dangerous, but rather, that its life-propelling nature is constantly embattled by the darker, anti-life forces within us. Now let's be clear: as pointed out by many, there's absolutely no scientific evidence for the existence of the death instinct. On the other hand, there's plenty of historical and philosophical evidence. With all the religious, scientific, and technological progress made by civilized man, it seems there's never been a society or a time free of some form of self-destructiveness. We, and perhaps men more so than women, kill ourselves one way or another — by war, cars, alcohol, drugs, suicide, or industrial accidents.

But we need not be Freudian nor metaphysical to appreciate and understand the relationship between sex and danger, which is why Kubrick's movie works just as well in contemporary New York City as did the original story in Freud's Vienna. Some time after I moved my office to a respectable professional building on Manhattan's not-too-shabby Fifty-seventh street, I received a referral of a patient described to me as a TV executive with a marital problem. It turned out that while he was in fact a highly successful and well-liked TV executive, his problem wasn't strictly "marital." He was married all right, but his real problem was that he was addicted to cocaine, alcohol, and sex. This, unfortunately, is not such an unusual combination, and as I do with other such patients, I referred this man to long-term drug and alcohol rehab before exploring psychotherapy. But even though I saw him for only one session, this man will always remain in my mind — for two reasons. First, a couple of minutes into the session, after openly telling me about his problems, he informed me that there was a "confidential S & M referral service" in the penthouse office of my building. Second, shortly after coming out of rehab, he was found dead from a drug-induced heart attack.

I suppose both points were memorable because they brought the coupling of sex and danger closer to my habitat. But the patient's "tip" about the referral service upstairs also struck me, because it was an attempt to shock and challenge me out of my presumed role of the responsible, mature professional. Now this is not about S & M or sexual addiction any more than about sex itself. We all grow up with a sense that sex is a mysterious, forbidden pleasure, one which even adults do not seem comfortable with — after all, they don't talk about it openly in front of us children, and only allude to it in hushed tones or in guilt-laden jokes. It's in fact presented to us as a restricted, dangerous thing, or more accurately as a dangerous pleasure, or perhaps a pleasurable danger.

I think it's fair to generalize here that when men act out sexually, they in fact engage in an attempt to defeat danger with pleasure — the pleasure of orgasm. But they do so not only to prove their masculinity or to run away from it to the illusional safety of a woman's body. They also do it in a narcissistic defiance of their most profound limitation. Without doubt, man's ultimate limitation is his body. Yielding to the laws of science, it can never be perfect, and as we grow, it inevitably decays and dies. It is therefore the best — and the worst — place to try to defy our limits. And what can be a better bodily agent to carry out such defiance than the forget-all escape of sexual ecstasy?

This, in my mind, is the ultimate underlying dynamic of sexual addiction. Whether he's struggling to reverse and "rub off" an early trauma of sexual abuse or whether he's trying to escape from feelings of emptiness and meaninglessness, the sex addict is ultimately someone who's dedicated to the denial and mastery of physical vulnerability — by means of orgasmic conquest. Of course, the sad irony of this form of self-destructiveness is that if you live so close to the body, you are never too far from the ultimate truth of the very enslavement to the physical which you're desperately trying to deny.

It's precisely because the addict — the compulsive user of alcohol, drugs, food, money, or sex — is bent on controlling the uncontrollable, on beating unbeatable physical odds, that the first step in any successful 12-step program involves the renunciation of control. As we saw in the last chapter, this places the therapist as well as the family members or friends of the sexually self-destructive man in an impossible situation, because part of this man's destructiveness is directed toward them and is aiming to defeat their helpfulness. So if you're involved with a sex addict, you too must accept that you have no power over his compulsions.

And that the best thing you can do to help him is to examine your own reasons for being involved with him, your own reasons for being involved with someone who's committed to preserving his own illusion of physical invulnerability by means of destroying his and your shared, and very real, physicality.

Some people feel that the sexually addicted man is simply having fun at the expense of others, and that unlike the drug addict he is not truly self-destructive. While there are in fact important differences between substance abuse and sexual compulsions, this sentiment doesn't square with the fact that the sex addict often ends up risking, if not losing, everything that's dear to him. It also doesn't square with his torment of feeling enslaved by his sexual desires, and with the intense feelings of guilt, self-hate, and emptiness that never fail to flood his consciousness following the orgasmic relief.

Now while the masochism of severe sexual addictions is foreign to most men, as we've seen once and again throughout this book, the same cannot be said about the dynamics that underlie it, from the sexualization of danger to the defiance of physical limits. Similarly, sexual masochism or the erotic enjoyment of pain, just like sexual sadism, is to some extent an integral part of the basic physiology and psychology of sex. For example, sexual arousal, teasing, and the physical sensations when approaching the moment of ejaculatory inevitability all involve a loss of physical control, the intermingling of pleasure and pain, and the joyful subjugation of the mind to the body.

Sexual Acting-Out: The Paradox of Celibacy

As I think I've demonstrated in this chapter, men's sexuality has a certain paradoxical quality. On the one hand, all sexual disorders (and orders) reflect and contain nonsexual emotional problems having to do with important past and present relationships. To cope with this, we must desexualize sex and search — at least some of the time — for nonsexual solutions to the sexual problem at hand. On the other hand, nonsexual emotional conflicts seem to always have a sexual origin, and to cope with this, we must find and explore the sexual clues hidden in the emotions. This paradox is perhaps best illustrated by men who — consciously or unconsciously — choose a celibate lifestyle. Asexual on the outside, they can be intensely sexual inside, perhaps too much so to bring internal fantasy and external reality into alignment.

As I've also discussed repeatedly, inside this paradox, like a Russian doll, lies another paradox, that of the conflict of masculine insecurity. One patient, a twenty-eight-year-old Broadway actor, came to therapy because he realized that he had been so focused on his career and so overwhelmed by his early success that he had completely neglected his personal life. "I've never had a romantic relationship and I'm embarrassed to say it, but I never had sex," he said in his first session. "Isn't it time for me to lose my virginity? Also, after I masturbate, I become so exhausted that I'm practically incapacitated for about forty-eight hours. Don't laugh, but because of this I have a rule never to masturbate the day of a performance — which becomes a problem when you're in a regular show."

I was initially a bit skeptical about this patient's alleged incapacitation, but he had proof. "I recently masturbated the night before I was on the *Today Show.*" He smiled. "And I have the tape — I'm telling you, I was a mumbling idiot!"

"Okay," I said, "so let's explore what's so exhausting about it for you." Well, it turned out that what would fatigue this patient so much was not the masturbatory activity itself but rather the content of the fantasies accompanying it. In those fantasies he was fighting the battle of the sexes — alternating from ordering women around with "Get undressed," "Suck my dick," and "Tell me how big I am" to being a sensitive, pubescent boy who's seduced by a large, dildo-strapped, older woman.

Being a nice, wholesome kind of guy, this young man could not imagine acting on such fantasies of domination and submission in the real world. But he also couldn't imagine being turned on by anything else — which was why he was still a virgin. I suppose one approach to his problem would have been to encourage him to experiment with implementing his fantasies in reality — in role playing, with a prostitute, or whatever. My approach, however, was different. What I thought he needed was not sex, but rather, a nonsexual implementation of his fantasies: a caring relationship with someone who was feminine enough to affirm his battered masculinity, yet masculine enough to revive his repressed femininity. Arguably, that's what all men need. And sex, too,... but perhaps in that very order.

There's little doubt that my patients find it easier to talk to me about sex than they would to a woman. But the truth is that when we talk about it, it's no locker-room talk. If anything, it's girl talk. It's relationship talk. It's feeling talk. The thing is, we can only do that because, knowing that we are two guys, there is no doubt about our gender. But when a man is with a woman, his masculinity is on the line. So does this mean there's no hope for open male-to-female communications? On the contrary. The logic of the conflict of masculine insecurity dictates that men in fact do need to engage in some girl talk with a woman. But they can only do so if the woman can engage in a bit of locker-room talk with them. Which shouldn't be much of a problem because, psychologically speaking, men and women are fundamentally more alike than different — the seven male attributes notwithstanding. While by virtue of its subject matter this book has highlighted the differences between the sexes, my belief is that what unites men and women ultimately outweighs what divides them. And even that which divides them need not be polarizing. With a bit of love and a lot of work even our very opposite can become our best complement.

Notes

The notes to this book may be found on the author's Web site:

WWW.IFMENCOULDTALK.COM

Bibliography

Angrist, S. W. 1998. Business Bookshelf: "It Doesn't Grow on Trees." *Wall Street Journal,* 12/24/98, p. A7.

Becker, E. 1997. *The Denial of Death.* New York: Free Press.

Bernhard, T. 1993. *The Loser.* New York: Vintage International Vintage Books.

Bollas, C. 1987. *The Shadow of the Object: Psychoanalysis of the Unthought Known.* New York: Columbia University Press.

———. 1991. *Forces of Destiny.* London: Free Association Books.

Brandes, S. 1980. *Metaphors of Masculinity.* Philadelphia: University of Pennsylvania Press.

Chagnon, Napoleon A. 1992. *Yanomamo: The Last Days of Eden.* New York: Harcourt Brace Jovanovich.

Covey, S. R. 1989. *The Seven Habits of Highly Effective People.* New York: Simon & Schuster.

Dostoyevsky, Fyodor. 1972. *Notes from the Underground/The Double.* New York: Penguin Books, pp. 16, 25, 34.

Dweck, C. S., and Leggett, E. L. 1988. "A Social-Cognitive Approach to Motivation and Personality." *Psychological Review* 95, 256–273.

Ellis, C. D. 1998. *Winning the Loser's Game: Timeless Strategies of Successful Investing.* New York: McGraw-Hill.

Erikson, E. 1950. *Childhood and Society.* New York: W. W. Norton.

Fairbairn, W. R. D. 1952. *An Object-Relations Theory of the Personality.* New York: Basic Books.

Fogel, Gerald I., Lane, Fredrick M., and Liebert, Robert S., eds. *The Psychology of Men.* New Haven and London: Yale University Press.

Freud, S. All references are to the *Standard Edition of the Complete Psychological Works of Sigmund Freud,* volumes 1–24. London: Hogarth Press, 1953–1974. (SE)

———. 1900. *The Interpretations of Dreams.* SE, 4 and 5.

———. 1905. *Three Essays on the Theory of Sexuality.* SE, 7: 125–245.
———. 1915. *Instincts and Their Vicissitudes.* SE, 14: 117–140.
———. 1917. *Mourning and Melancholia.* SE, 14: 237–260.
———. 1920. *Beyond the Pleasure Principle.* SE, 18: 3–64.
———. 1924. *The Economic Problem of Masochism.* SE, 19: 155–170.
———. 1926. *Inhibitions, Symptoms and Anxiety.* SE, 20: 75–175
———. 1933. *New Introductory Lectures on Psycho-Analysis.* SE, 22: 1–182.

Gay, P. 1988. *Freud, A Life for Our Time.* New York and London: W. W. Norton.

Gray, J. 1992. *Men Are from Mars, Women Are from Venus.* New York: HarperCollins.

Greenson, Ralph R. 1967. *The Technique and Practice of Psychoanalysis.* New York: International Universities Press.

Guntrip, Henry. 1969. *Schizoid Phenomena, Object Relations and the Self.* New York: International Universities Press.

Horney, Karen. 1993. *Our Inner Conflicts: A Constructive Theory of Neurosis.* New York: W. W. Norton.

Isay, Richard A. 1986. "Homosexuality in Homosexual and Heterosexual Men: Some Distinctions and Implications for Treatment." In *The Psychology of Men.*

Kafka, Franz. 1989. *The Sons.* New York: Schocken Books, pp. 115, 162, 150.

Kernberg, O. 1975. *Borderline Conditions and Pathological Narcissism.* New York: Jason Aronson.

———. 1980. *Internal World and External Reality.* New York: Jason Aronson.

Kidd, R., and Wenzel, M. P. 1992. *Golden Sound Story Disney Beauty and the Beast.* Racine, Wisconsin: New York Western Publishing Company.

Klein, M. 1964. "Love, Guilt and Reparation." In M. Klein and J. Riviere, *Love, Hate and Reparation.* New York: W. W. Norton.

Kohut, H. 1971. *The Analysis of the Self.* New York: International Universities Press.

———. 1977. *The Restoration of the Self.* New York: International Universities Press.

Kundera, Milan. 1999. *The Book of Laughter and Forgetting.* New York: HarperCollins, p. 110.

Langs, R., ed. 1981. *Classics in Psychoanalytic Techniques.* New York: Jason Aronson.

Lewis, M. 1995. *Shame: The Exposed Self.* New York: Free Press.

Liebert, R. S. "The History of Male Homosexuality from Ancient Greece Through the Renaissance: Implications for Psychoanalytic Theory." In *The Psychology of Men.*

Masters, W., Johnson, V., and Kolodny. 1986. *Masters and Johnson on Sex and Human Loving.* Boston: Little, Brown.

McCarthy, B. 1988. *Male Sexual Awareness.* New York: Carroll & Graf, pp. 147, 196.

Miedzian, M. 1991. *Boys Will Be Boys.* New York: Doubleday.

Ovid. 1955. *Metamorphoses.* Bloomington and London: Indiana University Press, pp. 16–20.

Peck, S. 1978. *The Road Less Traveled.* New York: Simon & Schuster.

Ponte, L. D. 1787. *Don Giovanni.* Munich: Gerhard Stalling AG, Oldenburg (Deutsche Grammophon).

Ramo, S. 1970. *Extraordinary Tennis for the Ordinary Player.* New York: Crown Publishing.

Real, T. 1997. *I Don't Want to Talk About It.* New York: Simon & Schuster, pp. 163–164.

Reich, W. 1949. *Character Analysis.* New York: Orgone Institute Press.

Rycroft, C. 1973. *A Critical Dictionary of Psychoanalysis.* Totowa, New Jersey: Littlefield, Adams.

Shakespeare, W. 1899. *Macbeth.* In *The Works of Shakespeare,* vol. 9. London: Macmillan.

Soros, G., with Byron Wien and Krisztina Koenen. 1995. *Soros on Soros.* New York: John Wiley & Sons.

Stoller, R. 1975. *Perversion.* London: Maresfield Library.

———. *Presentations of Gender.* 1985. New Haven and London: Yale University Press.

———. 1985. *Observing the Erotic Imagination.* New Haven and London: Yale University Press.

Stolorow, R., and Atwood, G. 1979. *Faces in a Cloud: Subjectivity in Personality Theory.* New York: Jason Aronson.

Sullivan, H. S. 1954. *The Psychiatric Interview.* New York and London: W. W. Norton.

———. 1956. *Clinical Studies in Psychiatry.* New York: W. W. Norton.

Tolstoy, L. 1983. *War and Peace.* Oxford and New York: Oxford University Press.

Winnicott, D. W. 1958. *Through Pediatrics to Psycho-Analysis.* London: Hogarth Press.

———. 1965. *The Maturational Process and the Facilitating Environment.* New York: International Universities Press.

———. 1971. *Playing and Reality.* Middlesex, England: Penguin.

Woolf, V. 1956. *Orlando.* San Diego, New York, and London: Harcourt Brace, pp. 137–138.

Wrangham, R., and Peterson, D. *Demonic Males, Apes and the Origins of Human Violence.* 1996. Boston and New York: Mariner Books, Houghton Mifflin, p. 234.

Index

A Note About the Author

Alon Gratch is a clinical psychologist in private practice in New York. In his psychotherapy practice he sees patients for individual, couples, and group therapy. He has been on the faculty of Columbia University and has written for the *New York Times* and the *Wall Street Journal*. Dr. Gratch is also a management consultant, working with corporations in the areas of leadership, negotiations, and crisis management. For more information, visit www.IfMenCouldTalk.com.